W9-AXF-916

PUBLISHING
101

A First-Time Author's Guide to Getting Published, Marketing and Promoting Your Book, and Building a Successful Career

by Jane Friedman

FOR
WRITERS

PUBLISHING 101 © 2015 by Jane Friedman. Manufactured in the United States of America. All rights reserved. No part of this book may be reproduced in any form or by any electronic or mechanical means including information storage and retrieval systems without permission in writing from the author, except by a reviewer, who may quote brief passages in a review. First edition.

Print edition ISBN: 978-0-9863126-1-8
E-book edition ISBN: 978-0-9863126-0-1

To receive a free monthly e-mail newsletter from the author on how writers can succeed in the digital age, subscribe at http://janefriedman.com/free-newsletter

Edited by Jane Friedman and Mark F. Griffin
Interior and cover design by Jane Friedman
Production coordinated by Jane Friedman

To my writing professors Dr. William Baer and Margaret McMullan,
who first introduced me to the world of publishing.

TABLE OF CONTENTS

PREFACE
Why This Book Exists

Here is a brief history.

I have been working in the publishing industry, in some form, since the mid-1990s. In 2001, I began working for Writer's Digest, the No. 1 brand and community offering education, information, and services to writers in the United States.

In 2008, when I became publisher and editorial director of Writer's Digest, I started a blog called There Are No Rules. I posted 4-5 times per week, usually on trends in the publishing industry. After I left Writer's Digest in 2010, I continued the blog, then eventually decided to blog only at my own site, JaneFriedman.com, where I continue to post advice for writers related to the business of publishing.

This book is a compilation of my best blog posts since 2008, organized and stitched together as a guide for new authors. You'll notice it has a lot of subheads, bulleted lists, and numbered methods—a stylistic quirk of online writing and particularly blog writing. I also occasionally include articles or longform features I wrote for other venues, as well as Q&As others have conducted with me.

The end result, I hope, is an efficient and effective way to get my basic, 101 advice for writers, without having to navigate hundreds of links or figure out what information is outdated.

Welcome, and let's get started.

INTRODUCTION

The Dirty Secret About Writing Advice

As the former publisher of Writer's Digest, I've likely read more annals of writing advice than anyone else on the planet. I'm intimate with every cliché writers hear about how to succeed or fail. And experience has shown me that prescriptive, step-by-step advice sometimes offers a comfortable illusion: that you can reach success systematically or by formula. Such advice, especially when simplified, bulleted, and listed, pushes aside the complexity, difficulty and dilemma of what it means to undertake a writing life.

I have always advised writers in good faith, and would never suggest a writer undertake something harmful, obstructive, or a waste of time. If you were able to internalize all the (sometimes conflicting) advice from hundreds, even thousands, of writers—as I have—I do think you'd be a better writer for it, if only because you'd sooner recognize and maybe avoid the most common pitfalls, as well as recognize the most constructive attitudes. But the writing itself never gets any easier no matter how much you know or publish. The dilemmas never go away.

There are some technical things every writer should learn to do correctly. Formatting and submitting your manuscript is one. Queries might be another. Yet I know talented writers often break all the rules about queries and charm agents anyway. That's what a very talented writer does. But I can't say that when I'm teaching you how to write a great query. I can't teach the exceptions or pleasing eccentricities (or what can boil down to a matter of confidence or nuance). I teach the rules, even though there aren't any.

The most honest book I could offer would encompass the following dilemmas and contradictions:

Talent vs. Practice (or Discipline). Some people are born to be writers. Others seem to be blessed with the discipline to get better. Can you succeed without any talent? Which quality is more important? And how do you know if you have any talent to begin with? Certainly those with talent need to practice, too—or not?

Luck vs. Persistence. I've seen so many lucky writers—people who were at the right place at the right time. Yet the cliché is that luck favors the prepared. That feels true, though I've met a lot of prepared people who never seem to catch a break.

Confidence/Ego vs. Doubt. I've never met a writer who didn't have self-doubt, though not all will admit to it. We're waiting to be revealed as complete phonies. Yet without some measure of outrageous ego—a belief that you have something to say to the world—there's no way you could justify writing. Writing is not for the weak. The weak ones give up easily, sometimes with the first rejection.

Professionalism vs. Eccentricity. The writers who are business-savvy and have a flair for marketing & promotion almost always do well. Yet the writers we tend to fall in love with, and the ones we remember, can be the craziest, the most rude, or the most outrageous. Strong personalities sell, too.

Extroversion vs. Introversion. Extroverts network better and find more people to help them. Introverts are naturally suited to writing and often notice all those wonderful details that extroverts miss. Horrible stereotyping here, but still.

This book isn't about those things—it is (mostly) not philosophical. Rather, this book is about the basics of the writing business, and I've geared it primarily toward beginning or early career writers who want to get traditionally published.

You may seek the secrets to success and a positive spin on an industry in great upheaval. But just know that the longer I'm in the business, the more slippery it all looks. I know what works for some, but it never works for all. I would love to sit down with you personally, and put together a specific plan of attack based on your talents and strengths. I do offer such services, but I hope this book fills the gap in the meantime.

Thank you for reading.

CHAPTER 1
The Psychological Battle

I meet many writers who ask (essentially), "Read my writing and tell me what I should do—if I should keep trying."

I empathize if you're looking for some sign you have talent or that you'll eventually make it. It's especially tough to continue doing something when you receive no recognition or encouragement for it.

But what I find is that most reassurances, while offering a boost to a writer's ego, are ultimately external, fleeting, and momentary. You need an essential fire inside, or an attitude, that carries you the distance. This attitude is defined by the following:

- Seeking feedback from professionals, and avoiding defensiveness and protectiveness of your work
- Being invested in the writing process and the meaningfulness of what you're doing
- Having patience with the process, and not rushing
- Taking advantage of every possible growth opportunity, and not being resistant to change
- Being proactive rather than waiting to be discovered.

It's a kind of wisdom that comes only from knowing yourself and what you want. As Bob says in *Lost in Translation*, "The more you know who you are, and what you want, the less you let things upset you."

My hope is that every writer I meet will not ask, "Read this and tell me what to do," but "This is my mission, how can I improve and grow?"

Your Family and Friends Are Wrong

Time for a little tough love. To all those writers who say:

- My family has encouraged me to write this story
- I had this idea while talking with friends, and they thought it was brilliant
- My [insert close friend or family member name here] absolutely love my stories
- I read my work to my students, they think I should get it published.

You need to ignore what these people are telling you. You need to write because you can't do anything else—because you would suffer if you didn't. Your motivation to write has to come from within.

Family members are supposed to encourage and support you, to act as cheerleaders during the long periods of rejection. There are some unusual cases where your family/friends can offer critical feedback as insightful and careful readers, and you can make excellent use of it. But for most writers, you must not and cannot rely on your family and friends to give you this feedback, even if they are your target audience. And you especially can't rely on them to tell you that your work deserves publication—or to give you any kind of business-of-publishing advice.

You Hate Your Writing? That's a Good Sign

One day, I received a message from a close friend, a struggling writer, that announced he was finally writing again. He commented, "We'll see if I end up hating it, as I have every single thing I've ever written before. I do hope to get over this at some point."

Every successful writer has had to overcome that feeling. It's an important feeling. It's a valid feeling. And if a writer *doesn't* have that feeling (at some point), I get worried. Why?

It's the Ira Glass principle: You have to produce a lot of crap—stuff that you know is crap—before you can produce anything good. (If you haven't watched Glass's series on storytelling on YouTube, be sure to set aside 15 minutes to do so.)

Unfortunately, writers in the depths of this "crap phase" will often wonder if it's worth their time to continue. That struggle—that feeling that you're wasting your time—is a sign that you're probably on the right path. But most people quit, not realizing that nearly every writer who does excellent work went through a phase of years where they had really good taste, but they produced total crap.

What's most important is that you can perceive that gap—that gap between what you know is quality and the lesser quality you achieve—and that you understand that gap is temporary. You *do* get better.

That's not to say you become less critical of your work. Great writers will always be critical of their own work because they have good taste. It doesn't get any easier, as just about every successful author will tell you. But that's not a reason to quit.

3 Questions Every Creative Person Must Ask

Here are the three dilemmas that come up again and again when I talk with writers about the business of publishing, and they are dilemmas that I can't solve. They boil down to three questions you have to ask yourself—and be able to answer honestly—to find a path that's your own, not mine.

1. Are you creating primarily for yourself or primarily for an audience? Almost all of my advice is based on the assumption that you want to entertain, inform, or increase your audience. Not everyone is concerned with this, nor should they be.

If you're producing work for an audience, it means:
- playing by at least some rules of the industry
- caring what others think of your work
- interacting with your audience and being available to them
- doing things not for your art, but out of service to your audience
- putting on a performance, or adopting some kind of persona
- marketing and being visible

If you're creating for yourself, it means:
- the act is worthwhile regardless of who sees your work
- fulfillment comes from your struggle with the practice, not from making your work public or receiving feedback

Of course, you may be creating for both yourself and an audience. But some artists who say they are producing work for an audience aren't willing to make the sacrifices required to do so. Which means there's another level to this. Are you creating for an audience, or creating for an audience that earns you money?

Once money enters the equation, you have to start sacrificing more of what you want, and bend to the demands of the market. (Or find a generous patron or foundation!)

What is it that you truly want out of your creative endeavors? Do you really know?

2. How much of yourself are you going to share? And which part?
Let's assume you do want an audience (of any size). It necessitates some kind of persona. Deciding not to have a persona (removing yourself from visibility, Pynchon style) is also a persona.

You can't imitate someone else's persona. You can only be yourself. Some of us think famous people are (or ought to be) aloof and distant, so we imitate aloofness, even when it has nothing to do with our personality.

After I give talks about digital marketing, relationship building, and social media, inevitably one person will come up and say, "I don't want to be visible online. I just want people to read my stories."

That's a rather boring proposition in this day and age.

So you have to ask yourself—even if you're shy or think you're boring— what part of yourself are you going to share and put on display? It's got to be something, so let's make it interesting. Let's really dive into the fiction of who you are—or aren't. Make up something you can believe in, so others can believe in it, too. (That's what we all want, most desperately. Meaning.)

3. What is your killer medium? Speaking only for myself, the book form is not my killer medium. (What you're reading right now originated as a blog post!) My killer medium is the workshop or the conference keynote. It's the ability to answer any question thrown at me. It's my desire to be of service in a personalized way.

The book is often assumed to be the most authoritative and important medium, but that's only because we've all been led to believe that—through a culture that has created The Myth about the author as authority. But it's a Myth, neither good nor bad. Just a belief system that, increasingly, we're all moving away from.

Creative people too often pursue mediums that have been pushed on them by other people, and because it's the well-worn path.

5 Things More Important Than Talent
Let me tell you a little story about my own writing life.

I have a BFA in creative writing, and when I was in college, I desperately wanted the professors to tell me if I had talent. I was never brave enough to directly ask the question, but I hoped they might take me by the shoulders one day, look me in the eye, and say: "Jane, you can't waste this gift, you must write!"

Now that I'm a professor, I realize just how irrelevant that question is. I see both talented and untalented students, but the ones who impress me are the ones who are motivated and driven to do the work—the ones who push hard despite obstacles. I also clearly see who has a positive attitude, and who is apathetic.

So far, these other qualities have mattered more than talent.

Let me tell you the five questions I find more relevant and meaningful than "Do I have talent?"

1. What makes you remarkable? Everyone of us is remarkable. We each have a unique set of strengths and weaknesses. For some of us, it takes a while before we realize what it is we *really* want to do, what we're doing here, and what we have to contribute in this world.

But each of us does have something remarkable to contribute, and I hope you're gifted with the knowledge of what that is. If not, keep asking the question.

2. What's your community? Your environment, and the people who surround you, are vitally important. Relationships matter. So what I want to know is: Who is your support network? Who is encouraging you? If you don't have anyone positive around you, you need to change that.

3. What risks are you taking? It's the old cliché: Nothing risked, nothing gained. Playing it safe as a writer will lead to mediocre writing at best. If you're not failing, you're not shooting high enough. Which leads me to the question below.

4. What do you do after you fail? Everyone fails. That's not the important part. What's important is what you do next. Are you learning? Are you growing? Is your experience making your heart bigger? Or is it shrinking you down, making you small? Beware of cynicism and bitterness, because if these emotions stick around too long, they will poison your efforts.

5. How do you deal with change? The only thing I know for sure is that publishing will change. Are you going to tighten up and resist, or will you look for the opportunities?

If you're frustrated with where the industry is headed, or how you're being treated by this editor or that agent, consider these words from Joseph Campbell: Is the system going to flatten you out and deny you your humanity? Or are you going to be able to make use of the system for uplifting and positive purposes?

Determination Versus Talent

I tend to side with people who believe determination is more important than talent. To be clear about the definitions, let me explain what I mean when I use the words "talent" and "determination"—as well as "skill."

Talent. I define this as what you're born with, what doesn't change.

When you have talent, it may lead nowhere if you don't have any way to cultivate or nurture it. The unknowable thing here is exactly how much talent you've got. It's not quantifiable and I'm not even confident it can be separated from other qualities discussed below.

Skills. This (along with many other things) is what comes with hard work and practice. People can put in the same level of hard work and not attain the same skill level as others. People who have a talent or aptitude for something often gain skills faster and at a more expert level.

Determination. This is what helps you overcome challenges, delays, and bad luck. This keeps you in the game when you feel like everything is working against you. This keeps you on a path of growth and improvement before, during, and after failure. Some call this persistence.

What I've noticed is that most writers who haven't succeeded (and aren't sure if they can succeed) love to hear that determination or persistence is more important than talent. People who've already achieved some level of stature tend to argue for the importance of talent. Successful people have already been "selected" in some fashion, so they're liable to believe they have talent that others don't. (Maybe they do, and maybe they don't. It doesn't really matter.)

Here are 3 things I believe about talent.

1. Neither talent nor skill is always recognized. This is because there are too many variables that can stand in the way: background, upbringing, education, opportunities, network, relationships, resources, timing, luck, culture. That is, life stands in the way.

2. Everyone has some kind of talent—but so what? Why do we believe that talent ought to receive recognition or attention? No one has to work to get talent; it is out of our control. We are all born with strengths, with special qualities that help us flourish at something in life. I'm not going to think you're a better person, or more deserving of success, just because you have talent.

3. I admire people who work hard to do what they love. What's especially inspiring are people who overcome great odds, or who work harder than everyone else, to achieve great things. There is usually tremendous sacrifice in that. There is something that had to be lost or left behind. It takes guts.

So that's why I don't really give a damn about talent. Talent is common. Talent does not set you apart. Talent has little to do with your character or contribution to the world.

Placing Too Much Importance on Passion

It seems like the cultural myth these days is that we ought to be pursuing our passion; otherwise we will be unhappy. Unfortunately, through overuse, "passion" has become a cheap word—I'm starting to roll my eyes when I hear it. While I was on the admissions committee for the E-Media Division at the University of Cincinnati, that's when I first became numb to students who claimed, "[x] is my passion."

If true, who cares? Every other student has a passion, too. What matters is how that translates into action. Show me what you've done because of your passion. Show me through action that you really mean it and aren't flirting with it. Show me that you've struggled and remained resilient. Show me that you have discipline.

Author Robert Sternberg said, "Passion is the quickest to develop, and the quickest to fade. Intimacy develops more slowly, and commitment more gradually still."

I've taught hundreds of writers with passion. I teach few writers with commitment to do the best work possible. The only time when I find passion useful is when it helps you more easily put in the effort or the work required—consistently, over time—to become a master at your art or your work.

How Will You Deal With Rejection?

Many years ago, when I was working as an associate editor for a fine art imprint, I applied for the lead editor position on Writer's Market. I interviewed with three different people in the division. I wanted the job so badly that I would take long drives around town, just thinking about how much I wanted it.

I didn't get it. The hiring manager encouraged me to keep trying to transition to the Writer's Digest community if other positions opened up.

Within two weeks, a managing editor position with Writer's Digest magazine was posted. I thought: *They'll never hire me for that job. Why bother? I have no magazine experience.* And so I didn't apply. Another four weeks passed, and the job was still posted. I remember staring at the job description in the lunch room, finally snapping out of my self-pity, thinking, *Why the hell not? What have I got to lose?*

I got the job. The rest is history.

Of the thousands of writers (and creative people) I have met, all have failed at one point or another. No one is immune. That's why I so consistently preach patience and persistence. You'll need it when faced with failure, loss, and rejection (which are great teachers, by the way).

Thomas Edison once said, "Many of life's failures are people who did not realize how close they were to success when they gave up."

President Obama once said, "Making your mark in the world is hard. If it were easy, everybody would do it. But it's not. It takes patience, it takes commitment, and it comes with plenty of failure along the way. So the real test is not whether you avoid this failure, because you won't. It's whether you let it harden and shame you into inaction, or whether you learn from it; whether you choose to persevere."

I know right away when I meet a person who has been hardened or shamed into inaction. It can happen to all of us, at some point, especially when we're new to something.

You must move through it. The happy (and usually successful) people I meet have a resilience that you can sense when you talk to them—people who understand that failure, loss, and rejection are part of the game (no matter what game is being played).

Take the failure and shine a light on it, learn from it. It's taking you one step closer to success.

The Traps Beginners Fall Into

Sometimes writers express sentiments that make me want to issue a red-flag warning: *STOP. You are about to hurt yourself.* Here are four of the biggest ones.

1. If I can't get a deal soon, I'm self-publishing. Why are you in a rush? Does your book have an expiration date?

Even if your book is timely, should you invest in a book project that has a very short life span? Is a book the best format for something that's incredibly timely?

If you're the type of person who is initially interested in traditional publishing, are you sure that self-publishing will satisfy you? Are you hoping to use self-publishing as a way to attract a traditional deal? If so, be careful. Self-publishing is a full-time job if you intend to build a readership. Are you ready to take on that full-time job of marketing yourself? Do you know who you're marketing to? Do you know *how* to market?

If your back-up plan is self-publishing, it's likely you'll end up disappointed with the outcome.

2. I just want to get my book published. This is the sister attitude to No. 1. It leads to all kinds of bad decisions, such as:

- Signing with any agent
- Signing a bad contract
- Falling for scams
- Becoming bitter
- Partnering with a less-than-ideal publisher or service company
- Focusing on book publication when another medium would be better.

Believe me, you don't just want to get your book published. Aside from the incredible amount of work for minimal monetary gain, many authors experience post-launch depression. It's that sudden realization that, even though your book now exists, nobody knows except for you. Even experienced and seasoned authors with good marketing and publicity plans can get discouraged, even angry, at the lack of attention they receive. When most books land on the shelves, they rarely make an audible sound.

Before you call me jaded, I should clarify that I don't think publishing a book is meaningless or without reward. However, as Clay Shirky has said, "In a world where publishing is effortless, the decision to publish something isn't terribly momentous." We live in a world of information abundance, not scarcity.

So make sure that you have a deeper and lasting purpose associated with your desire to get a book published. Make sure it's part of a larger career path and contribution to the world. Don't focus on just one book.

3. Quality is subjective, and I don't need a professional editor. An editor is not a family member, a friend, an English major, or your writing group buddy. An editor is someone with professional training whose only responsibility is to ensure you produce the best book possible.

A lot of cutting corners happens with self-published books, and it doesn't make a good impression on either your readers or your future potential publishing partners. Yes, it's true that all publishers and content providers are guilty of putting out stuff that's horribly average, even poor. But let's not strive to be like them.

I know what your next question is: How do I find a reputable, credible, professional editor? How do you get your hands on the real deal?

I admit it's a challenge. I've offered critical feedback to dozens of authors who protested that their work had been professionally edited, but clearly it hadn't been. Whoever they hired was not really a professional. There are "editors" out there doing more harm than good, who don't have appropriate experience. I'll address how to find reputable help in a moment.

4. I just need someone to *really* pay attention. Your work is so unique, right? It's never been done before. Most importantly, it has your heart and soul in it.

You've been told to write this story by everyone you know. You've been told it deserves publication. The only problem is, you can't get anyone in the industry to pay attention to you. If only someone would pay attention, you'd have it made. Right?

Everyone thinks they're the exception to the rule, and if only their work could get distribution across all major retailers, bestsellerdom would be theirs.

Unfortunately, this type of thinking only leads to one place: It's always someone else's fault that you or your work isn't hitting the milestones you'd like.

Who Should You Trust to Help You?

You've probably heard the "Wild West" cliché more than once in reference to all the changes happening in the publishing industry. I've been working in and observing the media industry since 1998, and never before have I seen so many people or services focused on "helping" writers as now.

Why is everyone suddenly interested in helping?

- Lots of people do, in fact, need help.
- There's lots of confusion.
- There's some money to be made.

When you combine reasons #2 and #3, it produces a lot of unnecessary "help" that writers don't need, or that could waste their time.

Let's get clear about what writers need to do, in order of priority.

- Read.
- Write. (Practice. Do the work.)
- Get meaningful feedback from trusted writing groups, mentors, and/ or professionals.

After that, there is no one-size-fits-all path. People learn, improve, and get published in different ways. But before you decide you're going to pay someone to help you—at any point in your writing, editing, marketing, promotion, or publishing path—ask these questions.

1. Who's behind it? Do you trust who's behind it? Are there specific names attached? Do they have experience that applies to what you're trying to do? What's the bias (if any) of the people behind the service?

2. What's the business model? How do they make money? Almost every service has to turn a profit, and there's nothing wrong with that. For valuable or quality help that furthers our careers, we should be willing to pay.

3. Is it transparent? It's to your advantage that we now live in an age where businesses are expected to be transparent and frank. So take a good look at the services you might want to pay for, or the websites where you spend your time. Are they upfront about what they do, what they have a stake in, and how they make money? Are they upfront about how the work gets done? I favor the ones who have nothing to hide, as well as those with a point-of-view and distinctive personality.

4. Is it credible? Is it authoritative? Sometimes this is tough for a new writer to evaluate. If you don't know what distinguishes a trustworthy and experienced editor or service provider from an inexperienced one, then at the very least, look for success stories that match the kind of success you want. Look for testimonials and recommendations. Look for a track record and history of achievement in the areas where you need help. (Someone who just got into the business within the last year might be an opportunist. Or they could just be a very intelligent but laid-off New York publishing employee.)

There are a lot of people and services that want to take your money, or your time and energy. Sometimes you get back exactly what you put in. And others will never be worth it.

Bottom line, always make sure you need the help before you pay for it. Do your research before committing. Get second and third opinions. And have your eyes wide open.

Make sure the editor you hire can give you referrals and point to published works or authors they've edited. Any solid editor will likely have a waiting list, and they won't take just any work that comes their way. They're selective.

For places to find reputable help, start here:
- PublishersMarketplace.com
- Blurb's Dream Team collaborators (visit Blurb.com)
- Reedsy.com

Would You Benefit from Hiring a Professional Editor?

In their query letters, I see more writers these days claim their manuscript has been professionally edited. And it's no surprise. People inside the industry—like myself!—are known for emphasizing the importance of submitting a flawless manuscript.

Rather than a reassurance, though, queries that mention a professional edit can leave me feeling *less* confident about the work. I've heard agents say the same thing.

This seems grossly unfair, doesn't it? There are two elements at play.

1. Most writers don't clearly understand how an editor might improve their work (or to what extent). Writers must have a level of sophistication and knowledge about their work (or themselves!) to know where their weaknesses are, and how a professional might assist them. When writers ask me if they should hire a professional editor, it's usually out of a vague fear their work isn't good enough—and they think it can be "fixed." There are many different types or levels of editing, and if you don't know what they are—or what kind you need—then you're not ready for a professional editor.

2. Writers may sincerely seek professional help, but very few are willing to pay for it. You probably will not receive a quality review on your entire manuscript—that will actually affect your chances of publication—for less than $2,000.

Can you benefit from a professional edit? Maybe. Your work already needs to be very good and deserving of the investment. Even the best editor in the world can't turn a mediocre work into a gem. But they can make a good work great.

Asking Good, Specific Questions

When you're seeking advice from agents, editors, or other professionals, the better questions you ask (in any situation), the more you will learn, and the better quality responses you will get.

For example, when people e-mail or call me asking broad questions like:
- "How can I get published?"
- "How do I market my book?"
- "Should I self-publish?"

It makes me wonder what kind of response is expected, since hundreds of instruction books, courses, and videos are available on these very topics.

Such questions cannot be answered in a reasonable length e-mail or phone call, and posing such questions risks disrespecting the person you're asking. (It calls for a significant investment of their time, expertise, and energy.)

So, find out everything you can on your own—go as far as you possibly can through online and offline research. Then, when you hit a real brick wall, confusing issue, or dilemma, ask a very specific question that will help you take the next step.

That's the way to ask a question that respects a person's expertise.

Finally—especially when you ask for anything that would be considered a favor—you need to spell out exactly what you are looking for. Don't generally ask, "Can you help me out?" Ask specifically for what you want. People who are doing the favors shouldn't be expected to come up with what they should give you. Outline (even in a bulleted list) things that they can quickly say "yes" or "no" to, without thinking hard about it. Most people want to be helpful, but as soon as it becomes a complex task, they'll save their energy for something else (like paying work).

Don't Get Fooled by Bad Advice

As humans, we have a crazy predilection for thinking in black-and-white terms. Us versus them. New versus old. Print versus electronic. Particularly in blogs or online communities, battles erupt and people take sides, such as in the traditional publishing vs. self-publishing argument.

The truth is, though, that most of us are on a spectrum. Most of us strike a balance, or switch gears when we see that it's necessary for progress.

Playing to extremes is exceptionally helpful in getting attention. Writing a great blog post or developing a successful online presence is often about knowing how to attract attention, or be bombastic in a charming way. Talking about the gray areas within an issue—parsing through all the intricacies—isn't known for generating traffic. Boldness is.

You'll all pay close attention if I say: **You Will Fail Instantly If You Do XYZ!** But it's a huge snoozer if I say: **A Few Might Stumble By Not Considering XYZ.**

When you read writing advice online—or in any medium—please keep this dynamic in mind. The people who talk about the contingencies, who make allowances for differences? Those are the ones to pay close attention to.

The black-and-white advice? Take it with a grain of salt.

CHAPTER 2
Are You Ready to Face the Business of Publishing?

Nearly all unpublished writers have one thing in common that trips them up, every time. **They rush to submit their work before it's ready or before they are ready**—especially writers fresh with the excitement of having just completed their very first book-length manuscript.

Countless writers who pitch at conferences are so new to the business they don't realize their manuscript of 150,000 words is a tough sell for a first-time author. (Did you know?)

If you've just spent months (or years!) writing a manuscript, why rush it to an agent or editor, and why rush it to just ANY agent or editor? And why rush it if you're new to the publishing business?

There are two things to ask yourself after you complete a manuscript or proposal:

1. Is the book really done? Is it really the best you can make it? And have professionals (whether editors, agents, or published authors) encouraged you, because they see and know you are ready? Do you feel confident that it's ready to submit?

2. Are you informed enough about the publishing business to understand where to submit the work, how to submit the work, and what obstacles you might face? Does your work break the rules of the industry? (If so, that's OK, but know it going in.)

Let's explore these issues more in depth.

The Secret to Writing & Publishing That Should Be Taped to Your Wall

Much publishing advice seems like common sense:

- Have a great hook in your query letter
- Take out everything that's boring
- Learn how to pitch your work

Being able to do these well, however, requires a perspective that's difficult to learn and apply: *You must achieve objectivity.*

It's why the Rule of 24 is supposed to improve your writing overnight. (Sleep on everything for a day.) It imposes distance. But 24 hours isn't enough time when it comes to long and complex works such as book manuscripts. We need another kind of rule.

Have you ever heard that for each year of a relationship (or marriage), you can expect 1-3 months of recovery time when it ends?

Part of that recovery process is about achieving distance and perspective.

When you finish a significant manuscript or proposal that took a long time to complete, you need distance to assess it without feeling attached. And especially if you're trying to convince agents or editors why your work deserves publication, a great amount of distance is required.

This is my theory on why so many queries and proposals fail. The work itself may be outstanding, but the writer hasn't achieved the necessary distance to either evaluate or communicate the commercial merit of her own work.

Aside from achieving distance (which takes time and training), you should find and trust a few carefully selected critique partners, or professional editors, to tell you how to improve your work, or position it for the market. Even if you haven't had the time or willingness to take enough steps back, others can offer a really hard push.

How Close Are You to Traditional Publication?

Don't you wish someone could tell you how close you are to getting traditionally published? Don't you wish someone could say, "If you just keep at it for three more years, you're certain to make it!"

Or, even if it would be heartbreaking, wouldn't it be nice to be told that you're wasting your time, so that you can move on, try another tack (like self-publishing), or perhaps even change course entirely to produce some other creative work?

I've counseled thousands of writers over the years, and even if it's not possible for me to read their work, I can usually say something definitive about what their next steps should be. I often see when they're wasting their time. No matter where you are in your own publishing path, you should periodically take stock of where you're headed, and revise as necessary.

Recognizing Steps That Don't Help You Get Published

Let's start with four common time-wasting behaviors. You may be guilty of one or more. Most writers have been guilty of the first.

1. Submitting manuscripts that aren't your best work. Let's be honest. We all secretly hope that some editor or agent will read our work, drop everything, and call us to say: This is a work of genius! YOU are a genius!

Few writers give up on this dream entirely, but to increase the chances of this happening, you have to give each manuscript everything you've got, with nothing held back. Too many writers save their best effort for some future work, as if they were going to run out of good material.

You can't operate like that.

Every single piece of greatness must go into your current project. Be confident that your well is going to be refilled. Make your book better than you ever thought possible—that's what it needs to compete. It can't just be good.

"Good" gets rejected. Your work has to be the best. How do you know when it's ready, when it's your best? I like how Writer's Digest editor and author Chuck Sambuchino answers this question at writing conferences: "If you think the story has a problem, it does—and any story with a problem is not ready."

It's common for a new writer who doesn't know any better to send off his manuscript without realizing how much work is left to do. But experienced writers are usually most guilty of sending out work that is not ready. Stop wasting your time.

2. Self-publishing when no one is listening. There are many reasons writers choose to self-publish, but the most common one is the inability to land an agent or a traditional publisher.

Fortunately, it's more viable than ever for a writer to be successful *without* a traditional publisher or agent. However, when writers chase self-publishing as an alternative to traditional publishing, they often have a nasty surprise in store:

No one is listening. They don't have an audience.

If your goal is to bring your work successfully to the marketplace, it can be a waste of time to self-publish that work, regardless of format, if you're unable to market and promote it effectively through your network. Doing so will not likely harm your career in the long run, but it won't move it forward, either.

3. Looking for major publication of regional or niche work. The cookbook memoir that your local church ladies produced this year is probably not appropriate for one of the major New York publishers.

That may seem obvious when stated, but every year agents receive thousands of submissions for work that does not have national appeal, and does not deserve shelf space at every chain bookstore in the country. (And that's typically why you get an agent: to sell your work to the big publishers, who specialize in national bookstore distribution and mass-media marketing.)

Now, if those church ladies were notorious for producing the award-winning Betty Crocker recipe 20 years in a row, we'd be onto something with a national market. But few regional works have that kind of broader angle.

As a writer, one of the most difficult tasks you face is having sufficient distance from your work to understand how a publishing professional would view the market for it, or to determine if there's a commercial angle to be exploited. You have to view your work not as something precious to you, but as a product to be positioned and sold. That means pitching your work only to the most appropriate publishing houses, even if they're in your own backyard rather than New York City.

4. Focusing on publishing when you should be writing. Some new writers are far too concerned with queries, agents, marketing or conference-going, instead of first producing the best work possible.

Don't get me wrong—for some types of nonfiction, it's *essential* to have a platform in place before you write the book. The fact that many nonfiction authors don't typically write the full manuscript until after acceptance of their proposal is indicative of how much platform means to their publication.

But for everyone else—those of us who are *not* selling a book based solely on the proposal—don't get consumed with finding an agent until you're a writer ready for publication. While I'm not advocating reclusive behavior—writers need to socialize and start developing relationships with other writers and authors—I see too many writers developing anxiety about the publishing process before they've even demonstrated to themselves that they can commit to writing and revising thousands and thousands of words—before they put in the amount of work that creates a publication-ready manuscript.

And now we come to that tricky matter again. How do you know when you've written and revised enough? How do you know when the work is ready?

Evaluating Your Place on the Publication Path

Whenever I sit down for a critique session with a writer, I ask three questions early on:

- How long have you been working on this manuscript, and who has seen it?
- Is this the first manuscript you've ever completed?
- How long have you been actively writing?

These questions help me evaluate where the writer might be on the traditional publishing path. Here are a few generalizations I can often make.

Many first manuscript attempts are not publishable, even after revision, yet they are necessary and vital for a writer's growth. A writer who's just finished her first manuscript probably doesn't realize this, and will likely take the rejection process very hard. Some writers can't move past this rejection. You've probably heard experts advise that you should always start working on the next manuscript, rather than waiting to publish the first. That's because you need to move on, and not get stuck on publishing your first attempt.

A writer who has been working on the same manuscript for years and years—and has written *nothing else*—might be tragically stuck. There isn't usually much valuable learning going on when someone tinkers with the same pages over a decade.

Writers who have been actively writing for many years, have produced multiple full-length manuscripts, have one or two trusted critique partners (or mentors), and have attended a couple major writing conferences are often well positioned for publication. They probably know their strengths and weaknesses, and have a structured revision process. Many such people require only luck to meet preparedness.

Writers who have extensive experience in one medium, then attempt to tackle another (e.g., journalists tackling the novel) may overestimate their abilities to produce a publishable manuscript on the first try. That doesn't mean their effort won't be good, but it might not be *good enough*. Fortunately, any writer with professional experience will probably approach the process with a business mindset, a good network of contacts to help him understand next steps, and a range of tools to overcome the challenges.

Notice I have not mentioned talent. I have not mentioned creative writing classes or degrees. I have not mentioned online presence. These factors are usually less relevant in determining how close you are to publishing a book-length work.

The two things that *are* relevant:

1. How much time you've put into writing. I agree with Malcolm Gladwell's 10,000-hour rule in *Outliers*: The key to success in any field is, to a large extent, a matter of practicing a specific task for a total of around 10,000 hours.

2. Whether you're reading enough to understand where you lie on the spectrum of quality. In his series on storytelling (available on YouTube), Ira Glass says:

> The first couple years that you're making stuff, what you're making isn't so good. It's not that great. It's trying to be good, it has ambitions, but it's not that good. But your taste, the thing that got you into the game, your taste is still killer. Your taste is good enough that you can tell that what you're making is kind of a disappointment to you. You can tell that it's still sort of crappy. A lot of people never get past that phase. A lot of people at that point quit. … Most everybody I know who does interesting creative work, they went through a phase of years where they had really good taste [and] they could tell that what they were making wasn't as good as they wanted it to be.

If you can't perceive the gap—or if you haven't gone through the "phase"—you probably aren't reading enough. How do you develop good taste? You read. How do you understand what quality work is? You read. What's the best way to improve your skills aside from writing more? You read. You write, and you read, and you begin to close the gap between the quality you *want* to achieve, and the quality you *can* achieve. In short: You've got to produce a lot of crap before you can produce something acceptable by traditional publishing standards.

Signs You're Getting Closer to Publication

You start receiving personalized, "encouraging" rejections.

Agents or editors reject the manuscript you submitted, but ask you to send your next work. (They can see that you're on the verge of producing something great.)

Your mentor (or published author friend) tells you to contact his agent, without you asking for a referral.

An agent or editor proactively contacts you because she spotted your quality writing somewhere online or in print.

Looking back, you understand why your work was rejected, and see that it deserved rejection. You probably even feel embarrassed by earlier work.

Knowing When It's Time to Change Course

I used to believe that great work would eventually get noticed—you know, that old theory that quality bubbles to the top?

I don't believe that any more.

Great work is overlooked every day, for a million reasons. Business concerns outweigh artistic concerns. Some people are just perpetually unlucky.

To avoid beating your head against the wall, here are some questions that can help you understand when and how to change course.

1. Is your work commercially viable? Indicators will eventually surface if your work isn't suited for commercial publication. You'll hear things like: "Your work is too quirky or eccentric." "It has narrow appeal." "It's experimental." "It doesn't fit the model." Possibly: "It's too intellectual, too demanding." These are signs that you may need to consider self-publishing—which will also require you to find the niche audience you appeal to.

2. Are readers responding to something you didn't expect? I see this happen all the time: A writer is working on a manuscript that no one seems interested in, but has fabulous success on some side project. Perhaps you really want to push your memoir, but it's a humorous tip series on your blog that everyone loves. Sometimes it's better to pursue what's working, and what people express interest in, especially if you take enjoyment in it. Use it as a steppingstone to other things if necessary.

3. Are you getting bitter? You can't play poor, victimized writer and expect to get published. As it is in romantic relationships, pursuing an agent or editor with an air of desperation, or with an Eeyore complex, will not endear you to them. Embittered writers carry a huge sign with them that screams, "I'm unhappy, and I'm going to make you unhappy, too."

If you find yourself demonizing people in the publishing industry, taking rejections very personally, feeling as if you're owed something, and/or complaining whenever you get together with other writers, it's time to find the refresh button. Return to what made you feel joy and excitement about writing in the first place. Perhaps you've been focusing too much on getting published, and you've forgotten to cherish the other aspects. Which brings me to the overall theory of how you should, at various stages of your career, revisit and revise your publication strategy.

Revising Your Publishing Plan

No matter how the publishing world changes, consider these three timeless factors as you make decisions about your next steps forward:

1. What makes you happy. This is the reason you got into writing in the first place. Even if you put this on the back burner in order to advance other aspects of your writing and publishing career, don't leave it out of the equation for very long. Otherwise your efforts can come off as mechanistic or uninspired, and you'll eventually burn out.

2. What earns you money. Not everyone cares about earning money from writing—and I believe that anyone in it for the coin should find some other field—but as you gain experience, the choices you make in this regard become more important. The more professional you become, the more you have to pay attention to what brings the most return on your investment of time and energy. As you succeed, you don't have time to pursue every opportunity. You have to STOP doing some things.

3. What reaches readers or grows your audience. Growing readership is just as valuable as earning money. It's like putting a bit of money in the bank and making an investment that pays off as time passes. Sometimes you'll want to make trade-offs that involve earning less money in order to grow readership, because it invests in your future. (E.g., for a time you might focus on building a blog or a site, rather than writing for print publication, to grow a more direct line to your fans.)

It is rare that every piece of writing you do, or every opportunity presented, can involve *all three* elements at once. Commonly you can get two of the three. Sometimes you'll pursue certain projects with only one of these factors in play. You get to decide based on your priorities at any given point in time.

At the very beginning of this section, I suggested that it might be nice if someone could tell us if we're wasting our time trying to get traditionally published.

Here's a little piece of hope: If your immediate thought was, *I couldn't stop writing even if someone told me to give up,* then you're much closer to publication than someone who is easily discouraged. The battle is far more psychological than you might think. Those who can't be dissuaded are more likely to reach their goals, regardless of the path they ultimately choose.

The Value of Writing Conferences

It took me a long time to realize it, but your relationships can be among the most important factors in your career growth and success. For this reason alone, it's invaluable that writers attend conferences.

You may wonder: Doesn't social networking replace all that?

No. It's a supplement. It can help keep relationships strong after you meet in-person, or it can spark an in-person meeting. Preferably, you'll use both to establish a vital network.

Why you should attend conferences:

- Your education and insight into the industry advances exponentially. You'll gain an understanding that's often impossible from just reading about it.
- You meet agents and editors, and start to see them as real people.
- You may have an appointment or consultation with a publishing professional, and if so, it will shorten your path to publication. You can get the reasons, immediately, that an agent or editor may not be responding favorably to your work.
- You connect with a peer group, and find people who can be mentors for you, and/or trusted critiquers.
- You get time away from daily life to reflect on your writing goals and next steps.

Many writers are familiar with the reasons to attend conferences, but not all understand how to get more out of them. **Here are 4 ways you can superpower your experience.**

1. Select a conference where you can meet with a specific editor or agent who is absolutely ideal for your work (after lengthy and intensive research). Get an appointment—but only if you feel like your work couldn't be more ready to pitch. This is important.

2. During any formal appointments, plan to talk about 10-20% of the time. Before meeting, develop a specific list of questions that, if you had the answers, you would know specifically what your next steps are (for your project or your career) when you leave. Do not attend any appointment expecting to be offered a deal or representation. Go for the learning experience and the opportunity to have a professional consultation. That's what it is.

3. Closely study the backgrounds/bios of every speaker, agent, and editor who is attending. Be knowledgeable for any chance conversations you have; having this knowledge will also spark questions you could ask during

panels or social hours. Don't be the person who asks the obvious question you could've figured out by paying attention to the program. Delve deeper. Make your questions count.

4. It's been said before, but I'll emphasize it. **Don't miss out on any aspect of a conference. Participate fully.** Introverts are not off the hook. You never know who you might meet or what you might learn that could make a difference later.

CHAPTER 3

A Few Words on Craft

I was probably the only student in my 8th grade class to look forward to English period, and copying down grammar lessons.

My English teacher, Mrs. McKinney, was methodical, strict, and exact about every aspect of the language. She told us precisely how to copy down the lessons, and what kind of paper to use (Steno pads), and we had competitions to see who could diagram sentences the fastest.

Everything I know about grammar I learned from Mrs. McKinney; I never had another teacher who delivered the information so logically and comprehensively. I am eternally grateful.

But if I have a pet peeve with writers (both beginning and published), it's their unrelenting obsession & unforgiving attitude toward errors in grammar, spelling, and punctuation.

Whenever Writer's Digest posts about a grammar issue, it invariably receives the most comments (and fiercest arguments). Whenever or wherever we have a grammatical fumble, in print or online, it's like we've committed a cardinal sin.

I have one thing to say about this: *Lighten up!*

Here's why.

1. Every one of us, from the day we are able to speak, instinctively know the universal grammar. You wouldn't be able to converse with other people if you didn't know it. So why doesn't everyone have perfect written grammar? Primarily because we're all flustered by the rules and regulations surrounding the written word—which is in a state of flux, by the way. To learn more about this issue, read *The Language Instinct* by Steven Pinker.

2. Perfect grammar has nothing to do with great writing. Certainly, I will admit that people who are better at grammar often have more sensitivity for the nuance of language—and tend to be better writers—but for the most part, facility with grammar has nothing to do with storytelling prowess.

So, I hate to see a new/beginning writer worry about grammar, or even apologize in advance that their grammar isn't perfect. I really don't care as long as the language isn't getting in the way of understanding and enjoying the story.

The worry you invest in grammar is energy diverted away from more important aspects of your story, such as characterization and structure. Grammar is a surface-level issue that can taken care of separately, near the end of the writing process, and can even be corrected or polished by someone else.

How to Leave Stuff Out

When I was young, my mom spent hours working on a middle-grade novel. These were the days before word processing, so she used an old Smith Corona electric typewriter. It became a fixture on the dining room table.

Eager to follow in her footsteps, I conceived of my own novel. I bought a spiral-bound notebook and wrote on the cover, "The Adventures of SuperDog." On the first page, I wrote, "Chapter 1."

And so I began to describe how SuperDog came into existence. I mean, it was important to explain the hows and whys of how such a creature came to be, right? This took at least one page.

Then I started thinking of all the other questions his existence raised. How did he manage to buy and supply himself with food on a consistent basis? How did he come to have all of his resources? Where did his magical bone come from? What events led him to getting his powers? This consumed at least Chapters 2 and 3, from what I recall.

I was obsessed with explaining as logically and clearly as possible the ins and outs of this creature, and getting all the day-to-day questions settled, so that readers wouldn't be confused.

It was pretty boring—so boring, in fact, I stopped around Chapter 6 or 7. I can't even remember what the story conflict was. I was too obsessed with the proper setup.

I was too young to know it at the time, but the stuff I was writing was really prep work—character background, setting/environment details, world-building rules—stuff that I needed to know to write the REAL story, but not something I should dump in the first chapters.

My inclination with SuperDog is the inclination most writers have when approaching their first manuscripts: *I've got to show how this world came to be. I need to put in this explanation of why this person is how they are now. I need to show what everyday life is like. I need to … ZZzzzzz.*

It's OK to leave stuff out. You have to, because if you don't, you'll never get to the real story you want to tell. The how-it-all-came-to-be can be related as you go—and some of it can create tension, e.g., "Why IS Jeb so nervous whenever he's around Lucy? When will we learn what happened between them?"

Or: Think of it this way. When you first meet someone new, what do you tell them about yourself? What do they need to know right away? And what will you save for later? You don't have long to convey the whole story on the first date. A lot must be summarized and left to the imagination—and it's better that way at the start.

Perfecting Your First Page

Here are three of the best exercises or tasks you might undertake when thinking about your first page and how you can improve it before sending your manuscript to agents or editors.

1. What is the absolute latest moment in the manuscript you can begin your story, and still not leave out anything that's critical to the story problem? Most manuscripts I read should really start somewhere between page 5 and page 30. Be ruthless in evaluating your opening—have you dawdled in revealing the story problem? Ideally, you've seeded it on page 1.

2. What details do NOT relate to the story problem or the protagonist? We rarely need the complete biography of your main character on the first page. Let those details emerge as the story unfolds. Don't share the everyday, mundane details we could guess. Share the most unique, special, distinctive details—*the ones that really matter to the story and character from the start.* The No. 1 mistake for first pages is overwriting—or working too hard at "painting a picture." If you load up on every single detail, how am I supposed to know which ones are important? Be selective. Be artful.

3. Have you shown or described something that really ought to be quickly summarized (or "told")? Sometimes writers go into flowery description about something that should be flat-out stated. (This is an issue that will remain relevant on every single page of your book.) Joyce Carol Oates once said, "Storytelling is shaped by two contrary, yet complementary, impulses—one toward brevity, compactness, artful omission; the other toward expansion, amplification, enrichment." When it comes to impatient editors and agents, favor brevity and artful omission in your opening pages.

The Biggest Bad Advice About Story Openings

It's probably the most over-repeated and cliché advice—so much so that writers have come to hate hearing it: *Start with action.*

I've critiqued hundreds, maybe thousands, of first pages, and this advice is most to blame for story beginnings that leave the reader in a quivering mass of Why-the-Hell-Do-I-Care-About-This?

Here's why: *The action ought to have context—and be as grounded as possible in a character that we're already starting to love.*

If your opening scene has weak (or no) characterization, but tons of action, this may create a scene that:

- Lacks personality, voice, or viewpoint
- Delivers a stereotypical crisis moment that's full of action or pain, but without a center
- Offers an action scene for the sake of excitement, but without any real connection to the real plot, conflict, or story arc

The story beginnings that I find most compelling offer the following:

- A character I'm beginning to know and understand
- A situation that presents tension for an important character
- An indication of the larger story problem/conflict between characters

Here's a sample of an opening paragraph that does these things:

When she stepped from the Cessna my first thought was that a man can't help but fantasize about a woman like that even if he doesn't much like her. My second thought was that she didn't look the type to venture into the mountains of Idaho where the nearest road is more than thirty miles away and phone service probably twice that. She wore a turquoise blouse, charcoal skirt, and three-inch heels; not the kind of outfit I'd recommend for hiking and riding.

I've also read countless manuscripts that begin by describing a character writhing in pain. Mental pain, physical pain, emotional pain, you name it. For instance:

> John clenched his throat and tried to stop the flow of blood, but he couldn't. His skin became whiter and whiter, and he broke out into a cold sweat. He felt prickles all up and down his back, and his breathing became intensely labored. He squinted into the sun and wondered if this was finally going to be it.

> *[Two paragraphs later, after more pain description]*

> He felt certain he was going to die after getting trampled by a bull moose. He thought about his life as a whole, and was actually pleased at the thought he'd never have to suffer married life again.

Most writers think it is better to dramatize this opening moment of crisis—to SHOW the character in pain or agony.

In fact, it's usually better to come right out and tell, and get to the point quickly. You can grab my attention much more effectively by starting out this way:

> On his third Alaskan hunting trip, it finally happened. John was trampled by a bull moose. His wife tried calling him while it happened but he couldn't reach his cell phone. In that moment it became clear to him: He wanted a divorce.

This is an extreme example, but hopefully the point is made. Dramatizing (or showing) can slow down your first scene to an absolute crawl. It's hard to care about any character's pain until we know that character's conflict, motivation, and overall environment. Later on in the book, when we're on the edge of our seat, wondering what will happen to John, because we care so much about John—that's the time to show and dramatize, and keep us in suspense.

Think about some of your favorite openings in books you've read. Study them. How do they balance showing and telling?

CHAPTER 4
How to Get Traditionally Published

How do I get my book published? It's the most frequently asked question I receive. I'll start by offering the most critical information and address the most pressing questions.

Are you writing fiction or nonfiction?
Novelists follow a different path to publication than nonfiction authors. If you're writing a novel, you must have a finished and polished manuscript before you even think about how to get published. If you're writing nonfiction, you must write a book proposal (basically like a business plan for your book) that will convince a publisher to contract and pay you to write the book. More on that later.

If you're writing a hybrid work (personal vignettes mixed with instruction, or a multi-genre work that includes essays, stories, and poetry), then you will have a difficult time getting a publisher to accept it. Getting published is a step-by-step process of:
- Researching the appropriate agents or publishers for your work.
- Reading submission guidelines of agents and publishers.
- Sending a query, proposal, or submission package.

What is a query letter?
The query letter is the time-honored tool for writers seeking publication. It's essentially a sales letter that attempts to persuade an editor or agent to request a full manuscript or proposal. Almost no agent or editor accepts full manuscripts on first contact.

However, almost every agent or publisher will accept a one-page query letter unless their guidelines state otherwise. (If they do not accept queries, that means they are a completely closed market—closed to new writers or submissions.)

Most major publishers will not accept unagented work. This means many writers should query agents rather than publishers. (We'll discuss agents and query letters in-depth later in this chapter.)

How does one find an agent?

In today's market, probably 80 percent of books that the New York publishing houses acquire are sold to them by agents. Agents are experts in the publishing industry. They have inside contacts with specific editors and know better than writers what editor or publisher would be most likely to buy a particular work.

Perhaps most important, agents negotiate the best deal for you, ensure you are paid accurately and fairly, and run interference when necessary between you and the publisher.

Traditionally, agents get paid only when they sell your work, and receive a 15% commission on everything you get paid (your advance and royalties). It is best to avoid agents who charge fees, though standards are changing.

So ... do you need an agent?

It depends on what you're selling. If you want to be published by one of the major New York houses (e.g., Penguin, HarperCollins, Simon & Schuster, etc), probably.

If you're writing for a niche market (e.g., vintage automobiles), or have an academic or literary work, then you might not need one. Agents are motivated to take on clients based on the size of the advance they think they can get. If your project doesn't command a sizable advance (at least five figures), then you may not be worth an agent's time, and you'll have to sell the project on your own.

Do you have to "know someone" to get published?

No, but referrals, connections or communities can certainly help! See the related question below about conferences.

What about self-publishing and e-publishing?

Self-publishing or e-book publishing options will not get your physical book into stores or lead to many sales unless you're willing to put significant and persistent effort into marketing and promotion. Most self-published authors find that selling their book is just as hard—if not harder than—finding a publisher or agent.

To the credit of many who self-publish, independent authors can be fiercely passionate about their work and their process, and much happier and satisfied going it alone. But those who succeed and profit often devote years of their life, if not their entire lives, to marketing and promoting their work, and have a flair for entrepreneurship. In short: It's a ton of work, like starting a small business (if you do it right).

So, you can self-publish, but it all depends on your goals and what will satisfy you. To learn more about self-publishing, see Chapter 5.

What are the most important things to understand about the publishing industry?

Publishing is a business, just like Hollywood or Broadway. Publishers, editors, and agents support authors or projects that will make money and provide a good return on investment. It used to be that this return on investment could happen over a period of years or several books. Now, it needs to happen with one book and in less than one year.

Professionalism and politeness go a long way toward covering up any amateur mistakes you might make along the way.

Unless you live under a lucky star, you will get rejected again and again and again. The query and submission process takes enormous dedication and persistence. We're talking about years of work. Novelists and memoirists often face the biggest battle—there's enormous competition.

Never call an agent or editor to query or ask questions (or just chat) if you are not a client or author. Never query by telephone—and I wouldn't do it even if the guidelines recommend it. You'll mess it up.

Agents and editors do not want you (a non-client or author) to visit them at their offices. Do not plan a visit to New York and go knocking on doors, and don't ask an agent/editor for a lunch or coffee appointment if you don't have a relationship already. If you'd like to interact with an agent or editor, attend a writers conference.

When working with a traditional publisher, you have to give up a lot of power and control. The publisher gets to decide the cover, the title, the design, the format, the price, etc. You have to go through rounds of revisions and will likely have to change things you don't want to change. But you must approach the process like a professional, not a creative artist.

You must be an active marketer and promoter of your book. If you come to the table with media savvy or an established platform (audience or readership), you'll have an easier time getting that first deal.

For nonfiction authors: Don't go looking for a publishing deal because you're looking for the authority or platform that a book can give you. Rather, you must already have the platform and authority, and thus be qualified to write a book. *You* bring the audience to the publisher, not the reverse.

If you write fiction or memoir, the writing quality matters above all else. Read, practice, and polish. Repeat this cycle endlessly. It's not likely your first attempt will get published. It will likely be your second, third, or fourth attempt. Your writing gets better with practice and time. You mature and develop.

If you write nonfiction, the marketability of your idea (and your platform) matter above all else. The quality of the writing may only need to be serviceable, depending on the category we're talking about. (Certainly there are higher demands for narrative nonfiction than prescriptive.)

Think beyond the book. A lot of writers have dreams of publishing a book because it's a dream that's embedded in our DNA from an early age. We are trained to believe that authors have some higher authority or credibility, and that we've really "arrived" once we deliver that book into the world. But there are ways to be more successful, and spread a message to even more people, that have nothing to do with authoring a book. Make sure that your goals are best served by the book format. Increasingly, in our digital age, a book is a poor option (or the final format) for your message or service.

After how many rejections should you stop?

Some authors are rejected hundreds of times (over a period of years) before they finally get an acceptance. If you put years of time and effort into a project, don't abandon it too quickly. Look at the rejection slips for patterns or a direction about what's not working. Rejections can be lessons to improve your writing.

Ultimately, though, some manuscripts have to be put in the drawer because there is no market, or there isn't a way to revise the work successfully.

Is Your Work Commercially Viable?

Before you begin querying agents or publishers, you should have a reasonably good idea of how commercially viable your work is. Here are the key considerations.

Positive Signs of Commercial Viability
- For first-time novels: approximate length of 80,000 words
- Commercial genre fiction: romance, mystery/thriller, science fiction and fantasy, and young adult genres
- For nonfiction authors: visibility and proven reach to a target readership (otherwise known as platform)

Not as Commercially Viable
- Poetry and short story collections
- Essay collections, column collections, etc
- For nonfiction authors: Trying to write on health/medicine, psychology, or other professional fields when you don't have the authority or credentials to give professional advice (in other words, you're writing based on the experience of an "average" person)
- For most novels: length above 100K or length below 50K
- Memoirs crossed with self-help, as well as memoirs that don't have a fresh/distinctive angle
- Mixed genre works that can't be easily categorized

This is by no means a comprehensive list of all the possible reasons your work might not be commercially viable, but it covers most cases I see.

Writing a Novel Query That Gets Manuscript Requests
The following section focuses on query letters for novels; nonfiction book queries will be addressed in the book proposals section starting on page 50.

The stand-alone query letter has one purpose, and one purpose only: To seduce the agent or editor into reading or requesting your manuscript.

The query is so much of a sales piece that you should be able to write it without having written a single word of the manuscript. For some writers, it represents a completely different way of thinking about your book—it means thinking about your work as a marketable commodity. To think of your book as a *product*, you need to have some distance to see its salable qualities.

Before you begin the query process, **have a finished and polished manuscript ready to go.** It should be the best you can make it. For novels or memoirs, only query when you'd be comfortable with your manuscript appearing as-is between covers on a major chain bookstore shelf.

The 5 Elements of a Novel Query

Every query should include these five elements, in no particular order (except the closing):

1. Personalization: where you customize the letter for the recipient
2. What you're selling: genre/category, word count, title/subtitle
3. Hook: the meat of the query; 100-200 words is sufficient for a novel
4. Bio: sometimes optional for uncredited fiction writers
5. Thank you & closing

The First Paragraph of Your Query

How you should lead varies from writer to writer and from project to project. You put your best foot forward—or you lead with your strongest selling point. Common ways to begin a query:

- You've been vouched for or referred by an existing client of the agent's—or if you're querying a publisher, you might be referred by one of their authors.
- You met the agent/editor at a conference or pitch event where your material was requested (in which case, your query letter doesn't carry as much of a burden).
- You heard the agent/editor speak at a conference or you read something they wrote that indicates they're a good fit for your work.
- You start with your hook—a compelling hook, of course.
- You mention excellent credentials or awards, e.g., you have an MFA from a school that an agent is known to recruit clients from, you've won first prize in a national competition with thousands of entrants, or you have impressive publication credits with prestigious journals or New York publishers.

Many writers don't have referrals or conference meetings to fall back on, so usually the hook becomes the lead for the query letter. Some writers start simple and direct, which is fine: "My [title] is an 80,000-word supernatural romance."

Personalizing the Query: Why It Makes a Difference

Remember, your query is a sales tool, and good salespeople develop a rapport with the people they want to sell to, and show that they understand their needs. Show that you've done your homework, show that you care, and show that you're not blasting indiscriminately.

Will you be automatically rejected for not personalizing your query? No, but if you do take the trouble to personalize it, you'll set yourself apart from the large majority of writers querying, and that's the point.

Example of a Strong, Personalized Lead

In a January interview at the Guide to Literary Agents blog, you praised *The Thirteenth Tale* and indicated an interest in "literary fiction with a genre plot." My paranormal romance *Moonlight Dancer* (85,000 words) blends a literary style with the romance tradition.

The 3 Elements of a Novel Hook

For most writers, it's the hook that does most of the work in convincing the agent/editor to request your manuscript. You need to boil down your story to these three key elements:

1. Protagonist + his conflict
2. The choices the protagonist has to make (or the stakes)
3. The sizzle or the twist

Some genres/categories should add a fourth element: the setting or time period.

What does "sizzle" or "twist" mean? It's that thing that sets your work apart from all others in the genre, that makes your story stand out, that makes it uniquely yours. Sizzle means: This idea isn't tired or been done a million times before.

How do you know if your idea is tired? Well, this is why everyone tells writers to *read* and *read* and *read*. It builds your knowledge and experience of what's been done before in your genre.

When a hook is well written but boring, it's often because it lacks anything fresh. It's the same old formula without distinction. The protagonist feels one-dimensional (or like every other protagonist), the story angle is something we've seen too many times, and the premise doesn't even raise an eyebrow. The agent or editor is thinking, "Sigh. Another one of these?"

This is the toughest part of the hook—finding that special *je ne sais quoi* that makes someone say, "Wow, I've got to see more of this!" And this is often how an editor or agent gauges if you're a storyteller worth spending time on.

Sometimes great hooks can be botched because there is no life, voice, or personality in them. Sometimes so-so hooks can be taken to the next level because they convey a liveliness or personality that is seductive.

You want to be one of those seductive writers, of course.

Hook Construction

You have a few options. These are the most common ways to build the hook.

- "I have a completed [word count & genre] titled [title] about [protagonist name + small description] who [conflict]."
- Answer these questions: What does your character want? Why does he want it? What keeps him from getting it?
- [Character name + description] + [the conflict they're going through] + [the choices they have to make].

Whenever I teach a class where we critique hooks, just about everyone can point out the problems and talk about how to improve them. Why? Because when you're not the writer, you have distance from the work. When you do come across a great novel hook, it feels so natural and easy—like it was effortless to write.

But great novel hooks are often toiled over. To convey a compelling story in just a few words is the test of a great writer.

I often recommend brevity when writing the hook, especially if you lack confidence. Brevity gets you in less trouble. The more you try to explain, the more you'll squeeze the life out of your story. So: Get in, get out. Don't labor over plot twists and turns.

Examples of Brief Hooks

Every day, PublishersMarketplace.com lists book deals that were recently signed at major New York houses. It identifies the title, the author, the publisher/editor who bought the project, and the agent who sold it. It also offers a one-sentence description of the book. These hooks are inevitably well-crafted, and can help you better understand what hooks really excite agents/publishers. While your hook would/should probably get into more detail than the following two examples, these hooks help illustrate how much you can accomplish in just a line or two.

> Bridget Boland's DOULA, an emotionally controversial novel about a doula with a sixth sense [protagonist] who, while following her calling, has to

confront a dark and uncertain future when standing trial for the death of her best friend's baby [protagonist's problem] [a doula with a sixth sense? cool.]

John Hornor Jacobs's SOUTHERN GODS, in which a Memphis DJ [protagonist] hires a recent World War II veteran to find a mysterious bluesman whose music [protagonist's problem] — broadcast at ever-shifting frequencies by a phantom radio station — is said to make living men insane and dead men rise [twist]

Check for Red Flags in Your Hook

How to tell if your hook could be improved:
- Does your hook consist of several meaty paragraphs, or run longer than 200 words? You may be going into too much detail.
- Does your hook reveal the ending of your book? Only the synopsis should do that.
- Does your hook mention more than three or four characters? Usually you only need to mention the protagonist(s), a romantic interest or sidekick, and the antagonist.
- Does your hook get into minor plot points that don't affect the choices the protagonist makes? Do you really need to mention them?

The Key Elements of Your Bio

For novelists, especially unpublished ones, you don't have to include a bio in your query if you can't think of anything worth sharing. But it's nice to put in *something*.

The key to every detail in your bio is: Will it be meaningful—or perhaps charming—to the agent/editor? If you can't confidently answer yes, leave it out. In order of importance, these are the categories of pertinent info.

Publication credits. Be specific about your credits for this to be meaningful. Don't say you've been published "in a variety of journals." You might as well be unpublished if you don't want to name them.

What if you have no fiction writing credits? Should you say you're unpublished? No. That point will be made clear by fact of omission.

Many novelists wonder if it's helpful to list nonfiction credits. Yes, mention notable credits when they show you have some experience working with editors or an understanding of how the professional writing world works. That said: Academic or trade journal credits can be tricky, since they definitely don't convey fiction writing ability. Use your discretion, but it's probably not going to be deal breaker either way.

Online writing credits can be just as worthy as print credits. Popular and well-known online journals and blogs count!

Leave out credits like your church newsletter or credits that hold little to no significance for publishing industry professionals.

Should you mention self-published books? That's totally up to you. Sooner or later this information will have to come out, so it's all about best timing. Lots of people have self-published, and it doesn't really hurt your chances. If you do mention it, it's best if you're proud of your efforts and are ready to discuss your success (or failure) in doing it. If you consider it a mistake or irrelevant to the project at hand, leave it out, and understand it may come up later.

Do not make the mistake of thinking your self-publishing credits make you somehow more desirable as an author, unless you have really incredible sales success, in which case, mention the sales numbers of your book and how long it's been on sale—and at what price point.

Work/career. If your career or profession lends you credibility to write a better story, by all means mention it. But don't go into lengthy detail. Teachers of K-12 who are writing children's/YA often mention their teaching experience as some kind of credential for writing children's/YA, but it's not, so don't treat it like one in the bio. (Perhaps it goes without saying, but parents should not treat their parental status as a credential to write for children either.)

Writing credibility. It makes sense to mention any writing-related degrees you have, any major professional writing organizations you belong to (e.g., RWA, SCBWI), and possibly any major events/retreats/workshops you've attended to help you develop your career as a writer.

You needn't say that you frequent such-and-such online community, or that you belong to a writers' group the agent would've never heard of. (Mentioning this won't necessarily hurt you, but it's not proving anything either.)

Avoid cataloguing every single thing you've ever done in your writing life. Don't talk about starting to write when you were in second grade. Don't talk about how much you've improved your writing in the last few years. Don't talk about how much you enjoy returning to writing in your retirement.

Just mention 1 or 2 highlights that prove your seriousness and devotion to the craft of writing. If unsure, leave it out.

Special research. If your book is the product of some intriguing or unusual research (you spent a year in the Congo), mention it. These unique details can catch the attention of an editor or agent.

Major awards/competitions. Most writers should not mention awards or competitions they've won because they are too small to matter. If the award isn't widely recognizable to the majority of publishing professionals, then the only way to convey the significance of an award is to talk about how many people you beat out. Usually the entry number needs to be in the thousands to impress an agent/editor.

Charming, ineffable you. If your bio can reveal something of your voice or personality, all the better. While the query isn't the place to digress or mention irrelevant info, there's something to be said for expressing something about yourself that gives insight into the kind of author you are—that ineffable you. Charm helps.

It's okay to say nothing at all about yourself. If you have no meaningful publication credits, don't try to invent any. If you have no professional credentials, no research to mention, no awards to your name—nothing notable at all to share—don't add a weak line or two in an attempt to make up for it. Just end the letter. You're still completely respectable.

Don't bother mentioning these things (as a novelist). Unless you know the agent/editor wants to hear about these things, you don't need to discuss:

- Your social media presence
- Your online platform
- Your marketing plan
- Your years of effort and dedication
- How much your family/friends love your work
- How many times you've been rejected or close accepts

Sometimes you might mention your website or blog, especially if you feel confident about its presentation. The truth is the agent/editor is going to Google you anyway, and find your website/blog whether you mention it or not (unless you're writing under a different name). Keep in mind that having an online presence helps show you'll likely be a good marketer and promoter of your work—especially if you have a sizable readership already—but it doesn't say anything about your ability to write a great story. That said, if you have 100,000+ fans/readers on Wattpad or at your blog, that should be in your query letter.

Example of a Solid Bio

A professional writer for more than 30 years, I've had short stories published in literary journals such as Toasted Cheese and The Missouri Review. My first novel manuscript was a finalist for a James Jones Fellowship. I am co-founder and editor of the online literary journal Cezanne's Carrot, and also write the blog Writers In The Virtual Sky.

Close Your Letter Professionally

You don't read much advice about how to close a query letter, perhaps because there's not much to it, right? You say thanks and sign your name. But here's how to leave a good final impression.

- **You don't have to state that you are simultaneously querying.** Everyone assumes this. (I do not recommend exclusive queries; send queries out in batches of three to five—or more, if you're confident in your query quality.)
- **If your manuscript is under consideration at another agency**, then mention it if/when the next agent requests to see your manuscript.
- **If you have a series in mind**, this is a good time to mention it. But don't belabor the point; it should take a sentence.
- **Never mention your "history" with the work**, e.g., how many agents you've queried, or how many near misses you've suffered, or how many compliments you've received on the work from others.
- **Resist the temptation to editorialize.** This is where you proclaim how much the agent will love the work, or how exciting it is, or how it's going to be a bestseller if only someone would give it a chance, or how much your kids enjoy it, or how much the world needs this work.
- **Thank the agent, but don't carry on unnecessarily,** or be incredibly subservient—or beg. ("I know you're very busy and I would be forever indebted and grateful if you would just look at a few pages.")
- **There's no need to go into great detail about when and how you're available.** Make sure the letter includes, somewhere, your phone number, e-mail address, and return address. (Include an self-addressed stamped envelope for snail mail queries.) I recommend putting your contact info at the very top of the letter, or at the very bottom, under your name, rather than in the query body itself.
- **Do not introduce the idea of an in-person meeting.** Do not say you'll be visiting their city soon, and ask if they'd like to meet for coffee. The only possible exception to this is if you know you'll hear

them speak at an upcoming conference—but don't ask for a meeting. Just say you look forward to hearing them speak. Use the conference's official channels to set up an appointment if any are available.

Query Letter Red Flags

Here is an overall list of things to double-check in your query letter.

- If it runs longer than 1 page (single spaced), you've said too much.
- Avoid directly commenting on the quality of your work. Your query should show what a good writer you are, rather than you telling or emphasizing what a good writer you are.
- On the flip side: Don't criticize yourself, or the quality of the work, in the letter.
- Don't editorialize your story for the agent/editor, almost as if you were writing a review of the work. ("In this fast-paced thriller," "in a final twist that will change your world," "you'll laugh, you'll cry, …"
- Do not explain how or why you came to write the story, unless it is really interesting or integral to the work.
- Do not talk about how you've wanted to write since you were a child.
- Do not talk about how much your family and friends love your work.
- Avoid heavy use of adjectives, adverbs, and modifiers. In fact, try creating a version of your query without *any* modifiers, and see what happens.
- When it comes to selling fiction, you don't have to talk about the trends in the market, or about the target audience. You sell the story. (However, for nonfiction queries, you do talk about trends and market, which is why some writers are confused over this point.)

Tell me more about exclusives—what are they?

This is when an agent responds positively to your query and asks for an exclusive read on your manuscript. That means no one else can read the manuscript while they're considering it. I don't recommend granting an exclusive unless it's for a very short period (maybe 2 weeks).

In non-exclusive situations (which should be most situations): If you have a second request for the manuscript before you hear back from the first agent, then as a courtesy, let the second agent know it's also under consideration elsewhere (though you needn't say with whom). If the second agent offers you representation first, go back to the first agent and let her know you've been made an offer, and give her a chance to respond.

Should I compare my book to another title, or compare myself to another author?

This can be helpful as long as you do it tastefully, and without self-aggrandizement. It's usually best to compare the work in terms of style, voice, or theme, rather than in terms of sales, success, or quality.

Is it better to query via e-mail, if allowed?

Yes. E-mail can lead to faster response times. However, I've heard many writers complain that they never receive a response. (Sometimes silence is the new rejection.) This is a phenomenon that must be regrettably accepted. Send one follow-up to inquire, but don't keep sending e-mails to ascertain if your e-query was received.

How can I format the e-mail query properly?
- Write your query in Word or TextEdit. Strip out all formatting. (Usually there is an option under "Save As" that will allow you to save as simple text.)
- Send the query without any formatting and without any indents (block style).
- Use CAPS for anything that would normally be in italics.
- Don't use address, date headers, or contact information at the beginning of the e-mail; put all of that stuff at the bottom, underneath your name
- The first line should read: "Dear [Agent Name]:"

Some writers structure their e-queries differently than paper queries (or make them shorter). Consider how much the agent can see of your e-query on the first screen, without scrolling. That's probably how far they will read before responding or hitting delete. Adjust your query accordingly. Usually the hook should go first, unless you have a strong personalization angle.

I have an e-mail address for an editor/agent who doesn't accept e-mail queries. Should I try them anyway?

You can try, but you probably won't receive a response.

How soon can I follow up if I don't hear back?

Try following up 2-4 weeks after the stated response time. If no response time is given, wait a couple of months. If querying via snail mail, include another copy of the query. If you still don't hear back after one follow-up attempt, assume it's a rejection, and move on. Do not phone or visit.

Is it OK to tell agents/editors to visit my website for more info?
Avoid this. Agents should have all the information they need to make a decision right in your query letter. (Of course, most of them will Google you anyway and check out your online presence to get a sense of how you might be to work with.) It's OK to list your website or blog as part of your contact info; just don't tell agents in the body of the query to visit your site for more info, or to read your book at your site.

Should I send a synopsis with the query?
Only if requested in the submission guidelines. (There's more to come on the synopsis.)

Additional Query Resources
If you'd like to read more on the art of query letters, my favorite online resources are:

- QueryShark: an opportunity to get your query critiqued + read others critiqued
- Agent Rachelle Gardner's website
- Former agent Nathan Bransford's website and guide to query letters

To identify the right agents or publishers to query, these are the best resources:

- PublishersMarketplace (subscription required)
- WritersMarket.com (subscription required)
- AgentQuery: free listings of literary agents

Don't forget to look at agency websites as you begin to select and customize your queries and submissions for each agent.

The Nonfiction Book Proposal

A book proposal argues why your nonfiction book (idea) is a salable, marketable product. It is essentially a business case or a business plan for your book.

Instead of writing the entire book—then trying to find a publisher or agent (which is how it works with novels)—**you write the proposal first**, which convinces the editor or agent to contract you to write the book.

Book proposals aren't something you dash off in a day or two. They can take weeks or months to write if properly developed and researched. A proposal can easily reach 50 pages, even 100 for complex projects.

New writers might find it easier to simply write the book first, then prepare a proposal—which isn't such a bad idea, since many editors and agents want assurance that an unknown writer can produce an entire book before they commit. (But having the manuscript complete does not negate the need for the proposal.)

That said, drafting a proposal first (even sketching it) can give you a better idea of what your book needs to include to make it stand apart from competing titles.

Note: You may occasionally hear someone refer to novel proposals, which includes a query or cover letter, a synopsis and/or outline, and a partial or complete manuscript—along with any other information the editor or agent requests. This bears little to no relation to a typical nonfiction book proposal.

When is a proposal NOT needed?

The easiest answer is: When the agent or editor doesn't require it in their submission guidelines. This can be the case with memoir, where the quality of the writing or manuscript holds more weight than the business case.

Generally speaking: When your book is more about information or a compelling idea, then you're selling it based on the marketability of your expertise, your platform, and your concept—and you need a proposal.

If your book will succeed based on its literary merit (its ability to entertain or tell a story), then it becomes more important to have a completed manuscript that proves your strength as a writer.

Producing a Salable or Marketable Nonfiction Book Idea

Usually some level of expertise is necessary to produce a successful nonfiction book, especially for fields such as health, self-help, or parenting, where no one will trust your advice without recognized credentials. Your background must convey authority and instill confidence in the reader. (Would you, as a reader, trust a health book by an author with no experience or degrees?)

Some types of nonfiction, especially narrative nonfiction and memoir, can be written by anyone with proven journalistic or storytelling skills.

It's probably safe to assume that your memoir is not salable unless you're confident of several things.

- Your writing must be outstanding. If your memoir is your very first book or very first writing attempt, then it may not be good enough to pass muster with an editor or agent.

- You must have a compelling and unusual story to tell. If you're writing about situations that affect thousands (or millions) of people, that's not necessarily in your favor. Alzheimer's memoirs or cancer memoirs, for example, are common, and will put you on the road to rejection unless you're able to prove how yours is unique or outstanding in the field.
- You need a platform. If you have a way to reach readers, without a publisher's help, then you're more likely to get a book deal.

Whether or not you need an agent for your nonfiction book depends on several factors:

- Are you writing a book that has significant commercial value?
- Do you want to publish with a New York house?
- Do you need the expertise and knowledge of an agent to get your proposal into the right hands?

If the answer to any of these questions is yes, then you should probably look for an agent. Projects that don't necessarily require agents include scholarly works for university presses; regional works likely to be published by regional or independent presses; and works with little commercial value.

How to Prepare a Book Proposal

For better or worse, there is no "right way" to prepare a book proposal, just as there is no right way to write a book. Proposals vary in length, content, approach, and presentation. Each book requires a unique argument for its existence (or a business case), and thus requires a unique proposal. For example, a coffee table book on dogs would be pitched differently than a scholarly tome on presidents, or an exposé on a celebrity.

However, these three questions will be running through the mind of every publishing professional who considers your project. Make sure, as a whole, your proposal effectively answers them.

1. So what? This is the reason for the book's existence, the unique selling proposition that sets it apart from others in the market.

2. Who cares? This is your target readership. A unique book is not enough—you must show evidence of need in the marketplace for your work.

3. Who are you? You must have sufficient authority or credentials to write the book, as well as an appropriate marketing platform for the subject matter or target audience.

Writing a nonfiction book proposal—a good one—requires not only sharp clarity about your idea, but also how that idea, in book form, is relevant and unique in today's market. Some authors have a very deep knowledge of the community surrounding their topic, and understand the needs of their audience. Others do not.

Either way, you'll have a much easier time writing your proposal if you take time to conduct market research beforehand, as well as develop an analysis of your existing reach to your readership. (Those methods will be discussed below.)

Before I detail the most common elements of a proposal, I want to emphasize again: Editors care about one thing only: A viable idea with a clear market, paired with a writer who has credibility and marketing savvy. Knowing your audience or market—and having direct, tangible reach to them (online or off)—gives you a much better chance of success. Pitch only the book you know has a firm spot in the marketplace. Do *not* pitch a book expecting that the publisher will bring the audience to you. It's the other way around. *You bring your audience and platform to the publisher.*

1. Cover page and the proposal's table of contents

Long proposals should have a table of contents.

2. Overview

A one-to-three page summary of your *entire* proposal. Write it last—it needs to sing and present a water-tight business case. Think of it as the executive summary.

3. Target market

Who will buy your book? What's the target demographic or ideal reader? Why will they spend $20 or more to read your book? Avoid generic statements like these:

- *A Google search result on [topic] turns up more than 10 million hits.*
- *A U.S. Census shows more than 20 million people in this demographic.*
- *An Amazon search turns up 10,452 books with "dog" in the title.*

These are meaningless statistics. The following statements show better market insight:

Three major sites focus on my topic at [URLs], and none of them have been updated since 2009. When I posted current information about this topic on my site, it became the leading referral of traffic for me, with more than 100 people visiting each day as a result.

Media surveys indicate that at least 50% of people in [demographic] plan to spend about $1,000 on their hobby this year, and 60% indicated they buy books on [topic].

The 5 most highly ranked titles on Amazon on this topic are now all at least 5 years out of date. Recent reviewers complain the books are not keeping up with new information and trends.

4. Competitive analysis

Researching for books similar to your own (or competitive titles) is usually the best way to begin writing your proposal. Fully understanding the competition and its strengths/weaknesses should help you write a better proposal.

To begin the research process, visit the bookstores in your area—the library, too. Go to the shelf where you would expect your future book to be placed. What's there? Study the books closely and take notes.

After you finish combing the bookstores and libraries, check specialty retailers that might carry books on your topic (e.g., Michaels for arts and crafts books). Finally, do an online search, beginning with Amazon; then try Google. Search any other sites that might be important to your book's audience.

Once you have a clear idea of the competitive landscape, you're ready to write the competitive analysis. This section describes the most important competing book titles and why yours is different or better. (Resist trashing the competition; it will come back to bite you.) Don't skimp here—editors can tell when you haven't done your homework.

Whatever you do, don't claim there are NO competitors to your book. If there are truly no competitors, then your book might be so weird and specialized that it won't sell.

Most importantly, don't limit yourself to print book titles when analyzing the competition. Today, your greatest competition is probably a website, online community, or well-known blogger. Your proposal should evaluate not just competing print books, but also websites, digital content, and online experts serving the same audience. Google your topic and the problem it solves. What terms would people search for if they wanted information or a solution? What turns up? Is it easy to get needed and authoritative information? Is it free or behind a pay wall?

Where do online experts and authorities send people for more information? Do they frequently reference books? Ask your local librarian where they would look for information on the topic you're writing about.

In many nonfiction topics and categories, the availability of online information can immediately kill the potential for a print book unless:

- You have a very compelling platform and means of reaching your target audience, and they prefer books.
- You already reach an online market and they are clamoring for a book.
- You are writing something that isn't best served through an online experience.

Many book ideas I see pitched should really start out as a site or community—even if only to test-market the idea, to learn more about the target audience, and to ultimately produce a print product that has significant value and appeal in its offline presentation.

5. Author bio and platform

Explain why you're the perfect authority or professional to write and promote the book. What gives you credibility with the audience or market? More on this below.

6. Marketing and promotion plan

What can you specifically do to market and promote the book? Never discuss what you *hope* to do, only what you *can* and *will* do (without publisher assistance), given your current resources.

Many people write their marketing plan in extremely tentative fashion, talking about things they are "willing" to do if asked. This is deadly language. Avoid it. Instead, you need to be confident, firm, and direct about everything that's going to happen with or without the publisher's help. Make it concrete, realistic, and attach numbers to everything.

Weak: I plan to register a domain and start a blog for my book.
Strong: Within 6 months of launch, my blog on [book topic] already attracts 5,000 unique visits per month.

Weak: I plan to contact bloggers for guest blogging opportunities.
Strong: I have also guest blogged every month for the past year to reach another 250,000 visitors, at sites such as [include 2-3 examples of most

well-known blogs]. I have invitations to return on each site, plus I've made contact with 10 other bloggers for future guest posts.

Weak: I plan to contact conferences and speak on [book topic].
Strong: I am in contact with organizers at XYZ conferences, and have spoken at 3 events within the past year reaching 5,000 people in my target audience.

The secret of a marketing plan isn't the number of ideas you have for marketing, or how many things you are willing to do, but how many solid connections you have—the ones that are already working for you—and how many readers you NOW reach through today's efforts. You need to show that your ideas are not just pie in the sky, but real action steps that will lead to concrete results and a connection to an existing readership.

7. Chapter outline or table of contents
Briefly describe each chapter, if appropriate.

8. Sample chapters
Include at least one—the strongest, meatiest chapter. Don't try to get off easy by using the introduction.

How to Submit Your Book Proposal
Check the submission guidelines of the agent or publisher. Sometimes you have to query before sending the proposal; often you can send the book proposal on first contact. The submission guidelines will also indicate any mandatory information that must be included in the proposal.

As far as *querying* with your nonfiction book project, you can usually pickup entire paragraphs from your book proposal overview and use it as the basis of your query letter. The query has to concisely answer the same three questions demanded of the proposal as a whole: So What? Who cares? Who are you?

Most Common Problems in Book Proposals
- You concentrate only on the content of the book or your own experience—instead of the book's hook and benefit and appeal to the marketplace.
- There's no clearly defined market or need—or a market/audience

that's too niche for a commercial publisher to pursue.

- Your concept is too general/broad, or has no unique angle.
- You want to do a book based on your own amateur experience of overcoming a problem or investigating a complex issue. (No expertise or credentials.)
- The proposed idea is like a million others; nothing compelling sets the book apart.

Very often, I find authors who have taken a very niche nonfiction book and attempted to approach an agent or big publisher. Consider if there's a smaller publisher that would be interested because they have a lower threshold of sales to meet. Big houses may want to sell as many as 20,000 copies in the first year to justify publication; smaller presses may be fine with a few thousand copies.

You may also have trouble getting positive responses because you're not pitching your work with a marketer's eye. Think about how you might interest a perfect stranger in your topic. Have you really tapped into current trends and interests when it comes to your book project, and are you framing it in an exciting way for a publisher (or agent)? Just because you're fascinated by your subject doesn't mean other people will get it. You have to know how to sell it.

The Question of Author Platform

If you want the best possible deal from a commercial, New York house, they will want to know:

- The stats and analytics behind your online following, including all websites, blogs, social media accounts, e-mail newsletters, regular online writing gigs, podcasts, videos, etc.
- Your offline following—speaking engagements, events, classes/teaching, city/regional presence, professional organization leadership roles and memberships, etc.
- Your presence in traditional media (regular gigs, features, any coverage you've received, etc.)
- Sales of past books or self-published works

You typically need tens of thousands of engaged followers, and verifiable influence with those followers (known as a platform) to interest a major publisher. Make sure that every number you mention is offered with context. Avoid statements like these: *I have 3,000 friends on Facebook* or *I have 5,000 followers on Twitter.* These numbers are fairly meaningless as far as engagement. You have to tell the story behind the numbers. For instance:

Better: More than 30 percent of my Twitter followers have retweeted me, and my links get clicked an average of 50 times.

Better: I run regular giveaway events on Facebook, and during the last event, more than 500 people sent their favorite quote on [topic] to be considered for the giveaway—and to also be considered for the book.

Show that you know your market in a meaningful way, show specifically how and where the market is engaged and growing, and show the engaged role you have.

Consider If Your Book Should Be a Blog or a Website

Some nonfiction topics actually work better when presented on blogs, websites, or communities/forums—where interactivity and an ability to freshen up the content at a moment's notice has more appeal to your audience.

Traditional houses are pickier than ever; producing anything in print is a significant investment and risk. They need to know there's an audience waiting to buy. And, given the significant change in the industry, authors shouldn't consider a print book their first goal or the end goal, but merely one channel, and usually not the best channel.

Additional Resources

For more help, I recommend Michael Larsen's *How to Write a Book Proposal*, the most definitive guide on the topic since the 1980s. It will step you through every single page of your book proposal.

For Memoirists

If you're writing a memoir, and it's your *very first attempt* at writing (or writing seriously for publication), odds are good that you won't yet be skillful enough to pass muster with an agent or editor.

Many people are sparked to write a memoir after they overcome great pain and adversity in their lives, as a means of catharsis, as well as to help others going through the same thing.

But just because you experienced something (and overcame personal adversity) doesn't mean a publisher will find your work marketable—unless you are a celebrity, have an amazing platform, or outstanding connections/endorsements.

So: Either put your blood, sweat, and tears into writing a kick-ass memoir that stuns people with its artfulness and well-crafted narrative ... OR ... get active online, offering support, encouragement, and advice on your own site/blog, or in communities focused on the challenge you overcame. If your true goal is to help people, this approach is likely to be far more effective and fulfilling than trying to publish a book.

The Most Common Memoir Challenge

For memoir, you use yourself as the lens through which readers see the world. You can change the focus or direction of the lens (your eye or your perspective), but it's not wise to consistently focus on the lens itself—or, the inner workings and specifics of your turmoil. It's much better to write scenes and describe experiences to evoke a feeling in the reader, rather than tell them how to feel, or to navel gaze.

Here are the most common flaws that I see in memoir manuscripts I review at conferences.

1. You have written a story focused on pain or victimhood—and nothing more. By far the most common problem is an unrelenting focus on the visceral experience of personal pain and anxiety—usually related to the death of a loved one, the tragedy of illness, or the short-term and long-term effects of abuse. You get extra (negative) bonus points if you wrote it as part of a grieving process, either at the recommendation of a therapist or as part of a therapy group.

Writing through grief and tragedy is a proven method to heal, but it is not a proven method for getting published. I say this not to be insensitive, but to bring needed attention to the fact that these stories are prevalent, and very few publishing houses are accepting them. This is especially true of stories of abuse, cancer, and caring for aging parents.

2. Your source material is a diary or journal. And you're using that as your rough draft, or the book is structured in that manner. Such materials are fine for inspiration and to remember vivid details. But very few diaries or journals are suitable starting places for a publishable memoir.

3. You want to tell about your experience as a means of self-help for others—that is, you mix the memoir and self-help genres. I have never seen this work on the page. You have to choose one or the other. Self-help is a better option if you have the credentials/authority to back up your advice. Life experience, or overcoming a personal challenge, is not enough expertise to help others, especially when it comes to physical and mental health.

4. You have no definitive story arc or story problem. Are you attempting to tell everything about your life, from beginning to end, starting with childhood, where you were born, where you went to school, leaving no stone unturned? Why? Are you sure it's essential to the story? Memoirs need a beginning, middle, and end, and there needs to be a story problem, just as you would find in a novel. And it needs to be told in scenes, and have characters. And you need to leave out a lot of detail.

5. The story is not told with a fresh or distinct perspective. You need to find the voice or perspective that makes the story compelling and offers vibrancy, and create an effective and engaging dramatic persona.

One of the more fascinating pieces I've read on memoir was in a July 2002 article in *Writer's Digest* magazine. W.W. Norton editor Alane Salierno Mason discussed the difference between the "I" memoir (which is all about the narrator) and the "eye" memoir (which is about point of view and relationship to the greater world as well as self).

Most people I meet are writing the "I" memoir, but it leads to a lot of talking and talking and talking (as Mason points out), and unless that talking is absolutely captivating, it's tough to take the project further than your own friends and family.

Writing a Novel Synopsis

The synopsis conveys the narrative arc of your novel; it shows what happens and who changes, from beginning to end. Sometimes agents require them as part of your submission package.

There is no single "right" way to write a synopsis. You'll also find conflicting advice about the appropriate length, which makes it rather confusing territory for new writers especially. However, I recommend keeping it short, or at least starting short. Write a 1-page synopsis and use that as your default, unless the submission guidelines ask for something longer. Most agents/editors will not be interested in a synopsis longer than a few pages.

Why the Synopsis Is Important to Agents and Editors

The synopsis ensures character actions and motivations are realistic and make sense. A synopsis will reveal any big problems in your story—e.g., the whole thing was a dream, ridiculous acts of god, a romance with an unhappy ending. A synopsis will reveal plot flaws, serious gaps in character motivation, or a lack of structure. A synopsis also can reveal how fresh your story is; if there's nothing surprising or unique, your manuscript may not get read.

Some agents hate synopses and never read them; this is more typical for agents who represent literary work. Either way, agents usually aren't expecting a work of art. You can impress with lean, clean, powerful language.

How to Craft a Synopsis

Start off strong; it will probably be similar to the hook that's in your query letter. Identify your protagonist, the protagonist's conflict, and the setting by the end of the first paragraph. Decide which major plot turns or conflicts must be conveyed for everything to make sense, and which characters must be mentioned. (You should not mention all of them.) Think about your genre's "formula," if there is one, and be sure to include all major turning points associated with that formula. The ending paragraph must show how major conflicts are resolved—yes, you have to reveal the ending! No exceptions.

General principles
- Tell what happens in an energetic, compelling way
- Use active voice, not passive
- Use third person, present tense
- Clarity, clarity, clarity
- Less is more—a good thing for you!

4 things you must accomplish, no exceptions
- Give a clear idea of your book's core conflict
- Show what characters we'll care about, including the ones we'll hate
- Demonstrate what's at stake for the main character(s)
- Show how the conflict is resolved

Common pitfalls
- Mentioning too many characters or events; *you have to leave stuff out!*
- Including too much detail about plot twists and turns
- Unnecessary detail, description, or explanation; every word must earn its due
- Confusing series of events and character interactions
- Writing flap copy rather than a synopsis (do not editorialize, e.g., "in a thrilling turn of events!")

A synopsis should include the characters' feelings and emotions. That means it should not read like a mechanic's manual to your novel's plot. You must include both story advancement and color. Think of it this way:

Incident (Story Advancement) + Reaction (Color) = Decision (Story Advancement)

Aside from mechanical plot descriptions, wordiness is typically the No. 1 problem in a synopsis. Here's an example of what I mean.

Very Wordy: At work, Elizabeth searches for Peter all over the office and finally finds him in the supply room, where she tells him she resents the remarks he made about her in the staff meeting.

Tight: At work, Elizabeth confronts Peter about his remarks at the staff meeting.

If you're seeking more insight into synopses, more than 100 synopses are critiqued by an agent at the Miss Snark archive on synopses writing. (Search for the terms "Miss Snark novel synopses" in Google.)

How Do You Know If Your Agent Is Any Good?

Oftentimes, writers shouldn't ask "How can I find an agent?" but "How can I find the *right* agent?" Here are some broad criteria for evaluating an agent.

1. Track record of sales. This is usually the No. 1 sign of whether you have a "good" agent: the characteristics of their client list and the publishers they have recently sold to. Are the publishers they sell to the types of publishers you consider appropriate for your work? Are the advances their clients command in the "good" range for you? These factors can be somewhat subjective, and are also based on your genre/category and your own sense of author identity.

Bottom line, ensure that your agent has experience and success in representing the type of work you're trying to sell. Most agents will list current clients on their site, or you can find records of agent-publisher deals at PublishersMarketplace.

If the agent doesn't have the experience or connections you would expect, then ask them about it (respectfully, of course). Publishing tends to be driven by relationships and reputation, and if your agent is trying to break into new business territory with your book, you might regret it later.

A note about new agents: Sometimes it's easier to get represented by a new agent who is trying to build a roster of clients. If you're a new author with a potentially small deal that wouldn't interest an established agent, then a new and "hungry" agent can work out just as well.

Even if an agent's track record is still developing, take a look at their previous experience in publishing (for example, were they formerly an editor?) and the experience and reputation of the agency they are associated with. If they're working at a solid agency with a track record, and/or have a long work history with the New York houses, these are good signs. Just make sure they haven't been trying to develop their list for a *very* long time.

2. Industry professionalism and respect. This can be tough for an outsider to gauge, but if they're treating you professionally, then it's a good sign. Timeless signs of professionalism: They get back to you in a timely manner, they communicate clearly and respectfully, their business operations aren't cloaked in secrecy, they treat you as an equal.

However: I have observed some unpublished writers who seem to be *very* demanding and have expectations outside the norm. What does *demanding* look like? Expecting to call your agent at any time and have a discussion, expecting daily contact, or expecting near-instant response. Remember: Most agents work for free until your book is sold. Their most immediate responses go to their established clients (who are bringing in revenue).

3. Enthusiasm. Do you get the feeling that the agent genuinely believes in you and your work? While agents are certainly interested in a sale, they're also interested in projects that excite them and clients they are proud to represent.

While it's not possible to put a quantitative measure on "enthusiasm," think of it this way: Your agent is going to be handling your publisher contracts, negotiations, and other financial matters (including payment to you) for the life of your work. You need to trust them completely. They champion your cause to the publisher throughout the life of the book's publication and resolve conflicts. You're entering into a meaningful business partnership, and fit is important.

Just as you wouldn't marry simply anyone, don't partner with just any agent.

Once you have an agent, here are some things that might happen.

It's now very common for agents to say, "I could have sold it 5 years ago." That's probably because it's true. I hope the agent is giving you more specifics about why this is the case. Is the market oversaturated on your topic? Are publishers demanding authors have bigger platforms? Have publishers cut back on their list? Are they unwilling to take even the smallest risk? Are bookstores not buying this category like they were before? Etc.

The agent might advise you what would make your book more marketable. If your agent is receiving the same type of rejection again and again, perhaps the industry won't support the type of book you're trying to sell. Or, if there is consistent publisher confusion about what your book is about, you and your agent should be having a conversation about how to address it. Publishers should be offering enough feedback so that your agent can discuss with you how your book or the proposal could be repositioned to sell. However, the agent's creative energy might be exhausted if he believes the project would take far more work and retooling to make a sale that's not worth his time. Or, he might not believe you're willing to reposition the book.

The agent should let you know what imprints/publishers he has contacted and has been rejected by. It's your right to know this information, especially after a long period of time has passed. You may also ask for the rejection letters, though your agent is under no obligation to provide you with specific contact information of editors and publishers.

While there are many well-meaning agents out there, it's true that some of them are amateurish, incompetent, or bad. Here are some issues to consider.

Did the agent help you improve your query, pitch, and/or proposal? A good agent will not take an author's query/proposal package without going through a revision process. There might be a handful of authors who can put together a crackerjack proposal, but they are few. An agent should be ensuring the pitch or proposal is primed for success, and this almost always requires at least one round of feedback or revision.

Your agent should not have to advertise for clients. Do not respond to advertisements from agents seeking clients. Also, if an agent contacts you, a red flag should go up. While agents do seek out clients, it's usually because an author has received recent publicity or attention (e.g., a personal essay or story of yours just appeared in a prestigious publication, or your blog was just ranked in the Top 10 by a major media outlet). A red flag should also go up if the agent makes all kinds of promises to you, praises you beyond reason, etc (and especially if these promises are followed up by a request for a fee).

People in the industry should recognize the name of your agent. Again, publishing is relationship driven, so editors and publishers should know who your agent is. If you can't find any online mention or reference to your agent, *and* they're not a member of AAR, that's a red flag. Check their track record carefully. See who they've sold to and how recently.

For more excellent information on how to tell a good agent from a not-so-good agent, visit the Writer Beware website and look for the section on literary agents.

Pitching Your Work at Writing Conferences

Most writing conferences offer opportunities to meet with agents or editors one-on-one and pitch your work, and I've read and listened to hundreds if not thousands of pitches. While I think it's important for writers to get out there and interact with and understand professionals in the business, I also think pitching can be a very difficult process. Here's why.

1. You may have little experience or practice in pitching, and walk into the pitches unbelievably nervous and anxious. All of that anxious energy usually detracts from the quality of the pitch. (So many writers fill the first few minutes with apologies for being nervous—not sure what to do, or what to say.) While it's a skill I wish more writers would practice (the art of persuasion or the art of selling), most writers expect their heart and passion to carry them. Sometimes it works, sometimes not.

2. You may consider the pitch a make-it-or-break-it moment—like awaiting the official verdict on whether your idea is worthy of further review and publication. The reality is that in-person pitches have about the same success rate as a cold query (less than 1% in my experience).

3. Because you are so focused on this mythic opportunity (and hearing that "yes" or "no" verdict), **you might miss out on the greater benefit of the pitch experience**—getting instant feedback on your project, or having a meaningful conversation about the market for your work. Such information can dramatically reduce future frustration and shorten your path to publication. Sometimes just five minutes of very insightful professional advice can change your perspective, approach, or slant. Plus flexibility and openness to change in today's publishing environment is important to long-term career growth and success.

4. Most pitch sessions don't offer enough time to have a solid conversation about your best path forward (next steps). At least 75% of the writers I meet with have a fuzzy or misdirected goal or path, and no clear idea of how to make progress. Ten minutes (or less!) probably isn't enough time to have a coaching session, plus most writers are so focused on the pitch they aren't in the right mindset to receive redirection. (Not to mention that such redirection can be a huge blow to a writer because it equates to rejection.)

5. Most writers don't experience the pitch process as part of the busi-

ness of being a writer. Most writers I meet experience the pitch as a highly intense, emotional, and personal process. Unfortunately, whenever engaging in a business conversation (which is what a pitch is), it's important to have some distance and perspective. That's why I always love meeting potential authors who have a business or marketing background, because they know that getting an idea shot down isn't personal, and they're more likely to be receptive to a conversation about marketability of a project and alternative routes to success.

Bottom line: Sometimes it's more valuable and important to know if you're headed in the right direction, rather than to succeed with a pitch.

But this mindset is tough to adopt. "Education" and "course correction" is not the dream. The dream is "get an agent" or "get published."

Unfortunately, when writers approach the pitch with so much of their personal life on the line, agents/editors (as human beings too) don't want to be the one to poke holes in your soul. It's better to say, "Sure, we'll take a look" … and then reject in business-like fashion after it arrives in the mail. But we knew in our gut when we heard your pitch it would not be ready for the market.

For all writers who walk away disappointed from a pitch, remember that success is rarely attained in those 5-15 minutes. Rather, it's all the years of work leading up to that moment, and how the years of work and experience (and your passion, your confidence) give you the smell of success.

Here are three tips if you find yourself in a live pitch situation.

1. Keep it short. Brevity is your friend! Just because you have three minutes (or 5 or 10) doesn't mean you should take up all the time. Never talk for as long as possible—it can take a mere 15 seconds to deliver a convincing storyline. The longer you talk, the less time the agent or editor is talking. And isn't that why you're meeting with them—to hear *their* feedback and reaction?

2. Focus on a character and the character's problem. When it comes to fiction, it's much easier to follow a pitch and remain interested when we can connect to a character and immediately understand their problem or conflict. Why are we going to care? What are the stakes? So what?

3. Stop at a moment of tension and wait. Rather than talk and talk (which sometimes happens because you're nervous), remind yourself that it's OK not to explain all the details or the final outcome. It's more effective to stop just as you've established the key stakes or tension, and wait for a reaction from the agent. Let them guide the discussion; find out what's caught their attention or what piece is missing.

Why Am I Getting Rejected?

Rejection is often the No. 1 area of pain, concern, and obsession for writers. More often than not, writers want to know WHY they've been rejected. Here are the most common questions I hear.

Why are editors rejecting my work when family and friends love it so much?

Your family and friends love you and see you in your work. An editor doesn't know you and is often more objective, especially when it comes to marketability. Publishing professionals have distance; you and your closest friends/family may not.

I receive lots of form rejections that have little or no feedback on my work. What might be wrong?

Reasons for rejection can be incredibly subjective (indefinable issues of taste), but you might consider the following possibilities:

- Something similar was recently published, or it's a category that's overpublished. You're not the only person with your idea, so your work may be rejected simply because someone else beat you to it. (This can often be the case with trendy nonfiction topics.)
- The timing is wrong. Editors change. Publishers cut back their lists. The market changes. Sometimes you need luck on your side.
- In the case of nonfiction: You don't have adequate credentials, or you don't have an attractive marketing platform.
- Your query letter, or the presentation of your materials, is not professional and/or does not meet submission guidelines.
- You are querying inappropriate publishers, agents, or editors.

May I submit the same manuscript more than once to an editor or agent who has rejected it?

Once you've been rejected on a manuscript (NOT a query—but a partial or full), you've more or less killed your chances with that particular person on that particular project—unless the editor or agent says they are welcome to receiving a revision. If there's no invitation to resubmit, then it's not likely that sending a revision is going to result in a different outcome. This is why it's critical to submit your manuscript only when you are absolutely confident it is the best you can make it.

How to Interpret Common Rejection Phrases

- "Doesn't fit our needs." This is the all-purpose rejection phrase that could really mean anything. It could relate to issues of professionalism, writing quality, or marketability. Don't try to figure out what it means—it's just a stock phrase that gets used again and again by everyone in the publishing industry.
- "Doesn't have sufficient market appeal." This means exactly what it says. Perhaps the market for your work is too small, indistinct, or weird. Or maybe your work lacks punch—it's not different enough, unique enough, or special enough for people to take notice.
- "Just couldn't get excited about it." If someone makes this comment about your fiction, it usually reflects a weak story, a weak protagonist, or little/no compelling conflict. Your story hasn't successfully and emotionally engaged the editor/agent.
- "The writing doesn't stand out." This probably means your writing lacks style, sophistication, voice—or your story is boring, unoriginal, or uninspired.
- "Not fresh enough." For fiction writers, perhaps your plot line is too cliché, your characters are too common, or your story is not compelling enough for publication.

After Rejection

Remember, getting rejected isn't special or personal. What matters is what you do after the rejection.

1. Keep submitting AND keep writing. Persistence is essential. Keep sending your work out. But most importantly, you should keep writing.

Once you finish a manuscript, the first thing you should do is start work on another project. Why? Because it helps create distance and perspective from the project you just finished—which will inevitably need to be refined and approached with a more critical eye.

2. Develop relationships and connections with people who can help you. More progress than you might think will depend on the willingness of others to help you and advise you. One of the most effective ways to develop relationships is to attend conferences and meet other writers, as well as editors and agents.

One of the most difficult aspects of getting published is querying cold. But once you've established a relationship with an editor or agent, then it's no longer a cold contact, but a person who may be compelled to pay attention because you made a good impression on them. Or, if you develop good connections with published authors, they can offer hard-won advice, even referrals to agents, if they believe in your work.

How to Get a Book Deal While Avoiding the Slush Pile

Writers who are new to the industry, or just have oddly shaped egos, will ask me, "How can I avoid the slush pile?"

Well, just by virtue of having something to sell that no one has asked for, you can't avoid the slush pile. But some people DO get approached without sending a single query or proposal.

Here are 5 tips on how to be one of those lucky people.

1. Get media coverage. This can be on a large or small scale, but of course, the bigger the publication covering you, the more likely you'll have agents and editors calling you within hours. Have you seen the movie *Julie & Julia*? Classic example of someone featured in the New York Times, then landing a book deal.

2. Get your work published somewhere that agents and editors scout for talent. For example: *Writer's Digest* magazine once featured 12 journals that agents read. Author and essayist Heather Sellers landed a book deal after publishing an essay in O magazine about 100 coffee dates to find true love. Writers who place an essay in the New York Times' Modern Love column are known to score book deals.

3. Have a major personality, opinion maker, or blogger recommend you in some form. You better bet that if someone like Seth Godin mentions you in his blog as some kind of amazing person, your popularity will skyrocket overnight. And I bet he receives so many solicitations for that reason that I feel very sorry for what his e-mail inbox must look like.

4. Develop a site/blog, or a community, or a tradition of content so significant, fresh, and original that it sparks #1 or #3. This is the dream for a lot of writers who start blogging or otherwise participate in social media. Just be careful that you're not the desperate, look-at-me writer whose intention to score a book deal becomes a big turn off. The strange thing about being proactively approached by an editor/agent is that they're most drawn to people who could not care less about them. (Remember how you can get romantically infatuated with a person who won't even toss a glance in your direction? Same principle applies.)

5. Cultivate a network of connections who champion you without being asked. From your end, it requires serious charm and also an idea or presence that's truly inspiring and compelling.

I don't like telling writers to sit around hoping for someone else to notice their brilliance. It doesn't happen that often. Most often, you'll have to learn how to pitch yourself effectively.

That said, there is considerable power in having a community and network of relationships that can come to your aid when you need it, and that can help you bypass the cold query process. In some groups or communities, there's a strong sense of giving back to others who are new and getting established. I do hear from many writers that their success couldn't have been possible without the tough love or generosity of an important mentor.

Also, as discussed, being online (and active in social networks) opens up more opportunities and chances to meet the right person who can help you. It also helps to clearly be a professional, solidly established, with an audience.

Not everyone is going to have the community-building and networking strengths. But every writer should consider at least one or two ways they can build a support network, become active in a community of like-minded people, and/or find a mentor. Getting published is much easier when you know a few people—who have the distance, experience, and savvy—to tell you how to navigate a tricky industry.

CHAPTER 5
Understanding the
Self-Publishing Path

What is your primary goal for self-publishing? That affects everything. It affects what advice I give you, it affects what service you choose, it affects how much money you spend, it affects the format, it affects how satisfied you are at the end of the process.

While I can't possibly cover every goal a writer might have in self-publishing, I'll cover the top three.

GOAL: I want the satisfaction of seeing my work in traditional print book form.

This goal assumes that, even if you don't sell any copies of your book, or see it distributed in chain outlets, you will be satisfied with just having your work in print.

If this is truly your goal, then the key question becomes: How much help or service do you need or want in making this happen?

Do you prefer to hire one firm to take care of every aspect of this project—a very hands-off approach?

It is possible to write a check, hand over a Word document, and get a printed book in your hands very quickly. AuthorSolutions is the biggest service provider today for that kind of result, if that's really all you want. Just don't expect any sales to come from it.

You can also hire full-service firms, that cost more money, but offer higher quality and more control, as well as a more meaningful level of author involvement in the process. (Girl Friday Productions is one example.)

Imagine your finished book in your hands. Imagine giving it to friends and family and colleagues. You never sell more than a handful of copies, and you never see it on store shelves. No agent or editor ever hears about it. Do you feel satisfied and happy?

GOAL: I want a book to convey my expertise and credibility in a specific field or profession, and to build my platform.

Self-publishing has always been a popular option for professional career and platform building—especially those who speak often, have a ready audience, and are experts in their field.

Often such authors (who are businesspeople, not writers) know more about their market and audience than a mainstream publisher, and the topic is too specialized to ever be seriously considered for trade publication.

In this case, the next important question becomes: How much profit do you want out of this?

If you want to maximize your profit from book sales, you should avoid full-service providers such as AuthorSolutions, since they collect a royalty on every book you sell. Instead, you should contract out all services yourself, or privately hire a professional to project manage the process for you—so that you control all property, rights and profits after the book is finished.

Imagine your book being available in your place of business, or through your website. Imagine it available at speaking engagements, and referenced by colleagues as a good resource. It is not visible outside of your own professional circle, and it is not marketed to a general audience or seen in stores. Do you feel satisfied and happy?

GOAL: I'm going to prove all those gatekeepers wrong and publish a book that catches the attention of the world—then I'll get a traditional deal!

This is probably the secret desire that a lot of self-published authors won't admit to having. In this scenario, while there is no "right" way to go about conquering the world, make sure you're brutally honest with yourself:

- Do you consider yourself an entrepreneur?
- Do you have marketing experience and savvy?
- Are you active online or with your community of readers?
- Are you ready to be business-minded about every aspect of your

writing career?

- Are you ready to spend money on people who can help you (e.g., freelance publishing professionals who know how to make success happen)?

You should be answering "yes" to most or all of these questions. Despite all the success stories, few authors make a living from their self-published work or go on to traditional book deals. If you envision yourself as a thriving indie author, you need to comfortably see yourself as a long-term entrepreneur. Not all authors are up for that.

Should You Self-Publish?

There's incredible emphasis these days on how authors have more power and control than ever in deciding how and when to publish. Technology has enabled us all to be active creators, publishers, and distributors, without needing anyone's permission or approval.

However, I worry that the continued proselytizing about self-published authors' empowerment is starting to become so pervasive that writers now assume there's no value that a publisher offers that they could possibly need.

Nothing could be further from the truth. Here are three reasons why.

1. Publishers push you to higher quality. Working with professionals should challenge you. It should raise the bar. You'll probably feel some doubts about the quality of your work. This is a good thing. Professionals usually understand and build off your strengths, and minimize the appearance of your weaknesses.

One of the first things I teach my writing students is you need someone you trust to push you—to tell you where things aren't working. Most people don't have that gift of being so distant from their work that they can see objectively where it's succeeding or failing. Even the writers who DO have that power usually have decades of experience and self-knowledge—from being pushed.

Yes, my argument does mean: To develop to your maximum potential, you need someone to create a little discomfort.

2. To compete amidst all the noise and distraction, you need the most professional quality possible. All of you who are about to say, "Publishers put out bad quality work all the time," stop right there. I don't care about them; I care about you. Since when did saying, "Since they screw up sometimes, then I have permission to screw up too" become a defense or a smart rationale?

Quality work that has a professional touch stands out. Way out. You think readers can't tell? There are subtle cues in every product and service we purchase—small signs that indicate quality. People may not be able to name them or point them out, but they feel them.

The disadvantage for independent authors is their lack of knowledge about what professional quality is or looks like. Traditionally published authors who go indie don't have this problem as much. They know the process; they know the huge improvements that can be made by a professional.

But people who haven't experienced that professional touch may not yet have a good measuring stick—which only further necessitates the involvement of a professional, whether on the editing, production, or promotion side.

3. Not everyone wants (or has the time) to immerse themselves in media, production, and technology. Some writers just don't have either the interest or the patience to do things on their own. They prefer a partner or professional assistance.

You may know how to cut your own lawn, but it doesn't mean you want to do it—and it's not illogical to hire it done if you have the resources. Tools do not make anyone an expert in anything.

Don't mistake me. I do believe in author empowerment and independence. You do not *need* a publisher. But some writers can greatly benefit from partnerships or professional assistance, in different ways, and at different times, in their careers.

What if you took a one-week class with me that focused on how to become a power blogger? If I taught you in one week what it might take you one year to figure out, would that be worth the investment? Maybe; it depends on your goals.

There are some things you can figure out on your own. There are other things you want to be taught by an experienced professional, to shorten the learning curve. And finally there are those things that you may never be great at, and that you hire help for.

Part of a successful career is understanding the difference.

Should You Self-Publish After a Near Miss?

Writers often ask if it's wise or helpful to self-publish their work if they have "near-misses" with agents or publishers. As you'll probably guess, I believe there's no one answer that works for everyone. But I'll try to help you come to the right conclusion.

YES: Go ahead and try self-publishing
- You know how to reach your readers (online or offline).
- You already have credibility with readers in your genre/category.
- You have a marketing and promotion plan, with achievable goals.
- You're comfortable being online and have already experimented with online marketing and promotion; you have an online identity and have participated in online communities.
- You have a current website and can update it yourself.
- You have an entrepreneurial spirit.
- You're in it for the long haul.

NO: Do not self-publish
- You don't know how to find or reach your readers (online or offline).
- You need physical bookstore distribution to be satisfied that you're successful (or that you're reaching your readers).
- You don't yet have your own website.
- You don't have a marketing and promotion strategy, but hope that someone will notice you.
- You don't like spending time online and/or dislike social media.
- It's your first manuscript and you don't want to see all that work go to waste. If that's the case, wait until you've written book #2 or #3 or #4 before you decide to release that first one. It'll still be there, trust me.
- You're looking for quick success and an agent.

Self-publishing does not kill your chances at a traditional deal later. But I wouldn't spend any significant money on self-publishing—whether print or digital—until you've developed a strategic plan to market to your target audience, and feel reasonably confident about the quality of your work.

10 Questions to Ask Before Using Any E-Publishing Service

With an avalanche of new services promising to help writers self-publish e-books even better and more profitably before, it's imperative that writers educate themselves about how these services typically operate—plus read the fine print of any new service before deciding to commit.

Note that when I discuss "services," they typically fall into 2 categories:
1. Single-channel, retailer-driven services (e.g., Amazon's Kindle Direct Publishing, Barnes & Noble's Nook Press, and Apple iBookstore)

2. Multiple-channel distribution services that often include some kind of formatting and conversion service; sometimes these distribution services sell e-books, too. BookBaby and Smashwords are two of the most well-known and recommended services.

- … and there are also other types of services, such as those offered by agents or even traditional publishers.

Here are 10 questions you must ask of any new service you consider using.

1. Is the service exclusive or nonexclusive? E-publishing services marketed directly to authors almost always operate on a nonexclusive basis. That means you can use their service to sell your e-book while also selling your e-book anywhere else you like (or using any other service).

There are two notable exceptions right now:

- **Self-published e-books made available for lending through Kindle Select.** Amazon asks for a 3-month exclusive if you join the Kindle Select program (which allows your book to be lent out to Amazon Prime users and those in the Kindle Unlimited subscription service).
- **E-books created with Apple's iBooks Author software (available only to Mac users).** You can still sell the e-book elsewhere, but not the specific version you create with the Apple iBooks Author software.

2. If it's exclusive, what's the term of the contract? If you're working with an agent to publish your e-book, you will likely be asked to sign a contract that has a six to 24-month term. This is simply to ensure that, after your e-book files are prepared, your cover designed, and all ducks put in a row, that you don't suddenly change your mind and take your e-book elsewhere. There are sufficient upfront costs that the agent needs to be confident of recouping their initial outlay. I recommend you not commit for longer than 1 or 2 years due to how fast the market conditions can change for e-books.

3. Do you control the price? While some services may have reasonable pricing restrictions (e.g, not allowing you to price below 99 cents), standard practice is to give the author complete control over pricing.

Caveat: Most e-book retailers mandate that you not offer more favorable pricing anywhere else (whether at another retailer or direct-to-consumer from your own site). Amazon in particular is known for carefully policing this and will automatically lower the price of your e-book if they find you pricing it lower somewhere else. (Some authors use this to their advantage and make their e-book available for free elsewhere so Amazon will then push the price of the Kindle edition to free, which is tricky to accomplish through other means.)

4. What's the upfront fee and/or how is the royalty calculated? While different services have different models, the fees should be transparent and upfront. For example:

- Amazon Kindle, Barnes & Noble's Nook Press, and Apple's iBookstore (and iBooks Author software) are all free to use. They make their money by taking a cut of your sales. Usually you earn 60-70% of your list price (assuming you price in the range they specify).

- Smashwords is free to use and distributes to all major e-book retailers except Amazon. Smashwords pays you 85% of your list price on sales directly through the Smashwords site, minus PayPal transaction fees. They pay you approximately 60% of your list price on sales through retailers (in other words, they take 10% after the retailer takes their cut).

- BookBaby offers conversion services and distributes to all major re-tailers. They offer two types of deals. If you pay an upfront flat fee, you earn 100% net of all sales—BookBaby keeps no commission. If you pay $0 upfront, then you have to give them a percentage of sales.

Always, always, always read the fine print in these cases. For instance, if you price your book very low (99 cents), and there's a 25-cent transaction fee for each of your sales, you've just cut into your profits even if you're earning 70% or 80% of list.

5. Are there hidden fees or charges? You can end up paying more than standard rates for conversion/formatting if your book runs very long, if you have an inconvenient file format that needs extra work (common with PDFs), if you have a lot of chart/table/image formatting, and so on. If your work has any kind of "special needs," expect a service to charge you more. (The best services, such as BookBaby, are very specific about what these costs will be.)

6. What file formats do they accept? This is critical to know upfront because it usually determines (1) whether or not you can use the service in the first place and (2) how much you'll get charged for formatting and conversion if that's a service you need.

A few things to know:

- Microsoft Word (or any text file) is commonly accepted. However: If you're publishing direct to Kindle or Nook (or use Smashwords, which is automated too), unless you "unformat" your Word docu-ment, it is likely to look like crap on an e-reading device when automatically converted to an e-book format. Most retailers' e-publishing services have extensive guidelines, preview programs, and other ways of ensuring things look OK before your e-book goes live.

- EPUB is the industry standard e-book file format. Later, I'll make recommendations for how to create your own EPUB files.
- Many conversion/formatting services typically offer you EPUB and MOBI files since that covers you on Amazon and just about any other e-book retailer.
- PDF is one of the most difficult file formats to convert to EPUB. Expect to pay.

7. Who owns the e-book files after they are created? It is ideal if you own the e-book files, and that is usually the case when you pay out of pocket for conversion and formatting services. In the case of some free services, such as Smashwords, you do not. (Why so? When you upload your Word document to Smashwords—the only format accepted—it goes through their "meatgrinder" conversion process to create a variety of e-book files. You then have access to those e-book files, but you're not supposed to turn around and sell them through other services.)

8. Are DRM protections or proprietary formats involved? DRM stands for digital rights management. DRM is supposed to prevent piracy, or illegal copying and distribution of your e-book after it is sold. However, I agree with those who argue that DRM is not reader- or consumer-friendly, and should not be used. The industry standard e-book format, EPUB, does not use DRM.

There are only 2 areas where you're likely to run into a proprietary format or DRM.

- Amazon Kindle uses a proprietary format with DRM. If you use the Kindle Direct Publishing program to publish your e-book, no matter what type of file you upload, they will automatically convert it to their proprietary, DRM-locked format. However, because their service is not exclusive, you can always make your e-book available in other formats through other services, without restriction.
- The Apple iBooks Author tool creates e-books in a proprietary format. No other device aside from an iPad or iPhone can view an e-book created by the Apple iBooks Author tool.

9. Where is your e-book distributed? If you're using services like Amazon Kindle Direct or Barnes & Noble's Nook Press, the answer is pretty simple: Your e-book is distributed only through those specific retailers. When you use a multiple-channel e-book distribution service (such as

Smashwords or BookBaby), then the mix of retailers they reach will vary. At minimum, you want to reach Kindle & Nook, since they currently make up about 85% of all e-book sales.

One common strategy among authors is to use Amazon Kindle Direct combined with Smashwords (which distributes to all major e-book retailers *except* Kindle). You can probably reach 95%+ of your market with that approach, if not 100%.

10. Can you make changes to your e-book after it goes on sale? If you're working directly with retailers (e.g., Amazon and Barnes & Noble), you can upload new and revised files as often as you like—they don't care. Same goes with Smashwords. However, if you're using a multiple-channel distributor other than Smashwords, you will likely have to pay fees to make changes.

Recommended E-Book Creation Tools
- Jutoh
- EasyEdit (for PC users only, produces Kindle-ready files)
- PressBooks
- Apple iBooks Author: produces image- or media-driven e-books, just be aware of the exclusivity they demand

The Future of Self-Publishing Services

The past several years have seen significant and well-publicized developments for self-published authors. It's probably not necessary to point out what the high-profile success stories are, but you've probably heard of authors such as Hugh Howey, JA Konrath, Amanda Hocking, and CJ Lyons.

A lot of ink—real ink and electronic ink—has been spilled on whether publishing will die, or books will die, or agents will die, etc.

But what about the impact on fee-based self-publishing services? I'm thinking specifically of the ones that focus on print-on-demand books, such as Author Solutions.

Let's discuss the history of these services first.

Print-on-demand (POD) became popular in the early 2000s, because it made self-publishing more affordable and accessible than ever before. Print-on-demand technology allows books to be printed one at a time, only after an order is placed, avoiding the necessity for an author to pay big bucks for a traditional print run that probably sits unsold in a warehouse somewhere.

In a publishing landscape *without* e-books, a POD service can make a lot of sense. The costs are low for everyone since there's no print run to pay for, and most inexperienced or new authors have no interest in learning to produce a print book on their own. A self-pub service package makes the headaches go away, and for not a lot of money, usually less than $1,000. (That $1,000 won't get you a well-edited, well-designed, or well-marketed book, but I'm strictly addressing the friction of, cost of, and access to production/distribution.)

Right now, Author Solutions is the biggest self-publishing/POD service company in the world, and was acquired by Penguin Random House (yes, a traditional publishing house). Over the last decade, they've bought up the most significant competitors, such as iUniverse, Xlibris, and Trafford. Their growth has been astronomical and reported on by outlets such as the New York Times, Wall Street Journal, and Inc. magazine.

To keep growing their business, they've been soliciting and establishing partnerships with traditional publishers, to set up new imprints that they exclusively service, such as Harlequin's Horizons and Thomas Nelson's West Bow.

But this is appearing more and more like a huge scramble to squeeze a few more profitable dollars out of a service that is no longer needed, that is incredibly overpriced when compared to the new and growing competition, and has less to recommend it with each passing day, as more success stories come from the e-publishing realm where author royalties are in the 70-85% range. (An author typically earns less than half that percentage for royalties on a POD book.)

Furthermore, the cat's out of the bag when it comes to the "value" of the package services you get from a fee-based company. Take David Carnoy of CNET, for instance, who plainly says:

> Buy as little as possible … Self-publishing outfits are in the game to make money. And since they're probably not going to sell a lot of your books, they make money by selling you services with nice margins. … it's better to hire your own people and work directly with them. Ideally, you should be able to meet with an editor, copy editor, and graphic designer in person—and they all should have experience in book publishing.

These days, service companies like Author Solutions are typically unable to tout any success stories, or show off the beautiful books they've produced, because what new or established author would pay for a service package when they've read about the success of an Amanda Hocking or a

JA Konrath, who have done exceptionally well without such help?

The answer is: No *informed* author.

That's why today's fee-based self-publishing company will be forced to change its service, the value of its service, and/or the price of its service—or otherwise become irrelevant (and die). Just how fast such services decline depends somewhat on how quickly e-books become the preferred format for a majority of readers.

Services like Author Solutions have reaped enormous profits from charging hundreds or thousands of dollars for their services, because until now, there wasn't a viable or cheaper alternative for an author who wasn't interested in learning the ropes of the publishing business.

We're now reaching the point where fee-based services can stay alive only by banking on the ignorance of authors—not that they haven't done so, to some extent, up until now.

But they can't continue to charge the same amount for the same service that has decreasing value over time, not when Smashwords, Barnes & Noble Nook Press, and Amazon's KDP charge zero. Not when Amazon's CreateSpace offers POD services for next to nothing. Not when an author can now, more easily than ever, find and hire quality help.

There will always be some level of demand for full-service, fee-based publishing companies. But not from the likes of Author Solutions. Their business model and customer value is based on an outdated model of the publishing industry.

CHAPTER 6
The Basics of Author Platform

Platform is one of the most difficult concepts to explain, partly because everyone defines it a little differently. But one thing I know for sure: Editors and agents are attracted to authors who have this thing called "platform," especially when it comes to nonfiction authors.

What Editors and Agents Typically Mean By Platform

They're looking for someone with visibility and authority who has proven reach to a target audience. Let's break this down further.

Visibility. Who knows you? Who is aware of your work? Where does your work regularly appear? How many people see it? How does it spread? Where does it spread? What communities are you a part of? Who do you influence? Where do you make waves?

Authority. What's your credibility? What are your credentials? (This is particularly important for nonfiction writers; it is less important for fiction writers, though it can play a role. Just take a look at any graduate of the Iowa MFA program.)

Proven reach. It's not enough to SAY you have visibility. You have to show where you make an impact and give proof of engagement. This could be quantitative evidence (e.g., size of your e-mail newsletter list, website traffic, blog comments) or qualitative evidence (high-profile reviews, testimonials from A-listers in your genre).

Target audience. You should be visible to the most receptive or appropriate audience for the work you're trying to sell. For instance: If you have visibility, authority, and proven reach to orthodontists, that probably won't be helpful if you're marketing vampire fiction (unless perhaps you're writing about a vampire orthodontist who repairs crooked vampire fangs?).

What Platform Is Not
- It is not about self-promotion.
- It is not about hard selling.
- It is not about annoying people.
- It is not about being an extrovert.
- It is not about being active on social media.
- It is not about blogging.
- It is not about your qualifications, authority, or experience, although these are tools for growing or nurturing a platform.
- It is not something you create overnight.
- It is not something you can buy.
- It is not a one-time event.
- It is not more important than your story or message (but hopefully it grows out of that).

Platform is not about bringing attention to yourself, or by screaming to everyone you can find online or offline, "Look at me! Look at me!" Platform isn't about who yells the loudest or who markets the best.

It is more about putting in consistent effort over the course of a career, and making incremental improvements in extending your network. It's about making waves that attract other people to you—not begging others to pay attention.

What Activities Build Platform?
First and foremost, platform grows out of your body of work—or from producing great work. Remember that. The following list is not exhaustive, but helps give you an idea of how platform can grow.
- Publishing or distributing quality work in outlets you want to be identified with and that your target audience reads.
- Producing a body of work on your own platform—e.g., blog, e-mail newsletter, social network, podcast, video, digital downloads, etc—that gathers quality followers. This is usually a longterm process.
- Speaking at and/or attending events where you meet new people and extend your network of contacts.
- Finding meaningful ways to engage with and develop your target audience, whether through content, events, online marketing, etc.

- Partnering with peers or influencers to tackle a new project and/or extend your visibility.

Some people have an easier time building platform than others. If you hold a highly recognized position (powerful network and influence), if you know key influencers (friends in high places), if you are associated with powerful communities, if you have prestigious degrees or posts, or if you otherwise have public-facing work—yes, you play the field at an advantage. This is why it's so easy for celebrities to get book deals. They have "built-in" platform.

Platform Building Is Not One Size Fits All
Platform building is an organic process and will be different for every single author. There is no checklist I can give you to develop a platform, because it depends on:

- your unique story/message
- your unique strengths and qualities
- your target readership

Your platform should be as much of a creative exercise and project as the work you produce. While platform gives you power to market effectively, it's not something you develop by posting "Follow me!" on Twitter or "Like me!" on Facebook a few times a week. Use your imagination, and take meaningful steps. It'll be a long journey.

Should You Focus on Your Writing or Platform Building?

Craft!
Platform!
Craft!!
Platform!!

It's a debate that might span eternity: how much time should you devote to writing versus platform building?

Excellent arguments reside on each side of this debate, which often boil down to: "Writing is all that matters," and "audience is all that matters."

But the truth is a little different for each of us (or falls somewhere in the middle), and that's why it's next to impossible to give general advice on platform. It varies based on the author and the work in question. But as a general rule: Nonfiction authors usually must pay heed to platform, while most beginning novelists do not.

Unfortunately, novelists too have frequently been advised to build a platform, the same as the nonfiction authors. This tends to put the cart before the horse and leaves fiction writers feeling justifiably confused about the issue. There's little way to build a platform when you don't have a single book or credit to your name. (The credible nonfiction author, on the other hand, usually needs a platform in place to prepare a convincing book proposal.)

This has been a preface to what I'd like to offer: a set of general guidelines to help any writer understand how to balance writing with platform building.

Balance is the key word here.

Focusing on your writing probably means spending 10% of your available writing time on platform activities. I never recommend abandoning platform activities entirely, because you want to be open to new possibilities. Being active online—while still focused on your writing—could mean finding a new mentor or the perfect critique partner, connecting with an important influencer, or pursuing a new writing retreat or fellowship opportunity.

Without further ado, the list.

When to Focus More on Your Writing

- If you are within the first five years of seriously attempting to write with the goal of publication
- For novelists: If you have not yet completed and revised one or two full-length manuscripts
- If you can tell that what you're writing is falling short of where you want and need to be
- If you see a direct correlation between the amount of writing you put out and the amount of money that comes into your bank account
- If you are working on deadline.

When to Focus More on Your Platform

- If you start to realize you're on the verge of publication
- If you have a firm book release date of any kind
- If you want to sell a nonfiction book concept (non-narrative)
- If you intend to profit from online/digital writing that you are creating, distributing, and selling on your own
- If you need to prove to a publisher that your work has an audience.

The Art and Business of Platform

In the nonprofit world, you'll frequently hear about "audience development," which concerns itself with outreach to people interested in what you do, and customizing that outreach based on a person's level of interest.

Audience development is difficult to strictly define because it involves not just pure marketing, but one-on-one relationships. It's not about selling (although the result is often sales); it's about creating an experience or community that engages with you over the long term. And that requires that you communicate with that community meaningfully and consistently.

One of the best summaries of audience development I've read is from Shoshana Fanizza, who has spent more than a decade in arts development:

> Audience Development, in a nutshell, is all about relationship building to achieve the "power of people" to support your art form. Consider it as building positive energy, people energy, to attract more support for you. Audience development does take time to see results. It is a building process. … You want to get to know your audience and connect with them. If they feel connected and cared for, they will want to become more involved. It will take effort and persistence, but you will see the relationships you build start to form a positive community around your art. This community is the key to succeeding!

I like introducing authors to the idea of audience development because it can be an easier way of understanding what we mean we talk about long-term platform building and reader engagement. You should take full ownership of reader engagement because it represents an investment in your lifelong career as an author. Don't rely on a publisher, agent, or consultant to find and "keep" your audience for you. If you find and nurture it on platforms and channels that you own, that's like putting money in the bank.

The Art and the Authenticity of Reader Engagement

When new authors ask me if they can just hire someone to engage with readers (e.g., on social media or elsewhere), they're often missing the point and the benefit of communicating with readers. Learning about readers directly and strengthening the connection leads to better marketing and promotion in the long term. When done well, it requires that you be present and be authentic. It's tough to do that if someone else is pretending to be you—and it can also prevent you from gaining insights into how to improve your future work.

However you decide to directly communicate with readers, it's important that:

- You enjoy the tools or platforms—so you stick with them for the long haul (plus readers can tell if you're not enjoying yourself).
- You're consistent with your voice and style, and that you don't adopt a "marketing voice" that might be a turn off to readers.
- You focus on what's satisfying and engaging for both you and readers.

People often respond well to playfulness, or when you're not taking yourself too seriously. Don't be afraid to experiment, have fun, and be human. Knowing yourself and feeling secure about who you are (and what you are *not*) goes a long way toward successful communication with your audience.

The Business of Reader Engagement

First things first: However and whenever you engage with readers, it should be on a permission basis. That means the reader has already indicated they want to hear from you—by liking you, following you, signing up for e-mails from you, etc. Based on the level of interest expressed, behave accordingly. For instance, how you behave and communicate with Twitter followers should be different than how you communicate with long-time subscribers of your e-mail newsletter.

Your communications will usually have 1 of 2 objectives:

1. Sales-focused, e.g., book-launch announcements
2. Relationship-focused (platform and audience development)

Sales-focused communications are typically tied to specific marketing campaigns, book launches, or other strategic initiatives when you're measuring their effectiveness and impact. (If they're not, consider why you're sending out sales messages without a strategy in place.)

When it comes to platform building, you'll be focused on relationship-driven communication (which often impacts the success of your sales communication). A few of the most critical tools include the following.

1. Your own website + Google Analytics. Your website is one of the best tools you have when making first contact with existing readers. You can use it to capture and communicate with your audience on a career-long basis through a blog or an e-mail newsletter, and you can analyze how people find you, what affects people's interest in you (and how/when they spread the word about your work), and what content is most popular with readers.

How do you find all this out? Both Google Analytics and e-mail newsletter analytics (more on e-newsletters next) will tell you a very pointed story about what your readers are looking for and what keeps their interest. You can uncover whether or not your social media accounts are having any impact on spreading the word (building buzz), and you'll learn what keywords people search for that land them on your content. This kind of data is invaluable when making hard choices about where to spend your time communicating with readers (especially when you need to focus on writing), what readers value in the relationship, and what they want to see more of.

Look at your website today, and ensure you're giving visitors an action step. What is it you want them to do when they arrive? Should they sign up for your e-newsletter? Should they get a free download? Should they follow you on Facebook or Twitter? If you're not prompting visitors to act, they probably won't.

2. E-mail newsletter. E-mail is not dead. It is still one of the most effective marketing techniques available anywhere, to anyone. And for authors, it allows you to communicate reliably and directly with your audience from one book to the next. You own the e-mail list, and you want the power of direct engagement with your readers without the danger of websites folding, platforms changing, or publishers merging.

Therefore, on your website (and anywhere else where it makes sense: Facebook fan page, writing conference engagements, etc): Ask people to sign-up for your e-mail newsletter. MailChimp is an excellent e-mail newsletter provider to use, free up to 2,000 names.

There are different types of content strategies for the e-mail newsletter; some authors only e-mail their readers one or two times a year, with a brief news summary or updates about new releases. Others e-mail more frequently and take time to send out useful content. For example, author CJ Lyons interviews an author and includes the Q&A in the newsletters she sends.

I prefer the useful content strategy, but whatever strategy you choose, don't let your list languish without making contact at least one or two times per year. Otherwise, people will forget they signed up, mark you as spam, and your efforts will have been in vain.

3. Social media sites or online communities that your readers frequent. Hopefully there is a sweet spot between:
- What social media or online communities you enjoy
- Where your readers reliably gather and communicate

- What mediums naturally complement your work

I advise experimentation until you figure out which sites or communities carry the most meaning and impact for reader communication (using analytics to help you determine the best choices). Once you identify which channel is effective for you, the big question becomes: What do you do there? Well, it's not about blasting buy-this information. To be an interesting person, you have to be interested in the world, and in other people. You have to be curious. So find ways to post and share about things that fascinate you or puzzle you. Post questions for other people to answer. Ask people to share something. You may not get it right at first, but remember: playfulness helps.

4. Customized communication and experiences. The people you reach (online or off) will all be at different stages of commitment to you and your work. Your communication must respect this and be segmented by audience as much as possible. There are two particular types of reader that deserve special attention and communication.

The new reader. To introduce new people to your work, I recommend the cheese-cube lure. Offer something for free (the first book in the series, a free chapter, a blog with cool content, a special digital download, etc). Cast a wide net with something broadly appealing. Then gradually move people into more serious commitments (by earning their trust), such as signing up for your e-newsletter or buying your book.

The true fan. For the readers who would buy anything you ever published, consider special communication and experiences only available to them. You know how your city symphony will have a VIP room with cookies and chocolate during intermission, for certain season subscribers? Think about what your VIP experience looks like, too. For some authors, that means earliest access and cheapest prices for their most loyal fans.

Strong reader relationships build unbelievable opportunities. Marketing and promotion ideas usually start by considering what reader relationships you have in place—or can build on. It's easier to start with reader relationships you have, rather than cold calling strangers when you need help spreading word of mouth. When you have a book coming out, share calls to action with your first circle of most devoted fans or supporters, and customize each communication to be appropriate to the level of commitment demonstrated by the reader. Never blast the same message to everyone; treat your long-time, loyal readers differently than someone new or casual.

If you're looking for a few models to follow, study the online presence of these authors:

- Claire Cook
- Cathy Day
- CJ Lyons
- Gretchen Rubin
- Andrew Shaffer
- Roxane Gay

How Much Does Platform Impact Sales?

There is a continuing debate over the impact of one's platform on book sales.

In one of the more interesting experiments I've seen, author C.S. Lakin decided to publish a genre novel (in a very particular genre, with a very particular formula) and release it under a pen name, to test whether a first-time author—one ostensibly without any platform—could sell a meaningful number of copies.

You can find a diversity of lessons in what Lakin did; one of the key takeaways (for me) relates to the role that genre plays in an author's success in achieving e-book sales through the largest online retailer in the world, Amazon.

Lakin commented that her purpose wasn't necessarily to prove platform unimportant, but the headline of the post and the comment thread (of course) point to a great deal of excitement over the early results: this first book by a platform-free author is selling 30-50 copies every day.

I agree with those who advise that fiction writers put a low priority on platform building, at least until you have some books to market and real seriousness of intent. By seriousness, I mean: you expect to earn money that will help provide a living.

But I also believe that paying even a little bit of attention to developing direct connections with readers (e.g., through having your own website) pays off over the long-term of your career. You don't do it for short-term gain; you do it to incrementally grow your name recognition and spread word of mouth—to help you better discover and engage with readers over 5, 10, or 20+ years.

Here's the thing about Lakin's experiment. I think it reveals platform hard at work, because Lakin happens to have a solid platform she can't hide, even with a pen name. Let me explain.

As far as my definition, I believe author platform has 6 key components:

1. Your writing or your content (in this case, books)

2. Your social media or online community presence and outreach
3, Your website
4. Your relationships (people you know, the kind of people who will answer your e-mails or phone calls)
5. Your influence (e.g., your ability to get people you *don't* know to help you out, listen, or pay attention)
6. Your actual reach (the number of people you can reliably broadcast a message to at any particular moment in time).

When people hear the word "platform," they often think about social media, or doing self-promotional activities. What they forget is that one's body of work is the entire engine behind any author's platform—it all starts with the writing and its appeal to a target audience—and also includes relationships developed in the process.

I haven't spoken to Lakin about this, but just looking at the surface of her experiment, here's what I see happening.

Social media outreach: Lakin used her own Twitter account, which has 44,000+ followers, to spread the word about the book.

Writing & content: Lakin is the author of more than a dozen other books. When she tweeted about her new book, she was appealing to people who already know and like her—and people who could help spread the word. (That said, I understand that perhaps her current fans may not be active readers of the genre in which she now writes under a pen name.)

Relationships: Lakin appealed to well-known author friends to write reviews of her work, which presumably offered social proof and credibility to her debut book. But how many authors without a platform have such relationships already in place?

There are other helpful factors, which some may not categorize as platform—and perhaps much of this truly boils down to our definitions of that word!—but that I find at least related to the strength of your platform. Lakin was having conversations with people about which genre to choose and was conducting some amount of reconnaissance—presumably drawing on relationships that are always part of any author's long-term success. And she is now discussing the experiment at one of the biggest blogs for self-publishing.

None of this is to downplay the value in Lakin's experiment and what lessons it holds for authors looking for keys to success. The most important point she makes (IMHO) is not to be taken lightly: the genre/subgenre you write in (or at least categorize your book by) affects success—and can carry a book's sales, at least in the short term—if you're following the conventions of the genre and playing well with Amazon. I just wouldn't be so quick to say, "This was a book published without an author platform," when we're looking at someone who is very experienced in the industry and has a network of valuable resources to draw upon.

3 Numbers That Matter to Your Platform

Every platform is different (we are all unique individuals!), but here are three specific numbers that can come in handy when proving the size, strength, or impact of your *online platform,* especially in a book proposal.

1. How many people visit your site monthly? This is easy to determine if you have Google Analytics installed. Check your dashboard and look at how many people visit your site in a month's time (the default view). See how that compares month-on-month, and year-on-year. Are you getting more visitors over time? What's the percentage growth month-on-month or year-on-year? This is hopefully a positive indicator that lends strength to your platform. Other Google metrics that can be important to your plat-form include:

- **What content is most popular on your site**, especially if it's highly ranked by Google's search engines. E.g., "My blog posts on how to bathe your cat are the most highly ranked for anyone searching *cat bath*." Or, "I receive more than 3,000 visits per month from people searching for *cat bath.*"
- **How long people stay on your site.** The longer people stay, typically the more compelling your content is. This is also called "site sticki-ness." Such visitors are more likely to respond to calls to action, buy things, click on ads, etc.
- **How people find your site.** There is no "right" answer here, just in-sightful ones. For example, if you claim to have impact on Twitter or Facebook (see #3 below), that probably means a good portion of your site traffic should come from those sources. If you claim to be visi-ble though search engines, your metrics should indicate meaningful search engine traffic. If your site is highly recommended by author-ities in your community, you should be able to prove it by showing your referral traffic.

2. How many readers can you reach directly via e-mail? Add the fol-lowing numbers:

- How many people subscribe to your site or blog via e-mail
- How many people subscribe to your unique e-newsletter
- How many people you would feel comfortable e-mailing personally

about a book or product launch.

This is the number of people you can reach directly via e-mail, and it's a number that's highly attractive to publishers. If you don't currently have a way of capturing e-mail addresses, then consider starting an e-newsletter, or offering an e-mail based subscription to your blog.

3. What level of engagement do you have through your online channels? (Or: What is your ability to get people to ACT?) One popular way to determine your engagement is to look at your Twitter or Facebook analytics. They tell you the level of engagement your tweets or posts receive and what percentage of your following you're actually reaching.

You can also use a service like HootSuite for social media updates. HootSuite provides you weekly analytics of how your posts "performed" in terms of clicks, replies, retweets, etc. That way, even if you have a modest following of, say, 1,000 people, you might be able to say that you engage 30-50% of followers in a single day. Having a ton of followers isn't as impressive as actually having their attention.

Track sharing statistics on your own site and through Google Analytics. I use the AddThis plug-in for my site, which publicly tallies the number of times an article is shared. This is very useful data to have on hand when making a platform statement about how well your content spreads. You can also use Google Analytics to help track how much of your traffic comes from social networks where you're active.

Consider this just the tip of the iceberg when it comes to all the different metrics you can collect related to your online platform. If you don't already have Google Analytics installed on your site, I recommend you start today.

Are There Limits to Literary Citizenship?

The backlash against Literary Citizenship is underway, and perhaps it was inevitable.

For those unaware of term, it's widely used in the literary, bookish community to refer to activities that support and further reading, writing, and publishing, and the growth of your professional network. In some ways, it's a more palatable (or friendly) way to think of platform building.

What I've always liked about the Literary Citizenship movement:

- It's simple for people to understand and practice. It aligns well with the values of the literary community.
- It operates with an abundance mindset. It's not about competition, but collaboration. If I'm doing well, that's going to help you, too, in the long term. We're not playing a zero-sum game where we hoard

resources and attention. There's plenty to go around.

In her piece "All Work and No Pay Makes Jack a Dull Writer: On Literary Citizenship and Its Limits," Becky Tuch raises a red flag on all this positive spin, and points to a downturn in publishers' marketing budgets:

> Who, then, must make up for this [economic] shortfall? Certainly it's not the owners and CEOs of publishing companies who lend a hand to writers in times of duress (in spite of the fact that their profits are derived precisely from those writers). No, it's writers who are expected to look after themselves and one another.

Tuch argues that writers are being exploited under the guise of marketing activities as "enriching" activities. She asks us to question and challenge this system, and the corporate publishers or corporate-culture machinations that have led us to the necessity of literary citizenship, and calls for "frank discussions about labor power and financial remuneration."

Here's a high-level summary of my own approach to this.

1. The disruption faced by publishing affects the entire media industry (and the world) and goes beyond economics. Publishing is not a specialized activity any longer. *Anybody can publish.* That's not to say anybody can publish well, but publication alone is not meaningful in and of itself in many cases. From the time of Gutenberg until roughly 2000, to print and publish something was to amplify it because of the investment and specialized knowledge required. That's largely not the case today (though for some print-driven work, it still is). To amplify something takes a different kind of muscle, and amplifying through print distribution is becoming less and less meaningful as 50% of book sales now happen online (whether for print or digital books). Publishers of all types and sizes are struggling with this disruption and what it means for their value to authors, readers, and the larger culture.

2. Authors can transcend publishers when it comes to reader loyalty. Most of us don't buy books because of who published them; we buy them because of who the author is. And if we don't know the author, we often buy based on word of mouth. Publishers try to encourage this word of mouth, but few have brand recognition or connections with actual readers, because they haven't traditionally been direct-to-consumer companies. They've sold to middlemen instead—bookstores, libraries, wholesalers.

In the last 5-10 years, authors have gained tools to connect directly with readers—tools that they've never had before—which give them tremendous power amidst the disruption. This is power that many publishers still lack.

Unfortunately, in the literary market, involvement with the readership is often seen as undesirable—writing for an audience or engaging with them is seen to lessen the art. ("I don't write for readers"—you've heard that one, right?) I won't address the problematic nature of this belief here, but this cultural myth is prevalent, and may be the subtext of some criticism of literary citizenship.

3. The abundance mindset trumps the victim or scarcity mindset. In Zen terms: are we going to see ourselves as part of the publishing world, or as acted upon by the publishing world (victims)? It may seem a slight and meaningless distinction, but it powerfully affects your outlook and how you decide what to do next—if you believe you are the person who has control of your life and work.

Also, we have to remember that when one area of the network or community suffers, it will invariably affect another part. We're already seeing shifts in the market that point to how publishers have to change—e.g., 25% of the top 100 books on Amazon last year were self-published, authors are successfully crowdfunding new books, and Wattpad has launched the careers of new, young authors, which uses a very different model than any we've seen before.

New business models are out there, and authors are finding the opportunities amidst the change. Benjamin Zander wrote in *The Art of Possibility:*

> The frames our minds create define—and confine—what we perceive to be possible. Every problem, every dilemma, every dead end we find ourselves facing in life, only appears unsolvable inside a particular frame or point of view. Enlarge the box, or create another frame around the data, and problems vanish, while new opportunities appear.

What frame are we using to look at the economic problem writers now face? I would suggest it's not useful to use the framework of, "Publishers are taking advantage of writers." Let's change the frame we're using—not to whitewash any potential unethical behavior, but to spot a productive way forward.

One of the more inspiring things I've read lately is Elizabeth Hyde Steven's *Make Art Make Money*, which is all about balancing business and art, as mastered by the late, great Jim Henson. I can't think of a better way to close than quote something she learned from studying his career:

We can walk into the world of business feeling we are on the turf of strangers, possible enemies. Or we can enter that world in a way that brings our own turf with us, so that we no longer feel defensive but expansive. With the realization of the power our art wields, we can become generous. When we do, we become compelling, enviable, impressive, and we have the ability to change things.

CHAPTER 7
Marketing and Promotion for New Authors

While all authors' situations are unique, they tend to experience the same disappointments during the traditional publishing process. The most common disappointment—and the one that can have the most damaging effects on the author-publisher relationship—is:

(Real or perceived): Lack of marketing and promotion support

What's even more frustrating is that all the old buttons publishers used to push don't work that well any more when it comes to making consumers buy books. And there's a whole new set of buttons that sometimes work, and sometimes don't.

However, these factors typically play a significant role in a book's success:

- Great content in the right package
- An author who knows and reaches their audience
- A publisher who places that book in every appropriate retail outlet
- A publisher who is able to get the attention of influencers and traditional media outlets
- Timing and luck

Also, for nonfiction especially, here's another criteria: your book needs to be a better vehicle for delivering information than what may be competing with the reader's attention online.

If you're still unpublished, here's how to get started (early) on the marketing process:

- Begin to establish your online presence (site, blog, social networks) and develop relationships with your target readership as well as influencers who recommend books. Make a dream list of online venues where you'd want your book reviewed or mentioned; start cultivating relationships with those sites or people.
- Identify groups or organizations that would be most interested in your book, and start a database of e-mail addresses and snail mail addresses.
- As you write and revise your work, think of ancillary materials or products that complement the work. Think of competitions or giveaways that would be interesting to someone who enjoys the book.

If you're working with a publisher on an upcoming launch date:

- It's vital you cut through the fog (with the assistance of an agent if necessary) on what the publisher will and will NOT do to market your work. If you're lucky, the publisher will be honest with you.
- Come up with a marketing plan that you can execute on your own. Remember: Marketing is not about shilling. It is about reaching people who would benefit or enjoy your work, and letting them know it is available. This often doesn't take money (e.g., advertising), but an authentic means of connecting with your target audience. You, the author, are the best person to know how to forge that connection. Your publisher may have professional inroads, but authors usually know the audience better.
- Tell the publisher what you will be doing, and identify areas where the publisher could be of great assistance to you. Publishers are much more likely to be helpful if you proactively show them your plan and ask them for what you want (as opposed to you calling up and demanding to know what they'll be doing to support your book).

Keep in mind:

- Publishers are most receptive to marketing your book during the 3 months before your book launch, and the 3 months after your book launch. Much longer before or after, and you may get ignored.
- Publishers will not be offended if you hire an independent publicist or firm to assist you. Yes, this can be a worthwhile investment if you have a very focused and realistic set of goals.

Why Don't Publishers Market and Promote the Books They Publish?

Why are publishers often accused of not sufficiently supporting their very own books? Wouldn't they benefit from it? Wouldn't it make sense? Aren't *they* supposed to be the experts here?

Here are a few reasons why publishers don't market and promote all of the books on their list:

- They don't have enough money, time, or staff.
- They have no means of directly reaching the target readership to let people know a book of interest is available.
- They can't measure the impact of their efforts, thus resources get pulled away from marketing.
- They hope the book finds its audience by simply being available and in stores. (Publishers are excellent at physical and retail distribution.)
- Did I mention they don't have enough money, time, or staff?

Now, you would probably advise: That means publishers should publish less. I agree. But that's not how publishing works. They try a lot of things and see what sticks.

Furthermore, publishers are known for putting most of their efforts behind A-list authors, or behind authors who receive a very large advance, or behind the book that receives the best response/commitment from the chain booksellers.

Every other title gets the "standard" treatment, which basically means a listing in the publisher's catalogue, advance copies to reviewers, some press releases—and done.

What still sells books? That's the nut everyone is trying to crack. Most people would say it's word of mouth. But how does word of mouth start? It's usually a mix of:

- Authors who already have established followings and can reach their readers directly
- E-mail promotions to a very targeted list (either a list that the author has cultivated or that the publisher is lucky enough to have)
- National media coverage or appearances
- Prominent reviews
- Recommendations by high-profile people (Oprah effect)
- Independent bookstore support.

Book Marketing 101—Or How to Generate Word of Mouth

The following section is a 2013 article I wrote for Scratch *magazine.*

It is possible, if not desirable, for an author to launch an effective book-marketing campaign without a publisher's support or assistance. Mainly, it requires time and energy. It may also require some monetary investment to hire a publicist, PR firm, or marketing consultant to advise and assist you. The good news is that, by the time your second, third, or fourth book comes out, you should have a solid base of readers to work from—a base that was developed from marketing activities associated with previous launches.

Remember that a comprehensive book-marketing campaign uses a combination of tactics to reach readers. It would be unusual to focus solely on social media, or solely on events, to generate word of mouth. The best approach combines online and offline components, and if done right, each amplifies and strengthens the other.

Author Events

Most authors know that the multi-city book tour is a thing of the past, but of course you can still find *New York Times* bestselling authors doing tours for their new releases. Chicago-based publicist Dana Kaye says such tours happen mostly as a favor to the bookstores, as a way for the author to give back to the community. But bookstores aren't always the best place for events.

Kaye says, "Any time you're trying to get people out of their house and go somewhere, it's very difficult. ... You're competing with many different things. However, more people are inclined to go somewhere if it feels like a party or an event, rather than just going to a bookstore and listening to an author read their work or talk about their work."

Many authors and publicists—and even the bookstores themselves—have caught on to this and now plan events in alternative venues, such as bars or clubs. Bookstores and other literary organizations sell tickets to author lunches held at restaurants, and the ticket price includes a copy of the book. Such events feel more social, and they avoid the lower perceived value and less compelling nature of the reading-signing format.

Kaye looks for ways to partner authors for events and tours, since that generally leads to better turnout and a better pitch for media coverage. For example, Kaye's firm organized and promoted the Young Authors Give

Back Tour, in which four YA authors, who had all published before 25, toured the country and taught writing workshops for teens. That angle got two TV appearances and a feature in the *Chicago Sun-Times.*

Even if the days of the traditional author tour are over, events still play an important role in an author's career. Kaye says: "Touring or doing an event is more about making a footprint. When you go to a city, it's not just the books you sell, but the people you talk to at the event. … It's about making connections with people. That being said, media is the primary reason you tour, even if that's becoming more difficult to pitch."

Working with Indie Bookstores

First-time novelist Marjan Kamali (*Together Tea,* Ecco, 2013) says her readings and bookstore events—some of which she planned herself—have energized her in a surprising way. "The reason they're so great is because I've been doing them at small, independent bookshops, which is who will have me. … It warms my heart to think there are these people out there who still love books, who know so much, who support authors."

Other authors feel the same way, and go out of their way to support their independent bookstore as part of their book launch or overall marketing campaign. Pete Mulvihill, owner of Green Apple Books in San Francisco, says that some authors adopt an indie bookstore to be their fulfillment center for anyone who wants to find an inscribed copy. He says, "We love when authors come by and sign books, whether there's an appearance or not, because it gives something we can offer that our major online competitor cannot. We'll most likely put it on our Facebook page or tweet about it. It generates a little more buzz. It tells people you're in town, you're a human, and that you care about indie bookstores. Even bookplates. You can send those to bookstores."

For her most recent book launch, Michigan author Loreen Niewenhuis made her travelogue, *A 1000-Mile Great Lakes Walk* (Crickhollow Books, 2013), available only from twelve Michigan independent bookstores for its first two months on the market. In an interview with Shelf Awareness, Niewenhuis said, "Authors … need to think about how they're getting their books to people. They need to think about how to make connections, not just about 'I need to sell my book.' How you sell your book is just as important."

Online Events

For her next book release, thriller novelist Jamie Freveletti, a client of Kaye's, is planning a live-streaming launch party using LiveLab Network. Freveletti says, "I did one streaming event with The Poisoned Pen bookstore, and I was surprised how many people logged in and watched it. People can be part of the excitement of it. It's just a fun thing to do."

But do online events sell books?

Kaye says, "We had a virtual launch [for a client] with several hundred people, but I didn't see the transition into sales. That's what I'd warn authors. If you're going to do an online discussion ... do something that's going to encourage book sales. It's a great way to interact with lots of people all over the world, but you want them to buy the book." Kaye recommends having an active buy link during the digital launch event, or providing a discount code to attendees to drive purchases.

It's always difficult to decide, however, which events might be worthwhile, since they are as much about creating word of mouth as selling books. A happy accident can always happen even if the sales aren't there. "My old boss Stuart [Applebaum] used to say we don't know if getting the word out about the book will sell the book, but we know they won't buy it if they've never heard of it," publicist Leslie Rossman says. "We're always looking for the critical mass of exposure for a book."

Traditional Media

Publishing insiders know that the number of media outlets available to pitch—on any type of coverage—has dramatically shrunk. Rossman, whose firm specializes in high-end radio such as NPR, says, "It's very competitive. It makes people very selective. There's fewer spots and that includes radio, TV, and print—and there's more syndication across the board."

However, when you do get a hit in the media, it tends to stick with people and make an impact. "If you're driving in your car, and you hear Terry Gross, that interview is going to resonate with you much more than if you're reading the interview online," says Kaye.

With persistence, authors can secure traditional media coverage without the publisher making the call. Katrin Schumann, the author of *The Secret Power of Middle Children* (Hudson Street, 2011), has been featured multiple times on the *Today* show, as well as on NPR and other media. When she started marketing her first book in 2008 with co-author Susan Callahan, she was totally unschooled in pitching, and didn't even consider TV a possibility. But Callahan had worked in marketing and understood the psychology behind it.

"She had this persistence," Schumann says, "continually knocking on your door in a slightly different way for the same thing. I realized that my instinctive approach was informed by the way I was brought up, which was polite. If they say no, they say no."

Over a year after their book launched, after repeated pitching, Schumann and Callahan got on the *Today* show. Schumann says of Callahan, "She didn't get overwhelmed and dispirited when encountering resistance. That's a key component authors don't take into account—the emotional rollercoaster of putting yourself out there continually and getting turned down, and not taking it personally."

Kaye's advice for authors who want to try pitching themselves is to focus on the quality of their pitch. Take the time to research media outlets, research what they're covering, and write a good pitch e-mail that shows how you fit into their editorial mission. Pitching doesn't require a special skill set or the contacts of a publicist.

However, Kaye says, it helps if you pick up the phone. "You have to not be afraid to call and get the right contact information, to do the digging." Kaye says authors can also ask their publisher for help; just tell them you'd like to reach out to a specific media outlet and are looking for the right person to contact with your pitch.

An effective and quality pitch process, however, can be time consuming, and this is where authors should evaluate where their time and effort is best spent, and if they can benefit from hiring a freelance publicist to assist them. Kaye says, "People ask, 'Can I do it on my own?' The answer is yes, if you have an extra eight hours in the day. Our job is to stay on top of what's current and stay on top of news stories. Most authors don't have time for that."

Online Marketing

It's the surest way to start a debate in a room full of writers: ask them about the value of social media and other forms of online marketing. On one side of the debate, you have those who argue that reader engagement through social media contributes to long-term career success and visibility. On the other side, you have people who have participated in some form of online promotion, and who found it a waste of time or a major distraction without meaningful impact on sales.

Leslie Rossman says that, when it comes to online marketing, much depends on what your starting point is: "How much energy do you want to invest in pursuing secondary media? Some people are interested in that because they want to build. Some people will not get top media, so they'll get something easy, and work up. If you're a self-published author, you would probably benefit from doing everything possible."

One of the biggest challenges for authors is deciding what types of online marketing will work for them strategically, and figuring out how to be effective in cutting through the noise without consuming huge amounts of their time. Then there's also the issue of actually enjoying themselves and the process.

Schumann, one of the leaders of Grub Street's Launch Lab, says that authors are taught to focus their energy in ways that feel productive and meaningful to them: "[Authors] feel like they have this mandate to do specific things, but those things don't feel authentic. They do them anyway—sometimes that's a reality—but sometimes you have a choice to say no, I'm not going to focus on that, I'm going to focus elsewhere. You can make those choices, as long as you don't make them by default. You're still in charge. It's better if you make really conscious choices about what feels comfortable for you."

When it comes to best practices in online marketing, the following themes emerged from my conversations with authors, publicists, and publishing industry experts.

Social Media (Facebook, Twitter, Etc.)

A gentle touch is encouraged. You're not a salesman pushing your book on people. Rather than focusing on ways to get people to buy your book—to achieve a short-term goal—approach social media as a long-term investment in your career. While book sales are important, you have to think about the big picture of what's sustainable. If a particular online activity saps your energy and becomes a drag, it's probably time to reassess and refocus. However, don't get discouraged if it takes time to understand or become comfortable with some online tools. Schumann says, "You don't master these things in one day, which can be really discouraging for authors. It takes some patience and perseverance and to be open minded."

If you're struggling to figure out social media, Rossman recommends taking a look at books or authors you admire. What does their activity look like? What blogs or websites did they appear on? What do they do on social media? Can you emulate those things?

Blogs

Regular blogging isn't necessary, but major blogs and websites can play an important role in spreading word of mouth, which means it can be worthwhile to write guest posts, do Q&As, or otherwise try to get featured by relevant bloggers who reach your target audience. It also helps to be an active participant or commenter on blogs where your readers hang out. Kaye says, however, to keep in mind that it's a small number of websites that actually have influence and traffic. If you do any marketing on a small blog or website, make sure its audience is a good fit for you and your book so you don't invest too much time for too little return.

Giveaways

Giveaways can work if done strategically. One of the most popular and effective venues for giveaways is Goodreads, a social media site for books and reading with more than 20 million members. One of the most important elements of the site—from a marketer's perspective—is the Goodreads star rating, which is based on reader reviews. Goodreads has been one of Kaye's favorite tools for getting the word out and generating pre-publication buzz. Kaye says, "As a society, we're very influenced by reviews. If there's not a lot of reviews [of your book], people probably won't buy it. The Goodreads giveaways are good ways to generate those early reviews that make a difference."

Since Goodreads will only do giveaways of physical copies, e-book authors—especially those who self-publish—have to look for other giveaway strategies. Amazon offers a special program for self-publishing authors called KDP Select. If you make your work exclusive to Amazon for 90 days, you can use 5 of those days for giveaways of your work. Independent authors typically use the giveaways to help generate reviews at Amazon, or to gain their book more visibility on Amazon overall. Some authors offer giveaways of a first book in a series when a new installment is about to launch, and enjoy a sales lift across the series after the giveaway concludes.

Another option is BookBub, a daily e-mail with more than 1 million subscribers that features limited discounts on e-books. For a fee—and if BookBub thinks your book is a good fit for its audience—BookBub will promote your e-book with a deep discount (usually setting prices of $2.99 or less) to a segment of its list.

E-mail Newsletters

Speaking of e-mail, newsletter lists that the author develops and owns can have a significant impact on sales and word of mouth. That's because it's easy for people to miss something that gets posted on social media, but just about everyone reads e-mail, even if it takes a long time. Kaye says,

"The e-mail list is the best way to engage your network." New authors may not have such a list ready for their first book release, but a recurring theme emerging from successful authors (both traditionally published and self-published) is that you should start building one through your own website, and at events, in preparation for future releases.

Parting Words of Wisdom

Kaye says she is constantly underestimating people's networks; if you build a network you can reach (either online or offline), they will come.

"A debut author did two events, one in St. Louis where she grew up, and one in Denver where she lives now. Because she was a debut author, I was very nervous," Kaye says. "She ended up having about 100 people come to each event, and sold even more books because people were buying multiple copies. That was very surprising to me. I really underestimated the people and the relationships really make the difference. If you make those connections, when it's time for your event, they will come out."

Freveletti experiments a great deal with all kinds of marketing to generate word of mouth, but, she says: "I can't keep up with every nuance of what's happening out there. But I can always call up a publicist and ask, 'What do you think of this?' They'll say, 'Oh, we tried that last year.' … And they save me so much time. The most important thing I can do is write. We all have to find this balance between marketing and writing."

A Key Book Marketing Principle

Most new authors, upon securing a book contract or planning a book launch, are advised they need to establish a Twitter account, a Facebook page, or [list social media channel here]. Why? To market their book, of course.

This presents an immediate dilemma: If the author is not already active on these channels, of her own interest and volition, she now has the mindset of using these tools to "market"—and the new author may have no idea what that means beyond telling people to like their page or follow them.

No one I know enjoys being a marketer on social media, not any more than people want to be marketed to. It poisons the experience, for everyone.

You might respond: Yeah, tell us something we don't know, right?

Yet authors continue to use social media—and their online networks—as blunt instruments, posting things that beg people to pay attention and become a buyer or follower. Unfortunately, asking for such attention on a social media network is likely to ensure you won't be getting any, except for those who already adore you or feel obligated to support you.

Here's the much better alternative to begging: When you develop a strategic marketing campaign for a new book, the first thing you should do is list all the people you know who will buy it without you asking, and would likely recommend it to everyone they know.

These are the people you send a round of personal and *private* appeals to. These are the people whose attention you already have. These are your most important relationships, relationships you probably treasure and nurture. Ask these people for specific types of help during your book marketing campaign, based on their own strengths or connections.

Do not make a habit of broadcasting general, blanket appeals for attention and help to strangers. Keep those broadcast messages focused on what strangers most want to know, and focus on how those messages serve them. (Example: "Don't miss the e-book giveaway on Wednesday only.") After you make your well-strategized broadcast, go back to your regularly scheduled programming of cat videos, gardening tips, or beer photos— that is, whatever you normally post about, why people enjoy seeing you in their newsfeed or stream.

None of what I'm saying precludes sending appeals to influencers who may have never heard of you. That's part of the game, too. But again, you should send personalized and *private* pitches if you're seeking their time or energy. Their attention is precious, and they value their audience's attention, too. You have to prove why you're worthy of attention in that personalized appeal. (What I'm describing is basically what you might hire a publicist to do on your behalf. You can do it yourself, too, if you have the time.)

So, I've just outlined two types of purposeful appeals:

1. Personalized messages to your trusted first circle, people who will buy your books without being asked.
2. Personalized messages to influencers, people who have an audience of their own that you'd like to reach.

Does this mean authors should never directly market their books or their brand through social media? No. But there should usually be specific strategy or reason for having what we call a "hard sell" message in your social media stream. It may involve breaking news (the book is now out!), a community conversation, or a special offer.

But social media is predominantly about "soft" marketing when it comes to authors and books. In my experience, the best marketing that can possibly happen centers on creating and strengthening those relationships (as in #1 and #2 above) that later come into play during a book launch. It's much easier to approach warm connections, or people with whom you've interacted over a span of months and years, than cold ones.

Especially for authors who live in a region that doesn't allow for much in-person relationship building, social media is invaluable for building those connections. It's also helpful for introverts who may find in-person networking more difficult.

So: Yes, you can use social media to help market your book, but try to forget about the typical way it's used or touted. Instead, focus on what you can help someone else with.

No. 1 Overlooked Skill for Every Writer

I wish they taught this skill to students in high school or college. Creative writing students especially need to spend a semester on it, but never do. You'd think publishers would deliver a 101 guide on it for their authors, though I'm not sure the publishers themselves always know anything about it.

The skill is copywriting. What is copywriting? According to Copyblogger, one of the top sites dedicated to the subject:

> Copywriting is one of the most essential elements of effective online marketing. The art and science of direct-response copywriting involves strategically delivering words (whether written or spoken) that get people to take some form of action.

Here are 3 primary ways that copywriting becomes essential to your success as an author.

Query Letters, Synopses, and Other Submission Materials
This is the classic form of copywriting that most writers engage in. A query letter is not a straightforward description of your work. It's a sales letter. It should be persuasive and seduce the agent into requesting your work.

And this is why writers struggle with queries, because they can't bridge the gap between writing to entertain (or inform or inspire) and writing to persuade. It's a different mindset, and it requires an ability to look at one's work as a *product* that has a *selling point*.

I once dated someone who spent 10 years in sales. What I learned from him is that it's not about succeeding on your first try or even with the majority of tries. It's about making the *highest number of tries* with the best prospects, then bouncing back quickly from rejection.

Unfortunately, most writers' egos are fragile, and they can't see the query process as one of the oldest practices in human history—a sales practice where rejection is commonplace.

So, adopt the mindset of a copywriter. You can't convince everybody, so just convince one person who's a good match for what you're offering. (But make sure you deliver the quality goods you promised!)

Website and Social Media Copy

This is one area where writers tend to have the most public failings. Online writing often boils down to copywriting, in these three forms.

1. Site and blog headlines. Every blog post requires a headline, and that headline demands your copywriting skills. Why? Go back and read the title of this section ("No. 1 Overlooked Skill for Every Writer"). Did it grab your attention, pique your curiosity, and make you want to read on in order to find out what that skill was? If the answer to those questions is yes, then that's effective copywriting in action.

Your post will be communicated across social networks and RSS feeds through its headline alone, without any other context. That headline must be strong and persuasive enough to garner someone's click.

Think about the titles of your site pages, too. Are the titles clear within a few seconds, telling visitors what content resides on your site? Don't count on cutesy, vague, or artistic headlines to spark curiosity. It most often leads to content that goes unread.

2. Effective tweets and status updates. Same principles apply here as with blog headlines. How do you catch people's attention in 140 words or less? Good copywriting. (See resources on the next page to learn the ropes.)

3. Your bio. There are many ways to write a bio, and many purposes for them, which can necessitate customizing them. But your basic site bio should help you achieve your immediate goals. If your site ought to lead to more freelancing gigs or speaking gigs, then your bio needs to give us a sense, within the first few lines, that you're an incredible freelancer or speaker. If your site ought to gather more readers around you, then speak directly to your readers in your bio. Think about who you hope will be reading your bio on a daily basis, and talk directly to them. Don't be aloof or stand-offish—at least not if you want people to contact you with opportunities or follow your updates.

Book Marketing Copy

If you're not working with a traditional publisher—and even if you are—then you need to learn how to write effective sales copy for your book—the stuff that's on the back cover, on your website, on Amazon, etc.

A few basics:

- Always have a headline.
- For fiction, never outline the entire story. You tease the reader; you raise questions that you don't answer. Here's a famous example from Alice Sebold's *Lovely Bones:* "My name was Salmon, like the fish; first name, Susie. I was fourteen when I was murdered on December 6, 1973." So begins the story of Susie Salmon, who is adjusting to her new home in heaven, a place that is not at all what she expected, even as she is watching life on earth continue without her—her friends trading rumors about her disappearance, her killer trying to cover his tracks, her grief-stricken family unraveling.
- In the case of nonfiction, you don't focus on yourself. Instead, detail all the ways the reader will benefit from the information in the book. For example, if I were trying to sell you a book about copywriting, I might say: *Learn the 3 secrets to writing effective copy every single time!*

Copywriting is a skill that you can learn and improve over time. Here are two of the best resources available:

1. Copyblogger.com They offer a free tutorial called 10 Steps to Effective Copywriting, which includes advice on writing headlines, the structure of persuasive copy, irresistible offers, and the No. 1 secret to great copy.

2. ProBlogger.com by Darren Rowse. This site offers specific tips to make money blogging—which means you need to become a great copywriter.

What Authors Forget About Marketing—Especially Those Who Dislike It

I think we can all agree that every author has a distinct writing voice or style, and that—over time—authors usually develop stronger and more confident voices.

What is acknowledged less often is how every author has (or should have) a distinct marketing voice and approach.

Sometimes, because we have less experience with marketing, or feel uncomfortable with the practice, we brace ourselves, even *change* ourselves, to engage in the activity.

This is good for no one.

Think about it carefully. Do you adopt a totally different persona or voice when it's time to market and promote? Of course you might put on your marketer's hat to brainstorm ideas about marketing strategy, but those ideas ought to be expressed and executed by the "real" you, not a stilted, rational, or smarmy marketer version of you.

If you're on the right path, it means you have a distinctive approach that can't be copied by anyone else. Let's look at a few examples.

John Green. Here's a YA author who capitalizes on YouTube videos as a marketing and platform device. He does it in partnership with his brother. Were these guys born to perform in front of the camera? Yes. Could any author pull this off? No.

Jeanne Bowerman. She's well known as the #twitterpimpangel. She talks about tequila a lot. She throws Rolos. She is unfailingly supportive and helpful to writers. She has a great story to tell about how she got where she is today. Is her story and approach replicable by any other author? No.

Chuck Wendig. For anyone active in the online writing community, you probably know Chuck already. He describes his website/blog as "unmercifully profane." He adds, "It is not for children. Frankly, it's probably not even for adults." Would a bunch of authors even *want* to pull off what Chuck does? No. But it works for Chuck.

I could give dozens of examples, and show you how an author's unique personality directly plays into their marketing and platform building approach. However, easier said than done. Why?

It takes self-awareness and honesty about who you are.

It asks that you focus on the people who will truly "get it" and be your biggest fans—meaning you don't try to please everyone all the time.

It requires that you focus *less* on the new shiny tools and *more* on creative and imaginative ways of sharing and delivering a message about your work.

Note: There is no personality type that makes you bad at marketing!

As you consider how to best develop your marketing voice and strategy, I recommend asking a couple trusted friends or advisers if they can envision you successfully doing X. Does X activity sound like you? Does it complement your values, what you stand for, how you prefer to operate?

If so, you're one step closer to developing your distinct marketing approach that's the best fit for you, your work, and your audience.

Before You Tackle Social Media

One of the most common questions I receive is: How can I use XYZ social media tool to market and promote my book?

Sometimes I feel like I'm being asked: How can I find Mr. or Mrs. Right who will make me happy for the rest of my life?

So many factors are at play, and one of the most critical is how interesting you are to other people. You might very well start by asking yourself, "What makes me interesting?"

Justine Musk has a fascinating post on this at her website, "The Importance of Being Interesting." That aside, here are three things you need to get right before you start trying to "get something" from social media (as opposed to just playing around, which is a meaningful goal in itself!).

1. Purpose comes first. Repeat after me: *Social media is a tool*. It works best when you have a purpose, direction, or strategy in using it.

Feeling lost already? See it as a creative or imaginative exercise. A blank page of paper is a tool. A pen is a tool. What you decide to do with them is a creative act. *It requires vision.* If you use social media *only* to market and promote a book, people will probably tune you out. (It's not a very creative approach!) Often, you need to express interest in others first—or offer a worldview.

So ask: What greater purpose might you serve? How can you be interesting, or of service, or entertaining? When you have a purpose, you'll not only be more effective, but you'll also enjoy yourself more, and stick with it longer. Andrew Shaffer is an excellent example of an author who uses tools for a greater purpose than just marketing and promotion. (See his Evil Wylie project, which started as a Twitter account.)

Don't expect that you'll get it right the first time. You'll have to experiment, and you'll have to be patient. This is good. You'll learn something from the process, even if you fail.

2. Great content (or entertainment) comes first. No amount of expert marketing can make a poor or mediocre product sell—or gain visibility—like a great one. If what you have doesn't meet the standards of your readers, you'll be struggling each and every day to spread word of mouth because people don't truly believe in your work.

You can tell what great content is because, when it comes to social media, everyone wants to share it. They want to comment on it. They want to "like" it. They want to be the one who made the cool discovery. They're excited and have that itch to post their opinion. Great content matched to the right audience inspires that.

3. Context comes first. The crowd who hangs out on Twitter is not the same crowd who hangs out on Facebook, or on LinkedIn, or on Google Plus, or on the Kindle Boards, or on the romance blogs. Of course there is some overlap between major social networks, but each tool will reach a different set of people. And each set of people will talk a slightly different language because they have unique perspectives and needs.

That means you're wasting your time if you decide to propagate the exact same message across many different channels. You'll also waste your time if your message never changes as time passes. Your message needs to fit the context, it needs to be timely, and it needs to be customized for each particular audience.

Sometimes you'll realize that a particular community is the wrong context for *any* message or contribution from you.

How do you know? Well, if you're paying attention (if *you're listening*), it's not tough to figure out. No one will comment, respond, share, like, or otherwise offer feedback. The community may even push you out. Or you may simply see no positive marketing impact (e.g., traffic to your site or a sales spike).

This may sound like "work," but describing all this in words tends to make it sound more complicated or time-consuming than it really is. If I spelled out every single step you might take to evaluate a potential social networking tool, I might never finish even after a year of writing! But when you use your head and your intuition, the creative strategy or answer will present itself to you.

The Marketing Paradox: Start Small to Get Big

Have the following thoughts ever crossed your mind?

- My book has a broad audience and could be enjoyed by anyone.
- I don't want to be pigeon holed—I want to attract all types of readers.
- If my book could get promoted on [big-name TV show], everyone would see how widely appealing my work is.
- When extra-terrestrials land, they'll become a new audience for my book!

Okay, maybe not that last one. But new authors often believe their potential audience is very broad.

I don't want to squelch anyone's ambitions, but this attitude does not make for a workable marketing strategy.

You may have dreams of reaching millions, but to reach millions, you have to start with the people who are your *target market* or demographic. Or, you have to think like a marketer:

- Define your target market.
- Position your book for that market.
- Develop an appropriate marketing mix for that target market (marketing mix defines where you plan to be active in reaching your audience)

If you try to be everything to everyone, you end up being nothing at all.

Professional marketers have long used the VALS psychographic segmentation to help them identify their target market and position their products.

While I don't think this approach makes sense for all books and authors, seeing this tool should help get you in the right mindset to define your market. Plus, what I want you take away is this: Even mass-marketed brands and companies have a target market. They are trying to appeal to specific people with each campaign.

Some authors want to remain free of genre labels, or want to be open to many types of readers. That's well and good—as well as a common and logical desire. But it's also one that you have to fight against when it comes to marketing.

Paradoxically, a strong marketing strategy and communication, especially for new authors, is to target as narrowly as possible and establish that core readership. You want to talk to the MOST interested people first—your best prospects—to avoid wasting time and energy in the initial stages.

You gain a large audience by starting with a small core, then letting the ripples grow. Don't try to go broad, then narrow. It usually works in reverse.

4 Ways to Immediately Improve Your Book Marketing Efforts

When I see bad book marketing out in the wild, I wish I could do something productive to help that author (or sometimes publisher!) see how they're wasting their time.

What is bad book marketing? It's whenever I receive:

- A tweet from a total stranger asking me to look at their book
- An e-mail from a total stranger asking me to look at their book
- A Facebook message from a total stranger asking me to look at their book.

And so on—I think you get the idea.

Here are 4 ways to immediately improve your book marketing efforts.

1. Use your website for hard selling. Do not lean on social media for hard selling. Social media typically works best for long-term awareness efforts, relationship building, audience development, and general networking. It is not terribly effective for repeatedly telling people, in your own voice, over and over again, "Buy my book." All of the information about why people might like your book—along with the hard-hitting sales pitch—should be on your website. If you don't have your own website where you control the content and presentation, it's next to impossible to have a successful book marketing campaign.

2. Brainstorm a list of all the *meaningful* relationships you have— people who you can count on to read your e-mails. Divide the list into three groups: (a) people who would probably like to be alerted to your new work, e.g., old classmates or coworkers, (b) people who have significant reach or influence with your target readership, e.g., a blogger or established author, and (c) your existing and devoted fans who may be willing to spread the word about your new work to their friends and connections.

For Group A, write a brief announcement and include a link to your website for all the book details.

For Group B, write a brief, **personalized** note to each person about your book promotion efforts, and offer 1-3 concrete ways they could help you— e.g., tweet about the book on a specific day, excerpt the book on their blog/site, run a Q&A, etc.

For Group C, write a brief, general note asking for support in any way they feel comfortable, and provide examples of what that support might look like.

If there are any influencers in Group C, consider moving them to Group B and writing something more personalized. **So few authors do any of this.** Taking the time to write personalized e-mails will dramatically increase support from your network. You shouldn't try to market and promote your book on your own; it takes a village, as they say.

3. Brainstorm a list of all the gatekeepers to your readers with whom you do not have a relationship yet—specific individuals and specific websites/blogs. For example, if you write romance, then popular romance review blogs would act as a gatekeeper. Do those blogs accept guest posts? Can you contribute to their community in some way? If you want to grow your readership, you'll have to work beyond your existing network. Find a way to help gatekeepers—rather than demanding something of them—and you'll find the whole process more successful AND enjoyable.

4. Invest in professional design and presentation for all marketing and self-promotion materials. This includes your website, your author photos, your book cover (the No. 1 book marketing tool, whether print or digital), your business cards, your Twitter avatar, your Facebook cover photo, etc. If you appear professional, that's half the battle. Amateur design hurts you tremendously in the long run—especially when it comes to gate-keepers and influencers. Sorry, but appearance matters, and a professional presentation shows that you take yourself and your work seriously.

How to Spend Your Book Marketing Budget

Authors often ask me how they should spend the limited budgets they have for book marketing and promotion. The following three factors are critical.

1. Who's your primary target audience? Don't spend a dime until you know who you're trying to sell to. You should thoroughly research your target readers' habits, where they spend their time online, and how they decide to purchase books. It does no good to spend money on a social media advertising campaign or a blog tour if your target audience doesn't use social media or read blogs.

2. How much of your audience do you "own"? If you have your own website or e-mail newsletter list (or other channel), then you "own" some part of your audience. You have the attention of a specific group of people who are already interested in your work. It might be desirable to invest in growing that "owned" audience, or you could improve the materials you use to market to them. If you do not "own" any audience, then you may want to invest in paid advertising, and convert people who respond to your advertising into an audience you own (by having them join your e-mail list, fan your Facebook page, etc). This is a long-term strategy that should benefit all books you publish.

3. What are your weak spots? Hopefully you have some idea of where your efforts are not what they should be. It might be your website or blog design, the copy on your website or blog, your skill level with social media or other tools, a weak network of contacts, or missing media that your audience might reasonably expect from you (e.g., podcasts or video).

These areas are likely worth investing in for most authors.

Get a website makeover. You could easily spend $2,000 (and a lot more) on an optimized site that's designed to (1) get people on your e-mail list and/or (2) introduce people to your books (and convince them to purchase). While I think a design makeover would be helpful in and of itself, this alone isn't sufficient. You usually need excellent online copy. While copy on your Amazon page is incredibly important for book sales, copy on your website is just as important. You don't own Amazon's customers. You can't analyze what happens on Amazon's site. But you do own and can analyze what happens on your site.

Hire a publicist for a specific book or campaign. This is probably a viable option only if one of your books is quite new, or if you (or the publicist) can identify a hook in your subject matter/expertise that appeals to media outlets. For $2,000–$3,000, you could hire a skilled publicist, with an excellent network of contacts, for probably one month to help garner mainstream media attention. Or, you could hire an expert to train you to be better at pitching all types of media (from bloggers to reporters). I do not recommend hiring a publicist or consultant if you already know and can get a response from the movers and shakers in your niche community.

Hire a digital marketing consultant. An expert can help ensure that (1) you are using effective and consistent messaging across all of your media channels (site, blog, social media)—and help hone your message, (2) your social media activity makes sense when viewed as a whole, and you're not missing any significant opportunities and (3) you aren't subverting your efforts or engaging in bad practices. A consultant can also give you advice on how to improve your influence, reach, and impact.

As you'll notice, all of these recommendations have the long-term view in mind, and aren't necessarily focused on selling one specific book.

I do not recommend the following investments:

- Broad, untargeted advertising (on any medium/channel)
- Press release blasts or any form of mass mailing and communication
- Buying friends, fans, or followers
- Physical review copy mailings of self-published titles—but do consider a pre-publication giveaway on Goodreads

A Critical Marketing Secret: Don't Go It Alone

One of my favorite bestseller stories is from Tim Ferriss, author of *The Four-Hour Workweek*. Just about everyone is curious how he managed to hit No. 1 on the New York Times bestseller list with his *first* book.

Here's what Tim says in his infamous post, How Does a Bestseller Happen?

Before I began writing [...] I cold-contacted and interviewed close to a dozen best-writing authors about their writing processes, followed by close to a dozen best-selling authors about their marketing and PR campaigns.

I asked several questions of the latter group, but one of the assumption-busting home runs was: "What were the 1-3 biggest wastes of time and money?"

This led me to create a *"not-to-do"* list. Number one was no book touring or bookstore signings whatsoever. Not a one. All of the best-selling authors warned against this author rite of passage. I instead focused on the most efficient word-of-mouth networks in the world at the time—blogs. The path to seeding the ideas of 4HWW was then straight-forward: Go where bloggers go. ... Build and maintain those relationships through your own blog, too.

Tim's first step is critical: He interviewed people who had achieved the level of success he wanted. He found out what worked for them. And he not only emulated it, but built critical relationships with those who were influential in spreading the word about his book.

You'll find this kind of story played out again and again.

Many times, when an author's marketing efforts fail, it's because they tried to go it alone. (Actually, even your writing efforts are apt to fail if you don't have a mentor or trusted critique partner who can give you honest and constructive feedback.)

Relationships are critical, and often when you see a successful author, what you see are only the *visible* aspects of their content, their online presence, and their credibility. What you can't see is all of the relationship-building and conversations that go on behind the scenes that contribute to a more impactful and amplified reach. Just because you can't see it doesn't mean it's not there. But I guarantee that no successful author has gone it alone.

A Few Words About Press Releases

This is part rant, part advice. It's frustrating to see authors *and publishers*—who probably have little time and resource to begin with—wasting their time by contacting bloggers (and others in the media) with dead-on-arrival press releases. Let's back up for a moment.

What kind of press releases do I receive?

I receive announcements primarily about new books, new products, and site launches. I also get information about author-experts who are available for interviews.

When I say "press release," I'm referring strictly to an e-mail announcement that is neither addressed to me personally (beyond an automated greeting line) nor is it seeking to serve me or my audience. It is looking to get something out of me: coverage on my blog or social network.

Why are the press releases I receive typically ineffective?
They are part of a huge and impersonal blast, hoping that a few hits will justify a send to hundreds or thousands of e-mail addresses. For instance, I receive regular blasts from book publishers announcing new releases. But it's hard to feel any excitement at receiving such an announcement when it is not tailored to me, my blog, or my audience. Such releases demand that I make the connection—that I figure out the right angle or fit.

Bad press releases:
- Do not address me personally
- Don't show awareness of my blog or site
- Are far too long, wordy, or boring
- Ask me to spend valuable time evaluating something I don't trust yet (e.g., "Review this book!")
- Put limitations on what I can or can't do
- Do not propose any specific action steps for me to take
- Focus on the author/publisher

In other words, I am not treated like a real connection. Here's an example of **a good e-mail** I received from a publicist. This was a cold contact, meaning we had never before been in touch. (This is an independent publicist, not a publicist working for a book publisher.)

Hi Jane.

My client, Rochelle Melander, has her 10th book coming out on October 18 from Writer's Digest Books. The title is *Write-A-Thon: Write Your Book in 26 Days* (and live to tell about it). Just in time for NaNoWriMo. Rochelle wrote the first draft of this book during NaNoWriMo 2009. We can offer you an excerpt for your blog plus giveaways of the book if that interests you.

Rochelle's website is www.writenowcoach.com for more info about the book. We have a press release, bio and book trailer ready to go. Review copies are available digitally and by mail.

Thanks for your kind consideration and I look forward to hearing from you.

This is short and to the point. It's clearly suited to my blog and audience since I regularly run book excerpts of new releases. It was easy to reply, and it felt like this would be an easy thing to run. Once I had a digital review copy in hand, I had control over selecting the best excerpt for my audience. And that's exactly what happened. Easy, fast, and satisfying for all.

Here are 5 reasons people might say "yes" to coverage of a book, product/service, website, or author on their blog.

- Strong, quality content that will appeal to their audience
- They don't have to "work" for the content or create it themselves.
- They believe in the author's message, or at least think it's worth considering/listening to.
- The content is not going to be duplicated on everyone else's site/blog.
- There's some control in selection of the content.

Yes, I pay more attention to appeals coming from people I know, or those who are referred to me by people I trust. But I'm happy to be pitched by strangers if I think their content or message is strong and suited to my audience. If I think the content is suspect, even if it's coming from someone I know and trust, I will either reject it or edit it until it's advice or instruction that I would feel comfortable delivering into people's inboxes.

Back to the rant: I've read trend pieces on whether or not the press release is dead. Sometimes I wish they would die, but I also realize they still have a role to play in disseminating official information quickly to specific media channels. But no publicist worth his/her salt ought to be blasting out mediocre requests for coverage to a list of near-strangers. It wastes everyone's time.

I'll always remember publicist Dana Kaye answering a question at the Midwest Writers Workshop, from a writer who asked her how big her contact list is. Kaye rightly pointed out that it's not list size that matters, it's the list quality. Who will actually read her e-mails or take her calls? Can she get people to pay attention? Does she have meaningful connections on that list?

That's where the real value lies—not in how many people you can reach with a generic message.

The Persistent and Damaging Myth About Introverts and Marketing

I'm getting frustrated with people who say they're bad at marketing & promotion because they're introverts.

Maybe this argument was more valid before new technologies came along—when marketing and promotion involved more "getting out there," networking at events and stores, or making phone calls.

But looking at how things work today, introverts should be over the moon at how lucky we are to live in an age when we can effectively market and promote by:

- staying at home
- using whatever tools suit our communication style best (e-mail, IM, Skype, Twitter, Facebook, etc.)
- crafting and controlling messages to our own satisfaction
- limiting interaction when needed

I've self-identified as an introvert since I was a child, and test as an introvert on the Myers-Briggs. I love this time-honored article about caring for the introverts in your life, and I know the horror of being told to "think faster." Some people just don't understand—it takes time to fully process what's being said, sort through knee-jerk reactions, thoughts, and feelings, then carefully and thoughtfully formulate a response.

But these tendencies of introverts …

- bad at small talk (but not necessarily shy)
- preference for small group conversation
- avoidance of huge social gatherings—or being drained by them

… these tendencies don't significantly impact our ability to be effective at online marketing and promotion. In fact, when you consider that "the only thing a true introvert dislikes more than talking about himself is repeating himself," you have the makings of a superlative online marketer!

These days, there's far too much bad marketing and self-promotion (that amounts to talking, in a very uninteresting way, about oneself), and not enough good marketing and self-promotion, which is about serving an audience.

Knowing your audience, reaching your audience, and engaging effectively with your audience is more about listening, understanding, curiosity, and good communication skills—not "extroversion" or "introversion."

So, my fellow introverts, you'll need to find a better excuse to explain why you're bad at marketing and promotion!

WIIFM?

How often are you asked a favor? How do you decide whether or not to extend the favor? You probably decide based on:

- The relationship you share with this person (or organization)
- WIIFM, or: What's In It For Me?

When it comes to marketing yourself or your work—or building your career—you have to assume there is no such thing as altruism. You must always identify & convey how the other person will benefit/gain by doing what you ask.

Here's what separates the classy people from the not-so-classy: Even when you have an excellent relationship with someone, a consummate professional (and a friend, too) will always position requests or proposals so that there's a gain for everyone.

Successful people have an excellent way of involving—early on—others who can have an impact on their success, and making them feel special, included, and benefited in some way—which results in future favors (or offers) when none have been requested.

Let's say you run a blog where you interview authors or review their books. If your recommendations carry weight in your community, and you highly and repeatedly recommend a certain author or book, you're offering support and publicity without being asked.

If the author notices and conveys gratitude (which they should), they will likely get in touch with you, and possibly open the door to a relationship or future requests.

But: Even if not, later on, you'll be much better positioned to ask this author for a cover blurb, or a referral, or some other favor in the future, assuming it's a good fit. (Sometimes these things are ALL about fit, or timing.)

In the social media community, the simple tenet of WIIFM can be forgotten. And as a result, you get a lot of people bashing social media. So, never forget that relationship building comes BEFORE favor asking. And there has to be a much bigger and better WIIFM when you approach people cold, without a solid relationship.

That said, sometimes people will offer favors if they are charmed by you, or like you, or are just in a good mood. But given how overwhelmed most people are these days, they usually appreciate and respond well to clear propositions with a straightforward action attached—and a benefit. Otherwise, you just become part of the noise.

The Giving-Stuff-Away Strategy

Whenever I hear an author or writer say, "Why would I ever give my work away for free?" I want to ask: "Do you not want to grow your audience?"

However, randomly giving your work away, without a pointed long-term goal, is not a way to succeed as an author. Knowing how and when to make an offer is key, and can be a strategic move during moments of your career.

Let's look at how this strategy applies to three different categories of author.

1. Unpublished Novelists, Memoirists, Essayists, and Poets

First ask: What you want to accomplish by sharing or posting your work online? Posting your work online isn't going to lead to a traditional book publishing deal—at least not by itself. Here are a few strategies that writers typically have in mind:

Test marketing and content development. The paint isn't yet dry; you're looking for direction on how to further shape the work, or abandon it. You can see this kind of activity on Wattpad.

Growing community and readership over the long-term. This requires pounding the pavement—through online networks AND off—to let everyone you know that your work is available to be read. It also requires you to be generous in reading and commenting on others' work.

Creative/multimedia experimentation. Posting creative work online, without any modification (just straight, looooong text), can be a weak approach even if you are test marketing or growing a readership. It's much more interesting to look at serialization, consider creative media spin-offs, or find aspects of your personality that can shine in an online format, or adapt your work so it blossoms in an online environment.

While I don't think you're killing your chances of traditional publication when posting your work online (no matter what your reasoning), there's not much point in doing so unless you have a strategy or goal in mind, and a way to measure your success. For example, I've seen novelists use serializations to build readerships for their email newsletters, get started on Twitter, and build an audience for other book-length work.

If you have no interest in marketing your work and connecting with readers after posting your stuff online, don't do it.

2. Published Novelists, Memoirists, Essayists, and Poets

It's essential for established or published authors to make some portion of their work available for free as a teaser, to increase fans/followers.

Fortunately, the more work you've produced, the easier this gets. You simply make your first book (or some of your early work—or most popular work) available for free. This allows you to cast a wide net to find readers, who then—assuming they like the free stuff—go on to buy full-length books.

3. Experts & Authorities (Nonfiction Authors, Published/Unpublished)

People working in nonfiction categories (who are *not* memoir driven) are under the greatest pressure to give away some form of their content. That's because, in today's world, the problem isn't insufficient information—it's TOO MUCH information.

What you'll often find is that nonfiction authors use their book as something that helps open the doors to other money-making opportunities (coaching, teaching, speaking, consulting, etc). Since content itself is not scarce, the nonfiction author must capitalize on what IS scarce in today's world, which is time, personalized attention, customization, and immediacy.

Also, it is near-impossible for most nonfiction authors to land a book deal unless they have a strong online presence, especially in popular how-to/information categories (e.g., health, self-help, business ...). And an online presence usually involves some form of content marketing, whether an e-newsletter, quality blog posts, digital downloads, and so on.

You Need Professional Headshots

I've been in the publishing business long enough to know and understand how important a professional photo can be (just like a professional website) in making the right impression. A professional photo can help:

- Show your seriousness of purpose, which can lead to trust
- Refine and distinguish the message you want to send about yourself
- Show yourself at your best.

A photo (professional or not) can also do not-so-great things:

- Give people the wrong feeling about you
- Trick or deceive (sometimes intentionally!)
- Show you at your worst.

It may be wrong to have this reaction, but when I see a great professional shot of someone, I immediately consider them more successful than someone who does not.

Also, in the online world, we often don't have a chance to meet everyone in person, so the image we hold in our head is whatever that person is willing to provide. And too often what is provided is not flattering.

Christina Katz, in *Get Known Before the Book Deal*, gives these reasons for having a professional headshot:

- Because you'll get the lion's share of publicity
- Because you communicate without words that you are a professional, camera-ready for visibility
- Because you get selected easier.

She offers these tips for what your photo should accomplish:

- Be as flattering as possible
- Catch you at your best angle, highlight your best features, and make you look like someone interesting to meet
- Reflect a professional quality (nothing distracting in the background, no one else showing in or obviously cut out of the photo, no poor lighting or shadows)
- Capture your essence so that people feel like they are meeting the person they expected
- Be sharp (as with all types of communication, clarity and technical excellence count)
- Be in context with your platform (if you write thrillers, you can be mysterious or look like the hippie girl next door, whichever is more compelling)
- Project confidence and success.

Don't Pay Money for BEA Book Promotion

This advice is for self-published authors, independent authors, and possibly traditionally published authors who seek to hire assistance in the marketing and promotion of their books.

Do not pay to have your book "promoted" at BookExpo America (BEA) by a third party. It is not worth the money, not even a little. I say this having attended BEA for seven years straight, as part of a traditional publishing house team.

Why?

1. Nobody is going to notice your book there. Your book is likely to be "promoted" with many other books, with no way of attracting attention even if someone did pause for a second within 50 feet of your book. Imagine setting a copy of your book down in the world's largest book fair, and expecting someone to not only notice it, but be entranced by it so much they can ignore 10,000 other things happening at the same time.

2. If you—the author—are not present to advocate for it, your book doesn't stand a chance. Services that offer to promote your book at BEA will not be hand-selling or promoting your book in a meaningful way. But they will be happy to cash your check and say that your book had a "presence" at BEA. If you want to satisfy your ego, go ahead. But it's not going to lead to sales.

BEA is a quality industry event, and it is a legitimate marketing and promotion opportunity for many authors and publishers. But I do not recommend any self-published or independent author pay a third party for BEA promotion.

Simple Tips on Finding and Working with a Book Publicist

I've heard a lot of nightmare stories from authors who were working with a book publicist and didn't get what they wanted out of the relationship or investment. Sometimes I think that happens because of misaligned expectations, or even a misunderstanding of what working with a book publicist can achieve or accomplish.

Put another way: When it comes to book marketing and sales, it's not always easy to say "Effort A led to Outcome B," especially if book sales gain momentum from word of mouth (that's still often the case), and authors don't have access to precise sales analytics. You can't always figure out how or why someone decided to visit Amazon or their local bookstore to buy your book.

A publicist is often seen primarily as a key to mainstream media coverage, but they also have tremendous value outside of that. They can cover marketing and promotion activities that you could do yourself, but they can often do it better, more efficiently or more knowledgeably. Their professional finesse may lead to a better impression and more sales in the long term, and leave you time to focus on other high-value activities. They can also help you avoid marketing tactics or campaigns that they know are problematic, or point you toward new, useful tools they've discovered. This is one of the key values pointed out by bestselling author Jamie Freveletti when I interviewed her; her publicist provides her with savvy guidance—and a person to bounce ideas off of—in a confusing and ever-evolving digital marketing age.

But let's go back to the beginning: why are nightmare stories about publicists so easy to find? Quite simply, because authors are expecting something that's not delivered. Here are some tips to avoid that situation.

- Make a list, in writing, of the specific outcomes you're looking for the publicist to achieve, and how that connects to what you are doing and what your publisher is doing. Share this with each publicist you might hire and ask for a proposal (along with their fees).
- Before hiring a publicist, research other campaigns they've worked on. Have they achieved the kind of results you're looking for? Talk to their past clients if at all possible.
- After the publicity campaign starts, you and the publicist will find that some aspects of the campaign are not working. This is common and a sign that refocusing is necessary. Talk it over with your publicist. Even better, have pre-determined check-in dates to talk about progress, what's working and what's not.

Pay Proper Attention to Your Bio

Lately I've noticed that some freelance and author bios are very short—sometimes not more than one line—and say little more than "John Doe is a writer."

When I made an observation on Twitter in regards to this phenomenon, Atlantic editor Alexis Madrigal suggested that it was a response to the "super long bio." Editor Glenn Fleishman said he fights with some writers to give him more than "So and so writes articles," and chalked it up to some people being shy or trained to be modest.

But there are other reasons for it, which involve writers modeling themselves after famous authors who can totally get away with a one liner. Fleishman said it's analogous to Japanese business cards, at least in the 1990s. Less info = more important.

So for some writers with short bios, it's an attempt to convey status. Other writers may be putting on that "mysterious" act—the romance of the introverted author whom you should never know *too* well, because that kills enjoyment of the work.

But as an editor and curious person, the message I take away from the writer of the short bio is: "I don't care about, nor do I need, you or your opportunities." A poor bio statement is a missed opportunity—unless you're

Jonathan Franzen or Oprah—to say something about yourself, explain what interests you, and lead people to more of your work.

At this point I should mention that a brief bio has never stopped me from investigating a person I'm super interested in. But it's an unnecessary stumbling block, and it's usually the people with the super-short bios who have no websites or easy contact information.

If you don't tell your story, who will?

Look, I know writers like to be mysterious, or want their work to speak for itself. But getting discovered is part of the game of every writing career, and unless more paid and amazing opportunities are landing in your lap than you can possibly accept, now isn't the time to use a mysterious one-line bio.

Now I'll get off my soapbox and offer some tips for writing a bio (or a number of bios) suitable for online venues. I do this exercise regularly with my university students.

1. Write the kitchen-sink bio. Start the process by writing a long bio if you don't have one. I like the five questions that Michael Margolis proposes to help you get started:

- Who am I?
- How can I help you?
- How did I get here (i.e. know what I know)?
- Why can you trust me?
- What do we share in common?

For authors specifically, I would boil this down to the following:

- Who am I?
- How did I get here?
- What do we share in common?

As any sensitive person would probably realize, these are fairly deep and complex questions that take time to answer in a way that's not overly earnest or self-absorbed. It helps if you think in terms of story or backstory, which writers happen to be pretty good at.

Here's an excerpt from Christina Katz's long bio:

A champion of mom writers while also maintaining her own prolific career, Christina's writing career tips and parenting advice appear regularly in national, regional, and online publications. Christina has been a "gentle taskmaster" to thousands of writers over the past decade. Her students go from unpublished to published, build professional writing career skills, and increase their creative confidence by working with her intensively over the years.

Here's another example, very different, at the start of Hugh Howey's long bio:

> Born in 1975, I spent the first eighteen years of my life getting through the gauntlet of primary education. While there, I dabbled in soccer, chess, and tried to write my first novel (several times).

While there is no single "right" way to write a bio, it should convey something of your voice, personality, or point of view. Howey and Katz both do that, with very different approaches. After reading just a few lines, you start to understand what you share in common with them.

Your long bio should probably be at least 250 words, and its primary home is on your website. You might not use it anywhere else or—that is—if done right, it will be too long for most other uses. It's for your fans, the most interested people, the editors, agents or influencers who read your work somewhere and are now scoping out your website or blog.

2. Create a short, capsule bio appropriate for running with your published articles. Take your long bio and start pruning. What are the most important things to keep?

- A broad picture of your experience and background
- External validators (where you've been published, where you've worked, awards you've won, anything that lends social proof); for authors, this usually amounts to your credits or publications
- A point of view or voice.

Let's look at Glenn Fleishman's bio, which is beautifully concise and tackles all of the above:

> Glenn Fleishman, @glennf, is the editor and publisher of The Magazine, a fortnightly electronic periodical for curious people with a technical bent. Glenn hosts The New Disruptors, a podcast about connecting creators and makers to their audiences, and writes as "G.F." at the Economist's Babbage blog. He is a regular panel member on the geeky media podcast The Incomparable. In October 2012, Glenn won Jeopardy! twice.

What constitutes point of view or voice here? We have some pretty distinctive words and choice of detail that conveys a POV: curious with a technical bent, geeky media guy, Jeopardy winner. All of these quickly signal to readers what Glenn is about.

On a personal note: Many of you know that I mention bourbon in my website bio. That little mention of bourbon offers a human touchpoint—that "something in common"—that has created unforeseen connections and opportunities. When I was invited to sit on a panel at the NEA, I was told that when they researched my background (by visiting my website), the mention of bourbon added a bit of personality that indicated I was probably not so bad to work with.

3. Customize your bio for each social media site where you're active. You get extra credit if you tailor your bio for each of your social media profiles. In some cases, this is necessary, like on Twitter, where you only get 160 characters and must come up with something original. In other cases, you might just copy-paste your short bio (from above), but since every social media community is different, it's best to focus on details that are most relevant to that particular community.

Where I think customization most benefits you:

Facebook. Why? People use this site for many different reasons, and it's impossible to predict who might end up reading the public parts of your profile. If you're sending out friend requests to people who may not know or remember you, that public bio becomes even more important. (I speak as someone who often looks for a Facebook bio note, but rarely finds it!) Long story short: it's a missed opportunity if you're using Facebook partly for professional reasons, but do not have a customized, public bio on your profile.

LinkedIn. This mostly depends on your day job and what role your professional career plays in your writing life, but LinkedIn bios should be far more, well, business-like—focused on business outcomes and achievements.

4. If your bio is often used by others, provide an easy cut-and-paste version at your website, on your bio page. This is important for anyone who is frequently speaking or doing events, who might often be mentioned in the media, or who otherwise has to frequently send out their bio for distribution. People who have to introduce you will appreciate having a 100- or 200-word version they can crib from and use in publicity materials.

A Checklist for Marketing Your E-Book

Knowing how to effectively market your e-book can be a challenge if you don't have any formal education or professional experience in sales and marketing. Plus, these days, the default strategy seems to be "I'll use social media." But that's not a strategy, it's a tool.

When I teach the basics of marketing communication to students, we start by discussing the marketing mix, also known as the 4Ps. Some say this model is outdated, but it's still a useful way to begin a discussion about marketing a product. This is *not* an exhaustive list of all the possible facets of the 4Ps, but it helps give you an idea of what comprises each.

Aside from having a quality e-book (**Product**), the other criteria for successfully selling an e-book are:

- List price (**Price**)
- Where and how the e-book is made available for sale (**Place**)—which includes your distribution and display within retail environments
- How you bring attention and visibility to your e-book (**Promotion**)
- Cover art (**Product**, but in some ways also **Promotion**, since it's a critical element of many promotional materials and sales pages)

Product

- Does your e-book have the same features or attributes as competitors in your genre/category? Consider story structure, chapter conventions, word count, illustrations, etc.
- Are there features you could add to make your e-book more marketable?
- Is it possible to launch with a series that will help with branding and repeat customers?
- Are you offering your e-book in the formats your audience most favors? Should you invest in additional formats to maximize sales?
- Does your e-book compete well against similar titles in terms of quality? Consider cover quality, formatting quality, editing quality, etc.

Place

Is it easy for readers to buy your book at their favored online retailer or for their favored device? Consider if it's wise to limit the places your e-book is sold for your own convenience or savings. If you limit its availability for marketing reasons, then ensure you're maximizing promotion or visibility through your primary distribution channel. For instance, if your goal is to push all sales through Amazon to get a higher ranking, make sure you're maximizing all of Amazon's tools and know how the ranking system works!

Price

- Have you chosen the right price for your reputation or brand that makes sense in your market? Most DIY authors are using the 99 cent and $2.99 price points in order to maximize earnings as well as opportunities for **promotion** (since higher volume gets you on bestseller & popular lists).
- Lower price points can communicate something different than higher price points. The higher the price, usually the higher perceived quality or greater expectation of quality or valuable information. Traditional publishers or bestselling authors can often charge more (at least for now) because they're known quantities.
- How will you use discounts as a strategic promotional tool?

Promotion

Coming up with marketing and promotion strategies is primarily a creative act and should naturally arise from your work's subject matter or themes, your own network of relationships, and your strengths in using particular media. I can't possibly offer a comprehensive or customized list of ideas here, but consider the following.

- Start with a selling strategy: How will you distinguish your book from others? What is your key selling point or hook? What will appeal to your audience?
- Develop a marketing plan by listing all the concrete channels you have available to you for marketing: e-mail addresses, your website/blog, your e-mail newsletter, social networks, online communities, organization/business affiliations, important relationships with influencers, teaching or speaking opportunities, and any other ways you touch potential readers. Create a timeline of action steps or tactics for each channel.
- Have you taken full advantage of your book's Amazon page as well as your Amazon Author page? Have you written the most compelling copy possible? Have you optimized your book for search/discovery on Amazon?
- Have you researched book bloggers who might review your book?
- Have you considered a blog tour, where you visit blogs that serve your target audience? Can your book be easily excerpted and offered up as

guest post content on specific blogs?

- Does your book's subject matter (or does your self-publishing approach) have a newsy angle that would merit coverage? Can you pitch articles to specific sites or media outlets that tie into your book's themes or release?
- Advertising is not recommended for authors without experience in researching target markets, writing good copy, and measuring impact.

A Final Word of Advice

If your book is not selling as well as you would've thought, given your existing reach to your audience, then look at each one of the 4Ps, and decide where your weakness might lie. Then develop a strategy to strengthen your position, and a way to measure your effectiveness. The only way you can improve over time is to analyze what works and what doesn't work.

Anecdotally speaking, I often see the most weakness in authors' key selling points; some people have a hard time getting past "Buy my book!" You'll have to be more imaginative than that to catch a stranger's attention!

Yes, Email Still Works for Book Marketing

I sometimes receive pushback from authors who question my suggestion that they harness the power of the email newsletter for long-term book marketing.

Or, in other words, isn't e-mail dead? Who reads e-mail any more?

Why do some authors, like Barry Eisler, decide to strike deals with Amazon? Partly due to their e-mail marketing power.

When I was publisher of Writer's Digest, our direct marketing relied predominantly on e-mail. Each e-mail sent could be tied to a specific amount of revenue it brought in, and each campaign was only as good as the open rate and click rate.

But, you might say, won't people see your calls to action via social media? Wouldn't people who would read your e-mail also see your social media updates? Maybe. Maybe not.

It may seem paradoxical, but the closer someone is to you, the more they may not respond to social media efforts because it's not as personal, or it gets mixed in with a lot of other social media noise.

Gatekeepers especially may favor a more structured or formal approach when a favor is being asked. (Speaking for myself, I prefer being contacted directly via e-mail rather than via Facebook or Twitter. But I still respond across mediums—and ask people to e-mail me directly when needed!)

Here are a couple of scenarios from personal experience:

- A former colleague was seeking monetary support for a charity run. I vaguely remember seeing his posts on social media, but it didn't tie into what I normally see him posting about, so it never registered. When I received an e-mail from him, explaining what he was doing and why my support mattered, I immediately gave a donation.
- Jeanne Bowerman raised more than $15,000 via Kickstarter to support the production of a film she's written. I'm sure I must've seen her posts about the film via Twitter, but I had never slowed down enough to understand what was going on. When I received an e-mail from her, with specifics on how I could help, I immediately did so.

Caveat: Everyone operates differently. Mileage may vary. Etc.

But if you have someone's e-mail address, and you've corresponded before on a personal level, there's an excellent chance you'll get a [more] favorable response from a direct approach.

Email Sins

One of the quickest ways to turn a potential reader (or influencer!) into an enemy is to send an unsolicited message via e-mail or a social network.

Here are 4 of the biggest e-mail sins.

1. Sending a regular mass e-mail to people who did not sign up to receive your messages. This even goes for content-based messages or links—something you might think is innocuous. It is not.

2. Sending a mass e-mail to your entire address book, or to every e-mail address you've harvested from your Facebook or LinkedIn contacts. It's tempting to say, "Just this ONE time." If the message is that important to you, take time to send a personalized e-mail to each person, or select a few influencers to contact instead. Don't be lazy.

3. Sending a regular mass e-mail from your personal e-mail account so people have no way to unsubscribe. The most basic courtesy you can offer is an automated unsubscribe function. That means people should NOT have to respond personally and ask to be removed. MailChimp is a free e-mail newsletter service with automated unsubscribe functionality.

4. Sending mass messages via Facebook or LinkedIn. It's just as bad as doing it via e-mail.

It might be perfectly fine to mass e-mail people who know you and love you (e.g., close family and friends), but if you're doing it with people you don't correspond with casually or typically, and they didn't opt-in, **that's called spam, and you should stop.**

Should You Pay Money for Online Advertising?

I rarely advocate authors spend money on advertising, in part because it takes a specialized skill set to do it well. Plus you have to know how to reach your **target market**, and some authors don't even know the definition of that term.

But if you think advertising might be helpful to you or your work, here's an introduction on how to do it well.

- Is your ad meant to build awareness or to make a sale? Most authors I know are interested in advertising to boost sales. If that's the case, keep reading.
- Does your ad have a call to action? You need one. A good example might be, "Download a free sample now," or "Read the first chapter."
- If your ad has multiple versions or multiple frames, make sure the call to action appears in every frame and version.
- Provide as much info as possible about the pricing or promotional offer. Discount offers and discount codes attract attention.
- Refer to deadlines or limits in quantity, if applicable. That will persuade people to take immediate action.
- An effective ad is well-designed and balanced. If your ad is more than just a text-based ad (i.e., a display ad), you should probably hire a professional designer to ensure it's easy to read and hangs together.

When people click on your ad, they should go to a landing page that matches the message in the ad, and offers more detail about the offer or product. Sometimes it is appropriate to link directly to an Amazon page. Just make sure that Amazon page has *all* the information it should (full book description, about the author, praise/blurbs, reviews, etc).

Other Tips

- If you have little or no experience copywriting, then gather as much feedback as possible from other authors and readers about the effectiveness of your message and call to action.
- Your ad needs to be targeted to an audience that will be receptive to your message. The biggest site is not the best; rather, choose a site that has a devoted fan base that you know will be interested in the type of work you've produced.
- Consider what other ads (or noise) you might be competing against on a particular site. The position of your ad also matters. If it's buried at the bottom of the site, or in a sidebar with a ton of other stuff, it might not

register with visitors. (This is particularly important if you're paying a flat fee for the ad, rather than a rate based on how many clicks the ad gets.)
- If you don't know what CTR means, or you can't define "conversion," you're probably not ready to start experimenting with online ads. Educate yourself fully before spending a dime.

Q&A with Jane on Book Marketing

How important is blogging for a writer's success?
Blogging is mostly overrated as a book marketing and promotion tool, and few writers have the discipline or stamina to do it for the length of time required for it to pay off.

However, a blog is probably the nonfiction author's No. 1 content marketing tool for their career—a career that presumably involves not just selling books, but also getting new clients, securing speaking engagements, teaching online classes, delivering new products, and increasing their profile as an expert.

Which leads to another question: What is "content marketing"? It's where you use content to provide value, build your brand, and gain trust with your readership over time. A blog is a form of content marketing, and it's generally the most well-recognized and understood by authors.

What are the elements of a successful author website and blog?
It should immediately communicate the author's name and/or brand and give visitors a specific call to action within 5-7 seconds, before they leave the site. What's a good call to action? It might be: read an excerpt of my book, listen to this interview with me at NPR, sign up for my newsletter, etc. Your call to action will change a few times a year, depending on your marketing initiatives or book releases.

Make your menu or navigation exceptionally clear to first-time visitors. Where can they find information about your books? How can they look at your blog or its archive? How can they contact you? Know what people look for when they visit your site, then make it easy for them to access it.

Do you recommend that writers participate in online forums, and if so, why?
Writers usually have two goals with this type of activity: being part of a writing community and being in touch with readers.

As far as the first goal, I recommend it insofar as it can be a valuable source of education, information, and encouragement. It might also have some marketing value, but you have to be careful that you're not marketing to the echo chamber of the writing and publishing community, rather than building your readership of non-writers.

For the second goal, participating in online forums *where your readers are* can be invaluable to understanding and anticipating their needs, serving them better, and—yes—marketing to them.

What about blogging communities? Can they help authors grow their readership?
I have limited experience with or knowledge of blogging communities, but my general impression is negative. (Every time one closes, such as Red Room or Yahoo Voices, I feel more steadfast in my critical POV.)

I *do* like multi-contributor blogs, into which I categorize Writer Unboxed, where I occasionally write.

What role does social media play in helping authors' books to succeed commercially? Asked another way, I find that authors can be reluctant to use social media. What is your advice in the face of their hesitation?
Social media helps authors in two primary ways.

1. It helps you maintain connections with readers and nurture that relationship over many years. While you may use social media at times to directly sell, like during a book release, the key value is in being in touch or communicating with people who are fans your work.

2. It helps you develop relationships with and reach influencers and others in your community who can help spread the word to their networks.

The question to ask yourself is: How, when, and where do you best engage with readers and others in the industry? There is probably at least 1 social network where that opportunity is richest and most meaningful for you. Focus on that network and do it to the extent that it energizes or inspires you. Forget the social media networks that feel like drudgery—that defeats the whole point of being there.

We know that email marketing is as important as social media. What advice do you give writers about growing their mailing list of avid and casual readers?
Make the email newsletter sign up very clear on your website; ideally it should appear on every page. Give readers a specific idea of what they will receive when they sign up for your list. Then deliver what you promise.

You once said in a blog post that writers must push their boundaries to incorporate new media into their marketing. (This isn't a direct quote.) At what point do writers need to pull back so they don't lose their focus on their writing goals?

When you find yourself going through a checklist of media initiatives, without any interest or enthusiasm, then it may be time to pull back and evaluate why you're doing it, especially if you're not seeing reader engagement. (Keep in mind that any new effort takes time to pay off—you have to show up consistently, find your voice, and improve. This can take 6-12 months for some people.)

I love to suggest writers experiment and question the mediums they may always default to; on the other hand, there's nothing wrong with pursuing what works—especially if it motivates you to produce more good work. You just need to be aware if you're clinging to certain things because you're afraid to change (while everyone else is moving ahead), or making good choices that build on your strengths and the qualities of your work.

How do you suggest that writers juggle their writing time with their marketing efforts in general?

This seems to be the question on everyone's mind these days, and I understand writers feel that they're under tremendous pressure. So when I hear this question, what I hear is: how can I relieve the pressure? How can I alleviate any stress or anxiety I have about juggling these things?

There is a very simple answer: Don't take it all so seriously, and detach from the crazy-making activities. In a moment of silence, I bet you know what you should be doing, so acquire the discipline, structure, and tools to make it happen.

For indie authors interested in finding an agent or publisher, what do they need to have in place aside from a killer manuscript?

It's immensely helpful to point to a growing and engaged readership devoted to reading just about anything you publish. Be able to demonstrate your efforts to cultivate and nurture that readership.

What marketing advice would you give a new writer just starting out?

Get your website established, even if it's just a shell, and begin improving it and getting better at honing your online brand, one day at a time. This is your home base for the entirety of your career. Get comfy.

CHAPTER 8
Author Websites and Blogs

It's not unusual for authors to be told by their publishers that an author website isn't necessary or effective. Publishers may advise authors that they're better off creating and maintaining a Facebook page instead.

But I consider it the No. 1 calling card for a successful digital-age author. In my experience of having a website *and* being active on social, I would feel hobbled if either piece went away. Social is more powerful with my website, and my website is more powerful with social. That's not to say there can't be varying strategies and tools for execution (and there have to be—every author career is different), but to say "no" to an author website for most authors? That seems like an opinion formed in 2005 that hasn't been seriously revisited or challenged.

But publishers aren't stupid or inexperienced. They shepherd thousands of new and experienced authors and know what sells books. What's going on here? Am I horribly wrong in continuing to advise authors to own and control their website as a long-term priority? Here's what I think is going on.

1. Publishers don't believe websites are effective for the time put into them—they create an unprofitable time sink. I can see how and why this might happen, since most authors are not educated on best practices of websites, what websites are good at, and how they integrate into a larger online presence. There's a learning curve that no publisher can be or wants to be involved in, so it becomes easier to say, "Don't bother (because you won't do it right)."

If the author decides to establish a website anyway, the publisher may be rightly concerned that the author isn't motivated or capable of maintaining it. Sometimes a bad website or out-of-date website can be more damaging than no website at all. Even if it is up to date, what if the author's website doesn't link to all retailers, and it offends an account? What if the author is saying or doing things that make life difficult for the publisher? (I experienced this to some degree at F+W Media, where the editors received requests from marketing: Please tell your author to change X on his site.)

What remedies might there be?

Educate authors. No publisher really wants to do this, though I think it's in their best interest. At the very least, publishers could write up a downloadable guide or record an hour-long webinar that's periodically updated.

Advise authors to use platforms that don't require technical knowledge to maintain. We're no longer living in the days of the webmaster; any individual who uses Word or Gmail can also learn to update a website. Some think WordPress is too complicated. But there are a range of solutions out there: SquareSpace, WordPress.com over self-hosting, even Blogspot will do.

Clearly advise authors what constitutes a waste of time. No author site should take so long to launch that it's out of date by the time it's live. And there's no excuse for an out-of-date site if you're using a platform like WordPress.

Bottom line: I think it's a mistake and a disservice to authors to make them think or believe a website is some sophisticated piece of technology that they can't handle or maintain. I expect more, and I've seen many writers, some over 60 years of age, successfully start and maintain their sites after being encouraged and educated in a positive and empowered way. This is part of being a capable author in the digital age, if you want to grow your career over the next 5, 10, or 20 years.

2. Publishers see better, clearer results from other types of activities, such as Facebook or Twitter social engagement, which may demand less of the author. It's important to start somewhere, anywhere. I also believe in the power of incremental progress; you don't have to launch and perfect everything at once. Start small, and build your skills and presence over time. A Facebook start for most authors feels doable and sustainable—and sustainability is key.

This also helps authors focus on social marketing and soft-selling, which—even if they don't know what that means—they might be more comfortable and successful at, if they're new to online media. Plus, more than 1 billion people use Facebook. An author, if invested in it, may reach more people there and fewer people at their site, at least initially. (Go where the fish are.)

Yet I have a hard time endorsing a social-only approach when you, the author, are at the mercy of the social media tool for reaching your audience. You can never control what Facebook or any other site does. And if and when it goes out of favor, you'll have to rebuild somewhere else—whereas with a website, you only get stronger and better over time, assuming you don't abandon it (and why would you, if you're still writing and publishing?). When I first launched my website, it was a shadow of what you see now. (I discuss that journey, in depth, in a 20-minute video on audience development you can find at my YouTube channel: youtube.com/janefriedman.)

Finally, Facebook is not an ideal setup for delivering straight-forward information. It's better at conversation and ongoing connections, rather than delivering things such as media kits, official author bios, event listings, book club materials, and so on. Sure, you can put those things on Facebook, but that's not an ideal setting for it, especially when people are typing your name or book title into Google. (And what about all those people who don't use social media?)

3. Publishers aren't sufficiently invested in the author directly reaching an audience on their own–or don't believe it happens at a meaningful enough scale, except for a minority. Agents and editors want authors with platform—which means authors who can directly reach readers. This mitigates the risk involved in publishing a book because there's a ready-to-go audience that the publisher doesn't have to find.

This presents something of a paradox. How can publishers seek authors with platform (which often involves an online presence that can be quantified) AND claim author websites aren't terribly effective? But I can see the rationale. If the platform is essentially established ahead of time—and that process probably took the author years—it's integral, but it's difficult for an author, on her own, to establish a meaningful platform from the time a book is contracted to the release date, especially if she's starting from ground zero. (Though, undoubtedly, the author will still be advised to participate in some range of online marketing activities, without being educated on what's good for the short-term vs long-term, and may not realize that getting on Twitter is kind of pointless if you're only doing it because your publisher said so.)

Put another way: Some authors are motivated and pretty good at the online and digital platform stuff (and at reaching an audience), and some aren't. And for those who aren't, the publisher may believe it's not worth bothering because the payoff won't be there in time for the publisher to see an impact on sales.

That seems rather focused on the short-term, or on the publisher's immediate return on investment rather than the author's long-term career.

I'd argue it's now the publisher's job to help authors connect with readers—to be marketing partners. And if they're going to be a valuable marketing partner, it means educating authors on how to do this stuff for the long haul even if the authors think they're "bad" at it—which requires authors undergoing an attitude adjustment, not a miracle injection of computer-programming know-how.

There could be another reason publishers aren't helping authors with this: it takes away their power if the author can reach readers without them. I don't honestly believe this is motivating publishers in their advice to authors, but when you see hybrid authors such as Hugh Howey, CJ Lyons, Barbara Freethy, and others who do well because they've made the investment of reaching readers directly, publishers have less negotiating power. Being in direct contact with readers (through your own site, blog, e-mail newsletter, wherever) is like money in your pocket, a long-term investment that pays off over time. Any of the authors I mentioned above would confirm this.

Sylvia Day, speaking at an industry conference in 2013, said that publishers have to offer "a comprehensive marketing plan that covers things that I'm not doing myself. I expect them to hit a market that I'm not already reaching. You need to find me a new audience, to broaden my audience. As far as digital is concerned, you cannot compete with what I'm doing on my own. You have to knock my socks off with a brilliant marketing plan to be my publisher."

There are probably two questions in this whole conversation that are most debatable and most difficult to answer, at least on a broad, general, and continuing level:

How much of an impact can an author website have on book sales over the long term, versus other strategies such as social media engagement, metadata optimization, Amazon promotion, Goodreads advertising, traditional media/PR, etc? This assumes that sales is the only or primary goal, and that other benefits are negligible (which is also highly debatable!).

Assuming the overall impact is meaningful, how many authors have the aptitude, patience, and/or perseverance to be like Sylvia Day? Can this be taught effectively, and if so, is it worth an author taking time and energy away from her writing? (And/or: Should an author spend money on someone else doing it?)

I say it's worthwhile (because I've experienced the benefits firsthand), but I understand why others say no.

Why a Facebook Page Can't Replace a Website

I've occasionally been asked by authors at conferences: Why not just use Facebook? Isn't that where everyone is spending their time already? Why would people visit my site? Why bother with all the effort of establishing a site, which, if it becomes dusty or out-of-date, could be more damaging than no website at all?

First, I'll address why it's a bad idea to use Facebook as a substitute for your author website.

1. People may leave Facebook. I remember the very first fan page I created for Writer's Digest—and it wasn't on Facebook or Twitter. It was on MySpace. Guess how many people visit that page now?

It may be hard to envision, but Facebook may eventually lose favor. Google Plus may become more popular, or it may be an entirely new site or technology not created yet. It's impossible to predict. But by choosing Facebook instead of an author website, you are favoring the short-term over the long-term. You are investing your time and energy in a platform that may not pay you back in several years' time. Maybe it benefits your current campaign or initiative—but you can never be sure it's going to benefit your second or third project.

In the meantime, your author website remains undone, and people who don't use Facebook become incredibly difficult to identify and reach.

2. Facebook is not under your control. This is pointing out the obvious, but authors don't take it seriously enough. You can never control what Facebook does—with its design, with its user interface, with your likes/followers, with its functionality, with its ad displays. You're limited in how you can optimize the experience, and your insights (metrics) are limited to what Facebook itself measures and decides to pass onto you.

Many people and businesses received a rude awakening when Facebook adjusted its algorithms so that only the most popular status updates would be seen by most fans of a page. If you want to reach ALL fans who've liked your page, you now have to start paying money.

That said, it's true that a site with 1 billion users has attractive qualities to anyone building an online presence. I'm not saying ignore Facebook, but realize you don't call the shots.

3. A website is the most effective way to deliver information to your audience. Your author website serves as a hub for all your activity—online and offline. Imagine the following scenarios:

- A potential reader hears about your book from a friend. They Google your name or book title. Where do they end up? If you don't have a website, they probably land on Amazon. That may not be a bad thing, but what if …

- A reader finishes your book, loves it, and wants to see if you have any book club materials, readings or events, or other opportunities to enrich the experience they've just had. They Google your book title. What do they find?

- A reader finishes your book, loves it, and wants to find other things you've written. That reader may explore Amazon, go back to Google and search for your author page, or find your Facebook page. Will they be able to find what they're looking for?

- Someone in the media hears about your book and wants to contact you. They run a Google search. What do they find?

- A conference organizer reads your book and thinks you'd make a great speaker. They run a Google search. What do they find?

- You probably see the common thread here. When people seek information, they often go to Google to search for it. People won't be inclined to visit Facebook when they have a specific goal or information they're seeking. Why? Because Facebook is a soft connection tool, for people to stay in touch in a very organic way. It's not about structured information delivery, but conversation and social engagement.

- A website, on the other hand, serves as a hub for all people who are interested in your work and are seeking more information or updates directly from you. It doesn't matter if they heard about you online or offline, people are trained to use their mobiles, tablets, and desktops to search for more information, and your author website is a 24/7 resource waiting for them.

I haven't even touched on the many other reasons an author website is essential to your long-term development as an author. They include:

- Developing an e-mail newsletter list that puts you in direct contact with your true fans (this is like money in your pocket, a long-term investment that pays off hugely over time)

- Making your other online efforts more effective—or making people aware of all the places you're active. For instance, the No. 1 way people find out about me on Facebook (and end up subscribing to my feed) is because they've visited my website or read my blog.

- Offering many ways for your fans to engage. Aside from having an e-mail newsletter, you may offer ancillary materials that fans would enjoy, such as additional chapters, resources, book club materials, etc.

But isn't a bad website worse than no website at all? It actually takes effort these days to have a bad website, given today's website building tools such as WordPress.

Sure, you may need to spend a couple hundred dollars every year or two for a developer to assist with a redesign or functionality add-ons. But for anyone with a long-term author career, this is one of the best and most critical investments you can make.

3 Reasons to Have a Website If You're Unpublished

When I tell writers it's mandatory they have a website, those who are unpublished will immediately ask, "But what do I say on my website if I'm unpublished?"

I'll answer that question in a moment, but this question assumes that there's no benefit to having a site unless it's to market, promote, and sell a book. But there are several good reasons to start a site even if you're not yet established.

1. Get over the learning curve. While it's easy nowadays to get a full-fledged site up and running in 24 hours, even with your own domain name (through services such as WordPress.com), you still need to learn new systems and become accustomed to new tools. Don't wait to start this process until the day you need a site. Educate yourself in advance. Start building a simple site today so you can have a killer site when it's most important to you.

2. Build awareness. In marketing communications, you have to distinguish between goals that are to (a) make a sale and (b) build awareness. At least half of the advertising you see is meant to build awareness rather than make a sale. Why? Because we're more likely to buy a product we've been hearing about—assuming a positive impression has been formed. Having a site (and participating in social media) helps build awareness of who you are and what you do. As positive impressions collect, it's an investment in your future success as an author or provider of services.

3. Open up opportunities. You never know who might visit or stumble on your site. You never know who's listening. You never know who's searching. When I had my own website that wasn't connected to my employer, many more opportunities opened up because it was clear how people could contact me, what I could offer, and who I was already offering it to.

I consider items 2 and 3 to be gravy. No. 1 is the biggest deal; get comfortable with the tools before you get into the serious work.

So, what do you say on your site if you're unpublished?

Keep it simple. You might need only 1-2 pages on your site, your welcome/summary page, and another for an extended bio. Your site should link to your other social profiles online (Facebook, LinkedIn, etc).

Don't belabor your unpublished status. You deserve to have a site if you're unpublished; it helps indicate your seriousness about your career. But you don't need to explain, at length, your journey to get published or your attempts to find an agent. Briefly describe the type of writing work you do, and leave it at that.

If you do have credits, list them. They don't have to be major credits. Local and regional publications count, as do blog posts and online articles. Link to anything that's available to read online.

You don't have to blog. I'll address blogging later in this chapter.

Include contact info or a contact form. A good head shot is nice, too.

Build a More Effective Author Website

Every published author's website should include these elements, whether on the homepage or elsewhere.

About/bio page. I recommend a brief, professional bio (250 words or less), and a photo. You can expand in many different ways, but a short bio upfront is very helpful and essential for those looking for the quick facts.

Information on your books, products, and services. You might have a separate page for each book or product, or you might combine everything together. Regardless, don't skimp on the details, and always include links to where your books can be purchased in both print and digital form. Ideal: A downloadable press or media kit for each book.

Social media integration. Let readers know where else you're active online, and make your site easy to share (using social share buttons).

Social proof. If you have notable media coverage, good reviews, positive testimonials, or a significant following on a specific platform (e.g., Twitter), let it be known.

E-mail/RSS subscription or sign-up. Make it easy for people to subscribe to your blog via e-mail/RSS. If you don't have a blog, then offer an e-mail newsletter. (Give people a way to stay connected!)

Here are mistakes I often see on author websites:

No way to sign up for updates. If people visit your site once, they may not ever return. But that doesn't mean they aren't interested in receiving news from you. Always offer an easy way for people to be notified when you have news or content to share.

Too many pages or paths. New visitors to your site will not likely visit more than a couple pages of your website. Make it clear on your homepage what's important by having a clear "call to action." (What do you most want people to do when they visit?) Don't build your site for you—build it for your future readers.

Heavy images, intro pages, Flash, etc. If your site takes a long time to load, or requires special plug-ins, or doesn't work on an iPad (Apple does not support Flash), you will lose a chunk of your visitors.

No clear contact info. Make it easy for people to e-mail you or find you on social networks. That's why you have a website, right?

Unfriendly to mobile devices. Nearly two-thirds of my new site visitors are on a mobile device. Thankfully, my WordPress theme is mobile-friendly. Is your website mobile friendly?

10 Ways to Build Long-Lasting Traffic to Your Site or Blog

While nonfiction authors might be rightly concerned with growing traffic to their site (as a part of their platform), novelists, poets, and other creative writers should probably treat their site as a critical tool underpinning career-long marketing and promotion efforts. Traffic will grow as you publish more; don't worry about driving traffic in isolation from that.

However, if you're actively generating content at your site (blogging) or doing something to attract attention online—and you're seeking traffic or readers—here are ways to get more eyeballs.

1. Make sure your social media profiles always link to your website. Twitter, Facebook, and other social media networks *always* offer—as part of your static profile—an opportunity to link to your homepage. Be sure to do so.

An advanced version of this strategy: Send people to a customized landing page on your website. E.g., you may want to create a special introduction or offer for people who visit your website from your Twitter profile, Facebook fan page, Goodreads page, etc.

If you blog: Be sure to link to new blog posts on each social media network where you're active. But don't *just* post a link. Offer an intriguing question, lead in, excerpt, or explanation of why the post might be interesting to people on that specific social network. While it may be possible to automate postings across your social networks whenever a new blog post goes live, it's more effective to give each post a personal touch based on what you know appeals to that particular community.

2. Include your website address on all offline materials. Whether it's business cards, print books, handouts, flyers, bookmarks, or postcards—any print collateral—don't forget to put your website address on it. It's helpful if you briefly explain what's at your site, e.g., "Visit my website to sign up for my free e-newsletter" or "Visit my website to download free first chapters from all my books."

3. Learn SEO 101 and its quirks for your content management system. SEO is search engine optimization. You want search engines such as Google to pull up your site whenever people search for terms relevant to you, your books, or your content. For most authors, the two most important SEO questions usually are:

1. Can people easily find my site if they search for my name?
2. Can people easily find my site if they search for my book titles?

Beyond these two questions, most authors don't need to worry much about SEO. (It becomes more important if you're trying to make money online or otherwise build a career based off your online content.)

However, you should have a basic knowledge of how SEO works, and whether your site is meeting basic requirements. The good news is that if you're using the very popular content management system WordPress, you're set up to have good SEO from the start.

4. Install Google Analytics and study how people find your site and use it. If your site is self-hosted, then you should have Google Analytics installed. If not, get started today—it's a free service and easy to set up.

After Google Analytics has collected at least 1 month of data, take a look at the following:

- How do people find your site? Through search? Through your social media presence? Through other websites that link to you?
- What search words bring people to your site?
- What pages or posts are most popular on your site?

By knowing the answers to these questions, you can better decide which social media networks are worth your investment of time and energy, who else on the web might be a good partner for you (who is sending you traffic and why?), and what content on your site is worth your time to continue developing (what content will bring you visitors over the long run?).

Speaking of e-newsletters …

5. Create a free e-mail newsletter. Whether you send it once a year or once a week, it's time to start a free e-mail newsletter so you can stay in touch with visitors to your site who specifically express interest in your updates. MailChimp is an e-mail newsletter service (free up to 2,000 names) that has a beautiful user interface and makes the process fun and easy.

Your e-mail newsletter, aside from having useful news or content, should link to your website. Your newsletter can point out (1) popular site or blog content & conversations that readers may have missed (2) free information or downloads you've recently offered and (3) anything else that's changed on your site that might have been overlooked.

6. Create free resource guides on popular topics. If you're a nonfiction writer, then this probably comes naturally: Put together a 101 guide, FAQ, or tutorial related to your topic or expertise—something people often ask you about. (The most visited resource on my site is Start Here: How to Get Your Book Published.)

If you're a novelist, this strategy may take some creative thinking. Good thing you have an imagination, right? Consider the following:

- If your book is strongly regional, create an insider's guide or travel guide to that particular region. Or think about other themes in your work that could inspire something fun: a collection of recipes; a character's favorite books, movies, or music; or what research and resources were essential for completing your work.
- If you're an avid reader, create a list of favorite reads by genre/category, by mood, or by occasion.
- If you have a strong avocational pursuit (or past profession) that influences your novels, create FAQs or guides for the curious.
- If you're an established author, offer a list of favorite writing and publishing resources that you recommend for new writers.

7. Create lists or round-ups on a regular basis. A very popular way to make people aware of your website is to link to others' websites. If you can do this in a helpful way, it's a win for you, for your readers, and for the sites you send traffic to.

In the writing and publishing community, weekly link round-ups are very common. But you can create such lists or round-ups on any theme or category that interests you enough to remain dedicated, enthusiastic, and consistent for the long haul—at least 6 months to 1 year, if you want to see a tangible benefit.

8. Do something interesting on your favorite social media site. Especially if you're not blogging, you may want to consider what creative project you might undertake on a community-oriented site. Consider:

- Daily themed notes on Facebook.
- Photographs or visuals on Instagram or Pinterest.
- Twitter chats or hashtag themed tweets. (Jeanne Bowerman's Script-Chat is a fabulous model to follow.)
- YouTube videos. (YA author John Green is a master.)
- Create reading highlights and snippets through Amazon highlights, Tumblr, or Goodreads (then distribute via Twitter, Facebook, etc).

9. Run regular interviews with people who fascinate you. Believe it or not, it's rare to come across an informed, thoughtful, and careful interviewer and interview series (or—not just someone looking to fill a slot or post generic content based on pre-fab questions).

Think about themes, hooks, or angles for an interview series on your site, and run them on a regular basis—but only as frequently as you have time to invest in a well-researched and quality interview. Such series also offer you an excellent way to build your network and community relationships, which has a way of paying off in the long run.

Check these interview series for an idea of what's possible:

- Other People with Brad Listi
- Interviews at The Rumpus
- The Creative Penn podcast interview series.

10. Be a guest blogger or interviewee on other sites. Whenever you guest or appear on other websites, that's an opportunity to have multiple links back to your own site and social network accounts.

A meaningful guest post means pitching sites that have a bigger audience than you, but they should also have a readership that's a good match for your work.

If you're not the type to write guest posts, then consider proactively offering yourself up to be interviewed as part of other bloggers' interview series.

A note of caution: Don't focus on guest post or interview opportunities strictly tied to the writing and publishing community (unless that is your true audience). You may need to research websites and blogs that feature authors or books similar to you in order to break out of the publishing industry echo chamber and find people who aren't writers, but readers.

An easy way to start this research is to Google similar authors or book titles—ones with the same target readership—and see what sites feature interviews, guest posts, or essays.

Whenever you make an appearance on another site, always promote the interview on your own social networks and create a permanent link to it from your own website.

While these are some of the most popular ways to build traffic to your site, there are many other ways. What has been successful for you? Share your experience in the comments.

3 Ways to Improve Your Author Website

To maximize the effectiveness of your author website, it's necessary to study the data behind how people find your website, navigate it, and use it. This is typically done via Google Analytics. On the day you install it, you'll immediately start collecting data on your website traffic and visitors; while you won't be able to see into the site's past, you'll start collecting and storing analytics data indefinitely.

Note: WordPress.com users cannot implement Google Analytics, and may find it difficult to get the level of data they need via WordPress's own analytics.

1. Analyze your "calls to action" on your static pages or post pages— or most popular pages. It's easy to get caught up in the appearance of your homepage, the front door to your website. In Google Analytics, take a look at your site content tab: your homepage may represent a small percentage of total visits. The long tail of visits may be spread over dozens or hundreds of pages if you have a blog.

For instance, on my website (which is very blog-centric), the homepage represents only 5% of my total pageviews. Most people visit a blog post and only a blog post. That means the page design template of my blog post page is critical.

So make a list of the most popular pages on your website (by using Google Analytic's site content overview), and imagine you're a new visitor to those pages. Then ask the following questions.

- If the goal of your website is to introduce people to your books, is it easy to see what your latest book is from your most popular pages?
- If you want people to subscribe to your blog, is it easy to immediately find the subscribe buttons or links from anywhere on your site (especially on the top half)?
- If you want people to sign up for your e-mail newsletter, is that prom-

inent on your most popular pages?

- If you want people to find you on social media, are those links immediately available?

Whatever No. 1 goal (or call to action) you have for new visitors, make sure it's clear regardless of what page they first land on; don't expect people to visit more than 1 or 2 pages of your website.

2. Start tracking the most popular outbound links. It's exceptionally instructive to understand how and when people leave your site. Google Analytics will give you data on exit pages for visitors, and if you set it up correctly, what links people click on.

When I discovered that my No. 1 most popular outbound link was to an article I wrote on nonfiction book proposals *at another site*, I immediately wrote a new post on the topic and replaced the link, to retain visitors longer at my site.

Knowing what people click on gives you in-depth insight into what interests your readers and at what points they're inclined to make a purchase (e.g., clicking on a discount code link to make a purchase at a retailer).

3. Install an SEO plug-in (if using a WordPress-based site), such as Yoast. WordPress is very SEO friendly right out of the box, so it doesn't take much work on your part to do good by the search engines.

But WordPress users also have access to plug-ins that help you do your absolute best on SEO. (I use one produced by Yoast.) It will not only help you understand SEO principles as you put together pages and blog posts, but it will give you additional functionality and fine-tuned control, such as being able to craft specific excerpts that are used in social-media shares and search engine display.

Do You Need to Rethink Your Website's Key Elements?

For 10 years, I've been analyzing website traffic—for my own site, for Writer's Digest, and for the *Virginia Quarterly Review*. Every site has different traffic patterns, but what I've learned is that the homepage is rarely the first page that visitors see. They often end up on a story page from a social media link, or they may visit through a "side door" after conducting a Google search and finding something useful in your archives.

Many writers (and businesses) spend a lot of time thinking about the homepage when they should be thinking about the areas that appear on every single page: the header, the sidebars, the footer, pop-ups, etc.

How you treat those areas (plus how you consider what goes on the homepage) means you'll need to ask yourself two questions.

1. For someone coming to my site very intentionally—a reader who knows my work and may be a fan—what are they likely looking for? And what do I want them to know?

2. For the drive-by visits, especially those that come through a "side door," what do newcomers need to know right away? What do I want to offer them?

Common Homepage Visit Scenarios

- If you're actively writing and publishing, people who end up on your homepage are likely seeking further information about your latest work or who you are. That's why the latest book cover (or project) should often be on the homepage and marked as such.
- Your bio page and contact page should be in the main menu, as this is another common reason for people to end up on your homepage.
- Homepage visitors may be seeking an overview of all the work you have to offer, so make it easy for them to find a page that offers the list in reverse chronological order. If you have a series, have the series title in your main menu.

How to Help Newcomers

- Have a tagline or description in your header—something that appears on every page—that clearly describes the kind of work you do. CJ Lyons makes it clear at her site: Thrillers With Heart.
- If you're actively posting new content or blogging at your site, you'll get most traffic to your posts, not your homepage. Make sure your sidebar offers a means to subscribe, to search your archive, or to browse by category. (Many established bloggers list their most popular posts in the sidebar.) Your site's main menu or navigation should make the content, themes, and depth of your site very clear.
- If you've been actively promoting something specific—whether on social media or traditional media—make sure your site refers to that something specific, or helps people find that something. This is also helpful if you get a really significant media mention somewhere; have a welcome message or post for those people. "Did you hear my interview with Terry Gross? Click here."

Maximize the Traffic You Get

- Most people who visit your site will never return. Offer them other ways to engage with you (or even offer them a free sample of something).

This is why social media icons are so prevalent on website headers/sidebars, and why professional authors have e-mail newsletter signups very prominent on every page. It helps better capture visitors at the moment they've expressed a glimmer of attention.

- Explicitly state, "First-time visitor? Start here." This is useful for sites with *lots* of content that can be overwhelming for the newcomer.
- Make the tough decisions: if people only spend 10-15 seconds on your site, what should they not leave without knowing? Your header and/or your sidebar area need to convey this quickly.
- If people reach the bottom of a page or post, they are *very* engaged. This is a prime opportunity to add a call to action, such as an email newsletter sign-up, or mention a book for sale.
- Remember: for active authors, who are frequently publishing, your strategy or focus may change every 6–12 months, which means your site has to change, too. A website is never something you launch and leave. It has to be updated to be effective.

5 Keys to Writing for an Online Audience

Online writing skills are critical, particularly since authors need to be increasingly adept at online marketing and promotion.

Here are 5 basics to keep in mind, whether you're writing for a website, blog, or social media—anything from Facebook to YouTube to Reddit!

1. Brevity is your friend. Less than 20% of text gets read online. Put your word count on a strict diet.

2. Make your content scannable. Why?

- Online readers are typically task-oriented
- Get to the point quick
- One idea per paragraph (even one-sentence paragraphs are OK)
- Add white space, subheads, lists, and/or quotes
- Headlines need to be literal. Speaking of headlines …

3. Clear and direct headlines get more clicks. If you want to be read, you need great headlines (and great subheads, too).

If people are confused by your headline, they won't click on it or read further. This even applies in situations where people know and trust the brand or author.

To ensure you haven't become lazy: Look at your last three headlines on the platform where you're most active. What message does it send? Is it a message compelling enough to hook a new reader?

You may object, "Literal headlines are *sooo boring!*" Sorry, but Google doesn't understand humor. Humor can't be searched. Leave cleverness and wordplay out of headlines, which are critical for SEO.

4. Categorize, tag, and annotate your content wherever you go. If you're using a popular blog or content management system (e.g., Blogger or WordPress), then you should be categorizing and tagging the content on your site. This helps both you and your readers find stuff.

When using other sites, such as YouTube, Flickr, or any social network, you have the same capability to categorize and tag. *Never forget to do so!* And while you're at it, take the time to write a full description of your content, plus add metadata, such as alt tags, captions, locations, dates, etc (your choices will depend on the content or site functionality).

Being thorough pays off—your content can be better searched and indexed. Which brings us to the final point.

5. If search engines can't find you, then you don't exist. Heeding points No. 3 and 4 help search engines locate your content. If you're a serious blogger, then I recommend investing in a WordPress theme with boosted SEO capabilities, such as Thesis or Genesis Themes.

I recently exchanged messages with a colleague who said that all of his company's book titles, blog post titles, and press releases were being routed through a SEO team for approval. While I think that's overkill (and potentially even damaging, but I won't get into that here), always remember that the keywords that go into your headlines, categories, and tags are critical for discoverability in the online world. You may have the best content ever, but if Google can't find it, then you're missing out on potential new readers.

A Final Note
Some longform content (the kind you find through Byliner or Longreads) aren't as beholden to these principles, at least not in the same way as blog-driven or social network content. There are always exceptions to every rule. But think long and hard before assuming you are an exception.

The Big Mistake of Author Websites and Blogs
One of the easiest ways for an author to get a site up and running is to use Blogger or WordPress. As convenient as this is, and as wonderful as I find WordPress, this can lead to a critical error: *Authors end up using a blog as their website, but aren't interested in blogging.* So their site looks like a neglected, un-updated blog or a lackluster website.

Both Blogger and WordPress can be used as effective site-building tools. But most new writers don't go the extra step of structuring their "blog" as a website. Let me explain.

Having a blog means you've got yourself a website. (Blog = site.) Blogging is simply a functionality or a way of presenting information or content on a website. A website may or may not feature a blog.

Blogger and WordPress systems focus on blogging functionality. They put the blog front and center, and assume that you are interested in blogging. If you are interested in having a site only, then you have to take steps to change the presentation.

You do not have to blog, and if you don't have much interest in the form, then please don't pursue it. As with any form of writing, it takes a considerable investment of energy and time to do it right and get something from it.

But I do recommend every writer have a website, and using WordPress or Blogger is a good way to do that for free and still conquer the learning curve.

So, how shall we transform your blog-focused site into something more appropriate? **We want to make the landing page static.** The landing page is what *first appears* when people visit your site.

While technically such a thing is possible in Blogger, it is not straightforward. (Search Google for tutorials.)

For Wordpress users, it is straightforward. Here's the process.

- Create a static page that will be your homepage; call it something like "Welcome."
- (Skip this step if you don't plan to make any blog posts.) Create another page where your blog posts will live. Most people call this "Blog," but you can name it whatever you want.
- Go to your Reading Settings in Wordpress. Where you see "Front page displays" select the option "A static page."
- You'll then need to select which static page is the "front page." Choose your Welcome page or whatever you created.
- For the "posts page," either leave it blank (for no blog posts to appear on your site), or choose the page you created, such as "Blog."

Take it from me: There's no need to blog to have a website. But please do set up your site properly to avoid the appearance that you do blog, but very badly!

Should You Hire Someone to Design Your Website?

In publishing, we often say how critical it is to hire a professional editor if you plan to self-publish. Or we say how valuable a professional publicist or PR person can be.

As someone who isn't trained as a designer (but who has worked with many designers over the years, and knows the benefit of great design), the following advice is going to sound paradoxical, yet ...

As a writer, you don't need to hire a designer or a design firm when you first start your own site or blog. Why? Three key reasons.

1. There are probably hundreds of solid design themes and templates available for standard WordPress sites. (I always recommend writers start their sites or blogs using WordPress and this is one reason why.)

To be confident you're choosing something with good design and functionality, you can pay for a premium theme (like Thesis), which usually run less than $100.

If you choose a different platform, the same principles apply. These tools have already been designed for optimal online reading and presentation. So: Avoid messing with the defaults too much. They are there for a reason.

(That said: There are some really awful design templates and themes available since nearly anyone can contribute/develop one. Try to have good taste.)

2. If you're just starting your site or blog, it will take time before you really know what you want it to do and what it should look like. Most people don't know how their site should "feel" for at least a few months or more. Once you've experimented—and started paying attention to other site/blog design—you'll start to form a vision and purpose. That's when a designer can make the most impact.

3. Unless you're launching a business or selling products, it's unlikely you need the "sleek" factor of a professionally designed site.

That said, here are a few considerations.

1. If you're already a successful author, and need to have a polished and branded site, hire a designer, by all means—especially if your author career is a significant part of your livelihood.

2. You may be so new to websites and blogging that you need the help and attention of someone who's not only a good designer, but a good teacher. This isn't so much a design consideration as a service consideration. It can help reduce frustration and beginner mistakes.

3. If you're undertaking an online-based authorpreneur approach, then you'll want to ensure your site reflects your unique qualities and mission. If you have a business plan and strategy——a definitive plan and set of goals—then design investment makes sense.

I see many unpublished writers (and other creative folks) hiring design help when they have an unclear idea of what they want their site to be, or what it should accomplish.

Until you have a clear idea of what you want to do with your site, a professional look and feel won't be much help. If you're in the process of establishing your online presence, the design templates provided with well-crafted systems like WordPress are more than sufficient for your needs.

And I can use myself as an example: My own personal site is designed entirely by me, using a free theme.

Blogging 101

Here's some beginning advice if you're totally new to blogging, about to start a blog, and/or feeling dissatisfied with your current blog.

Questions to Ask Before You Start

What will distinguish your blog? What's your unique angle? Most successful blogs have a very specific angle, topic, or audience. This makes it easier to attract attention and build a community around common interests or perspectives.

Your blog is a body of work, like anything else you might create. And here, I'm going to steal questions right from a talk that Dan Blank gave at the Writer's Digest Conference. Don't think: "I'm going to create blog (a thing)." Ask: What is my purpose? What are my goals?

The more time you spend blogging, the more value you build for readers over time and the more they find you. Your efforts will snowball. The only problem: You have to be patient. Are you willing to commit to blogging for more than a year? (It took me about 18 months before my blog was really going somewhere. It took that long to find my voice and the niche that I felt most strongly about, where I believed I had a unique contribution to make.)

Ideally, before you start a blog, you think about who'll send you traffic. Identify the notable community players, the people who you'll build relationships with.

Key Components of Your Blog

Aside from the blog posts themselves, you should also have the following:

Header/banner + tagline. It should be clear to new visitors what your blog is about and what they're going to get from it.

About page or bio. If your blog does its job, people want to know more about the person behind the writing. Don't make them search for this. I recommend creating a separate and detailed page that also includes contact information.

Calendar or archive. People new to your blog may want to dig around in your older posts. Make it easy for them to do so. Sometimes it's helpful to create a sidebar that tells readers what your most popular posts are.

Comment functionality. Your blog will grow, and you'll build relationships, through an easy-to-use comment system. Most major blog platforms (like WordPress) can help you streamline your comment system to automatically eliminate spam activity. (I recommend a combination of Disqus and Akismet if you're hosting your own site.)

Sharing functionality. Make it easy for people to share your posts on Facebook, Twitter (or just about anywhere else) through plug-ins like AddThis or Wordpress Jetpack.

Readability. If your blog or site is meant to primarily be read, then don't hamper readability by making the text too small, too tight or (worst of the worst) white type on a black background. Be aware that a lot of pop-ups, ads, or bad layout can also hamper readability and drive readers elsewhere.

For Each Post: Go Through This Checklist

Improve your headline. If people saw ONLY the headline (like on Twitter), would they feel compelled to click on it? Is it specific? Is it intriguing or provocative? Does it offer a benefit? Is it timely or relevant? Why will people click on the headline? Remember, that's often the only thing people see when they're surfing online and looking at search results.

Improve your readability. Consider adding more paragraph breaks (one-line paragraphs are acceptable), bulleted lists or numbered lists, images, subheads, quotes—whatever it takes to make your posts more scannable. Reading online is not the same as reading offline. If your post is very long, consider breaking it up into a series. Or, make it simple for people to save the post, print the post, or otherwise consume it offline. [This "rule" gets broken all the time successfully, but it requires the right readership and great content, among other things.]

Improve discoverability. Make sure each post is categorized and tagged, at minimum. If your blog platform allows for it, adjust what title, description, and keywords are attached to your post for search engine optimization (SEO).

To Grow Your Readership

- Update consistently and on a regular schedule.
- Frequently link to relevant blogs, resources, and sites.

- Try out a series or weekly feature.
- Interview people who interest you. Run Q&As.
- Comment on blogs/sites that have some relevance to your own blog.
- Allow readers to sign up for e-mail or RSS delivery of your posts. (Try Feedburner if this functionality is not already baked into your site.)
- Always post links to each new post on your Facebook page, Twitter, etc.
- Offer to guest blog for others. Provide them with even better content than usual.
- Be patient.

The No. 1 Rule to Grow Readership
Offer great content. Period.

What Should Authors Blog About?

The chain of events goes something like this:

An author's book nears its publication date (or perhaps the author is attempting to secure a traditional book deal). She knows she needs to market and promote the book and/or build a platform. She finds (or hears) advice that blogging is a good way to accomplish this.

She wonders: What do I blog about?

My unproven theory: We have many authors blogging poorly because of this series of events.

It's not dissimilar to authors ending up on Twitter or creating a Facebook page that ultimately fails to engage readers or sell books.

But then why do we hear all the time that these are good marketing practices?

Because it's true that blogging *is* a very effective marketing tool, when done well. I started blogging (in 2008) because it seemed like a fun creative outlet—a practice that would build discipline and better engagement with my community. Nearly 7 years later, blogging acts as the core of my platform and has largely made it possible for me to be a full-time entrepreneur.

So I'm not down on blogging, at least for myself. But I was willing to put in 7 years of effort, and I also improved as I went along. My best blog posts didn't start appearing until roughly 2011-2012.

You can be a quicker study than I was and be *a lot* more strategic. (Search for Chris Guillebeau's "279 Days to Overnight Success" for an example and excellent how-to guide.) Unfortunately, many authors pursue blogging without any understanding of the medium, and also as little more than a means to an end.

Meaningful blogging requires patience and persistence, as well as a willingness to learn what comprises good, compelling online-driven or online-only writing. It's not the same as writing for formal publication or in other genres/mediums—or even for websites other than your own.

I'm writing this *long* preface in response to the question "What do I blog about?" because the first answer may be: If you have to ask, maybe you shouldn't be blogging. In that, my position is somewhat stubbornly Zen: if the action is too forced or contrived, the blog may be doomed from the start. Or you may not stick with it.

On the other hand, I want to encourage experimentation. If you can approach this because it kind of *does* sound like fun, then let's spark your imagination as to what you might blog about.

Here are several models to consider, based on how challenging I think they are (assuming you want your blog to "pay off").

Easy: The Literary Citizenship Model
(See Chapter 6 for an in-depth analysis of literary citizenship.)

Blogging with the intent to promote literary citizenship opens up a lot of post possibilities, including:

- Informal book recommendations or reviews
- Q&As or interviews with people in the community (usually authors)
- "What I'm Reading Now" types of posts and other "media consumption" lists where you talk about what stuff you're watching, saving, listening to, collecting, etc.

Key benefits: You're building a great network of contacts as you build some excellent content at your site. Every author loves to get attention (or find a new fan) for their work.

Where the difficulty lies: Lots of literary citizenship activity exists online, in many forms. To get a large readership will require a unique angle or spin—although this is true of any blogging effort.

Easy-Medium: How-to Model
This is my model. Many seasoned authors have considerable advice and insight for others—and the audience of aspiring writers and established authors is massive. The downside: Connecting with other writers doesn't necessarily grow your readership; you end up in an echo chamber with other writers.

Key benefits: If you already teach writing or mentor other writers, you probably have some content you can re-purpose to fuel your early blog posts. Initially, you'll have no shortage of ideas, and your first readers will share your insightful advice on social media and help you build a traffic base.

Where the difficulty lies: In my experience, burn out. After a few years, it's tough to keep things fresh and interesting. Your readers, as they advance, may also outgrow your blog.

Medium: Behind the Scenes Model

You write about the research, people, news stories, or current events that play a role in the construction of your books or other work. You might also develop competitions and events that focus on reader engagement, such as having readers name your novel's characters, choose the best cover, etc. Presumably, readers will enjoy knowing more about the context and ideas that affect your writing and being involved in your future work.

Key benefits: For most writers, it feels natural to discuss the things that influence their work, and you will likely uncover and engage your most important fans.

Where the difficulty lies: You may run out of material quickly, and not have a very high frequency of posts. Or you may despise the idea of involving readers in your work.

Difficult: Personal Essay or Daily Life Model

Regardless of genre, some writers write short missives—that can extend into personal essays—that comment on what's happening day to day or that reflect on their personal life. This could also involve regular posting of specific media, such as photos or videos.

Key benefits: It can be a good creative outlet or practice, especially if you're committed to blogging on a schedule. Fans of your work may enjoy the intimacy (though some authors prefer to have an air of mystery).

Where the difficulty lies: Not everyone can write entertainingly about themselves (and some don't want to). For writers who aren't yet known, it will be hard (if not impossible) to interest other people in the details of your personal life, unless you're a superlative writer.

This is not an exhaustive list of what you could blog about, but it gives you an idea of the most popular options.

Please Don't Blog Your Book

It's been a trend ever since I worked full-time as a book acquisitions editor:

Blog-to-book deals. I acquired or oversaw the publication of more than a dozen bloggers-turned-book-authors. Sometimes it translated into book sales, sometimes not.

Point is: I know that blogs can lead to book deals.

However, I want you to think twice before you decide this is your path. Here are 4 reasons why.

1. Blog writing is not the same as book writing. Blog posts, to live up to their form, should be optimized for online reading. That means being aware of keywords/SEO, current events/discussions, popular online bloggers in your area, plus–most importantly—including visual and interactive content (comments, images, multimedia, links).

It seems almost silly to have to state it, but blogging (as a form of writing) holds tremendous merit on its own. Writers who ask, "Can I blog to get a book deal?" probably think of the blog as a lesser form of writing, merely a vehicle to something "better." No. A blog has its own reasons for being, and blogs do not aspire to become books if they are truly written as blogs.

Never use a blog as a dumping ground for material that's already been written for the print medium—or for book publication—without any consideration for the art of the blog.

2. Blogs can make for very bad books. If you dump your blog content into a book without any further development or editing, I'm willing to bet it will be a bad book (unless, of course, you wrote the book first and divided it into blog posts!).

It's true that many bloggers offer a compendium of their best writings as an e-book, for the convenience of their readers, or repurpose their blog content in a useful or creative way. That's not what I'm talking about.

I'm talking about lack of vision for how the content ought to appear in print, or how it ought to complement, extend, or differ from the online version. How can the content benefit from a print presentation? How does it get enhanced or become more special or valuable?

To give a couple examples:

Kawaii Not (a book that I oversaw publication for): This is an online cartoon that was adapted into a spiral, stand-up book, with perforations at the top of every page. The book was tremendously functional: Cartoons could be easily torn off and given to someone. We also included stickers.

Soul Pancake: This is a colorful activity-like book, based on the many questions and discussions that happen at a site of the same name. If you were to compare the site and the book, you would definitely find the same themes, styles, and sensibilities. However, the experience of the book and the experience of the site are two very different things.

I must admit, though, much depends on the genre/category of what's being written/published. For instance, when it comes to a book that's illustration-driven, there may be little difference between what's posted online and what goes into the book. But that's a book that sells based on its visuals, not its writing!

3. It's more difficult for narrative works to get picked up as book deals. This is a generalization, but most authors who ask me about this blog-to-book phenomenon are either memoirists or novelists. Unfortunately, it's very difficult to score a book deal with such a work. The blogs most likely to score book deals are in the information-driven categories (e.g., business and self-help) or humor/parody category (e.g., *Stuff White People Like)*.

Furthermore, I only know of memoirists who've scored blog-to-book deals, not novelists (remember, we're talking about BLOG form, not community sites like Wattpad). A couple examples of memoirish blogs that made the leap: *Julie & Julia* and *Waiter Rant*.

4. I love books that delve deeply into a topic and make no sense as blogs. I read hundreds of blogs each week. Much of my reading is done online, in fact. So nothing makes me more irritated than when I sit down to read a book—expecting something meaty, in-depth, and worthy of my full attention—than to find it reads more like a series of blog posts. Unfortunately, due to the blog-to-book deal (in part), this is becoming more common. (Also, some books now mimic the online world by chunking the content so the book reads "faster.")

In my mind, a book is a great medium for delving into those topics where the simplified, keyword-driven, ADHD world of blogging has no place. If I read a book and think, "I could've gotten this from a series of blog posts," then I consider it a failure.

Indicators That a Blog-to-Book Deal Might Work for You

- You're blogging in a nonfiction category, especially if your blog focuses on how to do something or solves a problem for people.
- You're focused on your blog for the joy of blogging, and you have the patience, determination, and drive to keep blogging for years. You won't get recognition overnight, and it takes time to develop a following. Ultimately, it's the buzz you generate, and the audience you develop (**your platform created by the blog**), that attracts a publisher

to you—not the writing itself (though of course that's important too!).

- You agree that the book deal isn't the end of the road, but another way to expand your audience for your blog (or services/community connected to your blog).
- If a blog-to-book deal path is appealing to you, then (again) go search for Chris Guillebeau's "279 Days to Overnight Success"; it's available for free at his website. He landed a book deal in about 1 year based on his blog. But he was laser-focused in his strategy and single-minded in marketing and promoting his blog to all the right people in the blogging community (not the publishing community). In other words, he has the mind and heart of an entrepreneur. Do you?

Self-Hosting Your Author Website

When it comes to establishing your author website, one of the more confusing topics is self-hosting: what it means, why it's advantageous, and when you should do it.

What Is Self-Hosting?

Sometimes it's easiest to describe what self-hosting is *not*. If your website has "wordpress.com" or "blogspot.com" (or the name of another service you use) in the URL, then you are not self-hosted. Rather, you are operating your site on a domain you don't really own that could be taken down tomorrow. You have very little control over what happens to your site in the long term, or how the site works, or what happens to it in the future. The functionality you get is limited, and the rules of that functionality can change at any moment.

Even if your site does not have "wordpress.com" (or similar) in the URL, that doesn't mean you're self-hosted. It's often possible to use a custom domain, or one that you've bought. This is called a "Domain Mapping Upgrade" at WordPress.com and costs $13/year. Blogger also allows you to use your own domain and doesn't charge.

For the purposes of this post, self-hosting is when you have access to all of your website files and the servers where those files are stored (that is, where they are hosted). You own those files and have the freedom to change them. You get to decide exactly how your site is built, from the ground up.

You might consider self-hosting as analogous to home ownership. When you own your home, you are responsible for upkeep, the utilities, the taxes, and the insurance. You have more freedom to customize your home and the property, but you also have the burden of responsibility when something goes wrong. When you rent and something goes wrong, it's someone else's problem—but you're also restricted as to what you can do as a renter, and you ultimately don't own the structure, though you may own the contents.

What Are the Advantages of Self-Hosting?
The biggest advantages for authors include the ability to:

- Implement a fully customized design—where you get to decide all the fonts, colors, page templates, headers, footers, column widths, stylesheets, etc. This is critical for long-term author branding, and most authors hire a website design firm to do this.
- Add plug-ins or tools to improve or extend your site's functionality, often at little or no cost to you. Some plug-ins are very lightweight and simple, and do things like add a notification bar or sharing buttons to your site. Others are very high-powered and complex, such as membership, online education, and e-commerce plug-ins.
- Add Google Analytics and gain access to Google Webmaster Tools to understand your website traffic and organic search traffic—and therefore understand more about your audience.
- Better monetize your site and activity, since you'll have 100% freedom to host advertising, add e-commerce tools (so people can buy off your site), and add specialized landing or splash pages for books or products.
- Better integrate e-mail newsletter sign-up tools and have full control and access to your readers via e-mail.

What Are the Disadvantages of Self-Hosting?
With great power comes great responsibility. You'll have to start thinking about:

Site security. Have you taken necessary precautions to protect your site from attack? E.g., make sure you use strong passwords and keep your site software and plug-ins updated.

Site backups. You're now responsible for site backups, which you'll need if your site should ever suffer from a bad update, a crash, or hackers. Some hosts offer backup services for an additional cost, or as part of your hosting package.

Site management. When your site goes down, it will become your problem to solve. When there's a bug or error, you have to troubleshoot or hire someone to help.

Some of these disadvantages can be overcome by selecting a hosting service appropriate for your needs and skill level. (More on this later.)

When Should You Use or Switch to Self-Hosting?

First, I should acknowledge you'll find more than a few prominent authors who (1) do not even have a website and (2) are not self-hosted. However, I don't think they're offering a best practice that everyone should follow. The truth is the large majority of successful authors *do* have a self-hosted website.

Here's when I think the self-hosting switch is merited:
- If you're actively publishing and marketing books to a paying reader-ship, and you want writing to be your primary source of income
- If you sign a contract for your first book with a traditional book publisher (and it's not the only book you plan to write)
- If you need or want to know "what works" in terms of your marketing energy and investment
- You're already feeling the limitations of wordpress.com/blogspot.com.

Here's when it may not be merited:
- You're unpublished
- You're "hands off" with your marketing; reader engagement happens if it happens
- You'd rely on social media or third-party sites for reader engagement (which means you accept the risks of using a third party)
- Writing isn't your primary focus and/or making money from writing-related activities isn't your focus
- You have a website that's not self-hosted, and you've never run up against any marketing, promotion, or reader outreach limitations.

What's the Process and Cost to Self-Host?

It's fairly straight forward.

1. If you don't have a domain name picked out or purchased, you'll need to do that before beginning the process. (For example, my domain name is janefriedman.com.)

2. Select a host for your site. I recommend selecting a host that has one-click installation of WordPress, since WordPress-based sites are generally the wisest for authors—they power more than 20% of the world's websites and have a robust developer community. That means you can easily find help or solutions when you need them.

3. If you have an existing site or blog, you'll need to export your content, assuming that's possible (for Blogger and WordPress, this is simple), then import that content into your new self-hosted WordPress site.

Hosts vary tremendously in cost and features, but for an average low-traffic site (fewer than 1,000 visits per day), you should be able to secure basic hosting for less than $100/year, often around $4–$7/month. For my host recommendations, plus a step-by-step video process, keep reading.

Choosing and Setting Up a Host for Your Site

I mentioned that some hosts offer one-click installation of WordPress, making it easy to get started. Those hosts include Bluehost, HostGator, and DreamHost.

These services offer inexpensive, beginner hosting plans that work well when you need to transition to a self-hosted environment, or are thinking about establishing your first author website. They are also accustomed to working with people with no technical background and offer 24/7 support.

To set up a self-hosted website using Bluehost specifically, visit this link to watch my video tutorial: http://bit.ly/WDselfhost

CHAPTER 9
The Key Principles of Online Marketing and Social Media

I've noticed a lot of authors and publishing professionals who discount the impact of online marketing and promotion. It usually goes something like this:

- People don't buy books because of Facebook / Twitter / [insert online community here].
- Or: Blogging/social networking takes a lot of energy, has little impact, and robs you of time better spent on publishable writing that earns you hard cash.
- Or: Your so-called friends and followers consist only of other people trying to sell YOU stuff.

Many authors have become disillusioned after not seeing any monetary impact from their blogging or online networking. "Show me the evidence," these people say, "that this effort actually amounts to sales."

Or, many of you have been on the receiving end of hard sells and shills—those annoying people who exploit every online connection they have in hopes of earning a buck.

I agree, those people ought to be spurned—especially because they are setting a bad example and turning people off to the tremendous potential of social media: the ability to efficiently and dynamically organize and connect with like-minded people for very little (or no) expense.

Social networking isn't a fad. It's an expression of what we love to do, which is socialize, have conversations, and form meaningful relationships with new people.

There are two reasons why I think some authors have found online marketing ineffective:

1. They tried to make something happen without a strategy and a hub.
2. They lacked the long-haul view, meaning they needed to see results too quickly, abandoned their efforts too quickly, and assumed failure.

What Action Do You Want People to Take?

Whatever it is you do online, consider what you want people to do or to think when you appear in their line of sight. When someone "sees" you online, I call that a single impression. Making an impression can mean the smallest of things, including:

- A Facebook status update
- A tweet
- A blog post
- A comment you leave on a blog or forum
- Whenever or wherever you leave a mark

If people are entertained, informed, or fascinated by something you've done online, they'll be curious and want to know more about you. **It is very important that you give them some place to go, or something to do.**

This is why I recommend every writer have a website, even before they have a book deal or a specific project to promote. You want to have a hub ready—a place for people to find out more, or sign up, or become a follower.

Some writers use Facebook or Twitter as their hub, at least in the early stages—meaning the only action you want people to take might be following you or friending you. This is fine.

Eventually, you'll need to up your game, and have them become a subscriber to your site/blog, or an e-newsletter. Or maybe you want them to download the first chapter of your book.

It really doesn't matter what it is you want people to do, as long as you are thinking in terms of what specific action would help you in your career at a particular moment in time. What are your goals for the next 3 months or 6 months or 12 months?

The action you want people to take (as a result of some impression) will change over time. It may even change frequently. That's OK.

But when it comes to online marketing and promotion, while not everything you do needs to be tied to audience development (that would get boring, tiresome, and unfun), you should have a path for people to follow.

This path underpins your presence on each facet of your online life, and leads back to the hub (where an action can be taken).

The longer you're online, the deeper and more effective you'll be. The more impressions you'll make over time, the more people will head to your hub. (You'll also be getting more comfortable, more savvy, and more in tune with what you need to do. It will be second nature.)

All this happens naturally; you couldn't stop it if you tried.

And that's why it takes patience. It's why quick and short online marketing campaigns (unless backed by a lot of corporate money and powerful connections) aren't effective for individual authors. You have to be in it for the long haul. That's how the payoff comes.

How do I know?

It's happened to me. I've received wonderful opportunities due to the long and deep tread of my online life. So I can testify with certainty: It works. But not overnight.

How to Avoid the Extra Work of Social Media

I often speak at writing conferences on the art & business of building a platform, which includes about 5-10 minutes of commentary on social media (out of a full hour). Frequently, during Q&A, most audience questions are about social media. People say that they aren't interested in social media nor do they see the benefit of the extra work presented by it—even though my presentation isn't actually *on* social media. Isn't that funny?

While I don't think social media use is mandatory, you can set up a significant challenge for yourself if you exclude it from your arsenal of tools. You might think you're just excluding it from your arsenal of *marketing* tools. Perhaps. But shift your perspective just a bit, and it turns out you're excluding it from your arsenal of *creative writing and publishing* tools.

Social media is a form of content, and can be seen as micro-publishing. Each post is sharing a tiny bit of your story, message or perspective—possibly something informative or inspiring. The posts might end up being part of a larger work. They might be daily creativity experiments. And they might offer you insight into how your audience thinks and engages with your work. Consider:

- Nonfiction writers who author blog posts (part of the social media universe, in my view) compile and edit them into a larger publication. Like this book!
- Artists or illustrators who post quick images on Pinterest or Insta-

gram and later publish a high-quality print book collection that includes some of those images.

- Fiction writers who post about their research and inspiration for a novel, giving readers a sneak peek of what's to come.

Or, think of it like this: You're micro-publishing and sharing things you're happy to give away, and that reach a very wide number of people, because they can spread freely. These things are your "cheese cubes"—but they're part of a much bigger cheese you have in store. The people who become invested in your work and your message will buy the premium cheese basket: the final, polished, very intentional work with the highest value.

Some author examples to consider:

- Debbie Ohi posts a daily doodle on social media; it's part of her creative practice.
- Jeanne Bowerman started a Sunday night Twitter #scriptchat to learn about scriptwriting, and ended up becoming an expert herself in the topic she set out to study.
- Robert Brewer issues a poem-a-day challenge to get himself and his community producing poetry.

I post publishing and media infographics on Pinterest to keep tabs on industry change, and use them as reference points in my talks, and also to benefit others.

Are these things "extra" work? Not really; in the cases above, they're the very heart of the creative work. They are digitally native forms that usually involve sharing the work before it's part of something final or cohesive. This is often rocket fuel for your art; see Austin Kleon in his recent release, *Show Your Work*. Social media doesn't have to feel like a drag on your time when it's not separate or devised in isolation from your "real work."

I'll leave you with the words of Richard Nash, who I interviewed for the Fall 2014 issue of Scratch magazine. We talked about writers who say (basically), "I just want to write," and would rather not be distracted by non-writing activities. He says:

> No one wants to just sit and write! Not even Beckett didn't want to just sit and write—seriously! If Beckett can't abide just sitting down and writing, then any writer can find emotional and cultural stimulation by engaging with society. The two are not mutually exclusive.

Whatever time limitations you face or whatever artistic goals you have,

I believe the really meaningful (platform-building) social media activity draws on the same creativity and imagination that's part of your "serious" work.

When Is Enough Enough?

A writer recently asked me to comment on whether there is anything to be gained from being active on more than two or three social media accounts. How extensive should you really get—and is it possible that "less is more"?

I interpret this question to mean: When is enough enough? And how do I make any effort worth my time?

Answering this question requires stepping back—waaaay back—and looking at how and why authors use social media in the first place. I'm going to focus on the three most common stages.

- Growing relationships in the community.
- Actively marketing a book (or product/service).
- Nurturing reader relationships.

Stage 1: Growing Relationships

This kind of activity is largely unquantifiable, but it's also where nearly every single person starts (at least if you're not a celebrity).

As you learn to use any social media tool, there's a "warming up" period as you understand the community, its language, and its etiquette. Most people begin by reaching out to the in-real-life people they already know on the network, then branch out and connect with people they haven't met in person before.

What's the purpose of this activity?

Well, why do any of us attend social functions? To have a good time, to learn and be informed, and to seek encouragement and support.

When does it reach its limits of utility? That's kind of like asking how many relationships, or how many friends, is too many. If it's starting to drag on your resources and time to do other things more important to you (such a writing), then it's time to re-assess.

While I don't recommend analyzing your social media use (from a numbers perspective) when you're focused on it being, well, *social*, it's helpful to check in with yourself on how the activity is making you feel. Energetic or drained? Positive or anxious? Empowered or jealous?

If you're experiencing more negative emotions than positive, it may be time to step back from the specific networks causing these emotions, or step back entirely until you identify what's creating bad mojo.

Stage 2: Actively Marketing a Book

You'll only be successful at marketing on social media if you've already been through stage one. No one likes a stranger barging into the room and hawking his wares. It's considered rude and the stranger is ostracized quickly.

But let's be honest: many people have been told to get on social media in preparation for a book launch, and have no interest in using it beyond the marketing and promotion utility. That people feel this obligation or burden is one of the greatest failures of publishing community, but I'm going to set that aside and instead speak to how to manage this stage authentically without rubbing everyone the wrong way.

Social media is excellent at building awareness and comprehension in the community of who you are and what you stand for. Over time, you become more visible and identifiable, because you show up consistently and have focused messages (let's hope). It's usually only after this recognition and trust develops that you can run a successful campaign that focuses on the sale—getting the community to buy. (For those who don't have these relationships or trust in place, here's a work around: Get your friends and influencers to help spread the word for you.)

If you do have your own solid foundation, then create a focused and strategic campaign, with specific start and end dates, for each social media network. Build in ways to measure if it's working or not. For example, it's easy to track how many people click on your links in Twitter, or retweet or favorite you. Facebook shows you the number of likes and shares. Over time, these simple metrics can tell you a lot about what people respond to, so that you can adjust and improve your updates. (At its heart, social media has a lot in common with strong copywriting. For lessons in copywriting, see Chapter 7.)

Regardless of your stage of activity—but especially during marketing campaigns—you should measure traffic to your website from social media. Does it make up a high or meaningful percentage of visits? If you don't know, this is a significant gap in your knowledge that is preventing you from really answering the question: How do I make it worth my time?

Here, my assumption is that the author website is the most important online presence of all, where the most valuable or interested readers end up. If you're seeing a lot of readers reach your site through a particular social media outlet—and those referral numbers are increasing month-on-month or year-on-year—it is indeed worth your time.

Stage 3: Nurturing Reader Relationships

For published writers (regardless of how you publish), social media becomes a key way to stay engaged with your audience, and nurture it for the long haul of your career.

Some people advise writers to get on social media before publication in order to grow their audience, and this can make sense for nonfiction authors who need to build visibility and authority in their field. For fiction authors, it can make little sense. How can you build readership around work that hasn't yet been made public? You can build relationships, and be part of a community, but you're not necessarily cultivating a *readership*. A potential readership, maybe. But there's a big difference here that's not frequently enough acknowledged, and also leads to a lot of frustration and claims that social media doesn't work.

But let's focus back on the primary challenge of stage three: this is when the real pinch comes into play, where authors have to balance time writing with time interacting with their audience. There's a lot of value to be gained from nurturing that connection, and it can even inform what you write next. Yet every author has to form a strategy that they are personally comfortable with and can sustain with reasonable comfort (with additional stress budgeted in for the marketing and promotion campaigns of stage two).

It's hard to prescribe a formula because (in my estimation) this comes down to your personality, your type of work, and where you're at in your career. Your priorities will change, and your social media use will fluctuate. That's natural and expected.

Getting Down to Brass Tacks: When Is Enough Enough?

If you want an answer that is truly quantifiable, then I would say: It's enough when you are maintaining or growing readership, as demonstrated by visits to your website or sales of your work.

How many social media networks does this take? It only needs to take one if you're very efficient and smart about how you use that network. Or it might be five, if you prefer diversity and experimentation. There is no single answer, but to increase the value of your activity, consider your sales funnel. (Apologies for the business term.) Your sales funnel reflects how you turn social media engagement into people who ultimately become readers. You can read more about sales funnels here. Just as anyone who's serious about quantifying their social media activity needs to have a website, you also need to consider the path readers take to find you, and how you can lead them down that path more quickly and effectively.

When or Why Social Media Fails to Sell Books

Social media isn't something you employ only and just when you're ready to sell. If that's your plan, then YES, you will fail magnificently. You will be ineffective when people can smell you shilling a mile away—when you show up only when it benefits you, when you have no interest in the channel/medium other than personal, short-term gain.

Social media is about developing relationships and a readership over the long term that helps bolster your entire career (and sales too).

When people claim that social media hasn't worked for them, I can usually guess why—because I see it used wrong every day, very directly (because it lands in my inbox or social media stream).

Here are scenarios when social media doesn't work to sell books.

1. It's not personal. None of us like impersonal message blasts. I'm going to assume you're already smart enough not to do that. But you can still be impersonal with a one-on-one message. How? You don't actually personalize the message, or think about the needs of the person on the receiving end. You might be using a stilted or sales-y approach that turns people off. You may send messages based on the bullhorn approach, where you yell, and everyone else is supposed to listen.

Instead, try something interactive, engaging, or personalized. Try being a human being. Don't change who you are or what you do when you market. Better yet, don't see it as "marketing," at which point you might turn on your fake marketing voice.

2. You're too noisy. Are you tweeting the same message every hour? Are you posting the same call to action on Facebook every day? Are you constantly on social media asking people to do something for you? It might be time to shut up. Instead, think about: creating new and valuable content, sharing interesting articles, answering people's questions, listening to what the community is saying.

3. You're hitting up the wrong crowd. When you're starting from ground zero, it can be tough to know who or where to go first. You might not know if Twitter or Facebook is better for calls to action—or you may find it's really about being on GoodReads for your particular book.

The best 2 pieces of advice I have: (1) Try to identify at least 2-3 other successful authors in your genre, and see where they're active. If you have a relationship with them, ask what has worked and what has failed. (2) Experiment widely at first, then slowly narrow things down to maximize return on time spent. Whenever possible, measure the impact of your efforts through analytics tools, e.g., Google Analytics or tracking links.

4. You're bad at copywriting. You must always have an answer to the question that your audience will instinctively ask themselves: What's in it for me? If you can't answer that question effectively, then you better be very entertaining. Good copywriting is something you can learn, and it's not about smarmy sales tactics. Rather, it's about being clear on what makes your stuff unique—its benefits and promises. You sell the sizzle.

5. It's working, but you're not patient enough for it to pay off, so you quit too soon. Whenever anyone asks me how I became so successful doing [insert social media tool here], I say two things: patience and persistence. I was never immediately successful with anything until I better understood it, knew what I wanted out of it, and what made sense for my audience. It took practice and paying close attention.

6. You're too sales-driven. You send Facebook messages or updates that plead: "Like my page!" or yell some version of "Pay attention to me!" WHY should I pay attention? Why do I care? What's in it for me? Or you tweet only to push your book, and that's clearly the only reason you're on Twitter. (Authors who get on Twitter because they've been told they should are automatically bound to fail. Stay off it, please, unless you're there for the relationships, or to inform others.)

Your social media involvement and platform building won't work as a one-time effort (though, of course, you might have a specific campaign for a specific book that's very strategic, which is excellent).

You have to be consistent and focused It has to be about more than selling books—or whatever your goal might be. It has to be about what you stand for, and who you are.

And, finally, you have to be willing to adapt and change your approach as online behavior and tools change. Yes, it's a bit of a game. But I hope you come to see it as a creative and engaging one.

5 Principles for Using Facebook

Facebook demands consideration from nearly everyone, because choosing to stay off it means stepping away from the social sharing and conversation of more than 1 billion people.

Yet choosing to play the game as an author or marketer—and use Facebook as a means to an end—can spell immediate failure if your friends and followers feel used.

No one likes to be marketed to on Facebook, at least not in that overtly obvious "Buy my stuff" manner. Yet to approach it with no strategy at all could mean missed opportunities or wasted time. (Add on to that: it's difficult to give advice about Facebook because it keeps changing—in structure, functionality, and effectiveness. So today's advice may become obsolete tomorrow.)

No easy answers.

But here are five principles that I use and mention when people ask me about Facebook.

1. Like attracts like. If you post helpful, interesting, or valuable stuff on Facebook, targeted to a particular sensibility, you will attract an audience who matches what you post—and will reward you for it through likes/shares. If you like to talk politics, or be argumentative, or complain, you'll attract the same.

This is a critical principle for just about all online activity, but particularly important on Facebook because people tend to treat the site like their living room. They're comfortable saying or doing anything.

If you don't like the activity or conversation surrounding you—or you're not getting the results you think you should—look at what you're putting out. Don't assume you need to increase your fan/friend count.

2. Fan pages take work to be meaningful. One of the biggest questions I get is: Should I start a fan page separate from my personal profile?

I like to respond by asking: Are you prepared to develop a content strategy for it? Are you prepared to spend time on it? Otherwise, there's no point.

Here are a few other questions to ask:

Would it make sense to allow people to follow to your personal profile instead? You can make any of your personal profile posts public, and your followers will see those posts in their news feed without being your friend.

Is there a huge divide between your personal friends and your target audience? If it's problematic to make public posts on your personal profile (maybe for some reason you don't want your friends to automatically see your public posts), then a fan page eliminates that problem. Think it through carefully, though. If your first step in developing your fan page is to blast your Facebook friends with, "Go LIKE my page!", that tells me there's no real divide (yet!) between your personal friends and target audience. (That's not a bad thing—your friends are often your first circle of supporters who love to know what you're doing and want to be supportive.)

Do you need the functionality of a fan page? One of the biggest reasons to start a fan page is to have app functionality and/or analytics/insights into your fans. You need to be rather advanced in your platform building and author career to benefit from the added features of a fan page (vs. using the personal profile subscribe function). As developed as my own platform is, even I don't see the need for it in my own career.

Would you prefer to shut down your personal profile but still have a Facebook presence? I see this happening more and more. You may be "done" with Facebook but realize the importance of having a presence for marketing purposes. A fan page is the solution.

3. Target your posts appropriately. For Facebook personal profiles, I've always advocated the use of lists, back when it was a hidden feature, and long before Facebook created automated lists.

It's still a good idea to create unique lists, going beyond the automated list feature. While it takes time, having people tagged by how you know them, where you met them, or what your connection is becomes invaluable when you decide who should see each Facebook post.

Why should you care? See No. 4 below.

4. Reduce the noise. A recent study asked Facebook users what they liked least about fan pages. One of the biggest annoyances: people or companies that post too often.

We've all done it: instead of defriending or unliking someone or something, we mute them instead. The end result is the same, though. That person or thing disappears from our news feed.

I'm a strong advocate of the "less is more" philosophy when it comes to content and social sharing. We all have too much to read anyway, so why bother sharing anything except the absolute best and most essential stuff?

What does this mean in practice? A few things:

Avoid automated posting, e.g., feeding in every last one of your tweets. While I've seen some people do this successfully (and some aren't active on Facebook anyway, and don't care!), it's one of the fastest ways to get muted. Plus, you're missing an opportunity to say something geared toward the audience you have on Facebook, such as asking a compelling question to spark a discussion.

There is no one "right" frequency for posting. It all depends on what you're posting about and your audience's appetite for your POV or personality. For some people, frequent posting (to the point of TMI) is their shtick, and if you want to ride that personality wave, go ahead. Just accept its limitations in terms of who you'll attract.

A little hand-holding goes a long way when you share links or content. Explain why you're posting it, or share a compelling quote from it, or otherwise introduce the content so people understand why it deserves their time. Be a thoughtful curator, not a blaster.

Don't practice the hard sell except during special campaigns. Facebook is a great soft-sales tool (building awareness and visibility). It is a lousy direct sales tool. Don't try to turn it into one, though of course you should mention important events like book signings, conferences, product launches, special promotions, sales achievements, successes, etc.

5. Always take a personal approach. I hate blasts regardless of platform, though I especially hate them on Facebook since I spend more time there and see them more often. Yes, please reach out to people on Facebook. But do it on an individual level, and be respectful of people's time. (More on this below.)

Marketing Tactics to Avoid on Facebook

1. Do not send a blanket invite to "events" that aren't really events. We've all been invited to participate in some "event" that didn't even have a physical location, and was a thinly veiled "Buy my book!" blast. Don't do that. You should also avoid sending invites to people who wouldn't in a million years attend your event because of location/geography/investment. In short, do NOT misuse the event functionality as a pure marketing play.

2. Do not invite your existing Facebook friends to be a "fan" of your page. I have no problem with writers creating fan pages to keep their "personal" page more "personal." But if someone is already a "friend" to you, they shouldn't have to be badgered to be your "fan." I say: Let those friends find it on their own, or allow them to ignore it.

In general, if you need to have a personal page AND a fan page, then don't solicit one group to join the other group. You don't need to reach them in BOTH places. (If so, I venture to say you're using Facebook too much like a hard marketer.)

Think about it: What do you really gain by having your personal friends also "fan" you—because if your personal page holds any meaning at all, then your real friends/family probably don't need to get the fan treatment. (I can already hear your arguments about creating unwanted "writer noise" for your family/friends. If that concerns you, that's what lists are for: filtering updates upfront, when needed.)

If you're sure that a fan page is the right approach for you, grow it gradually, over time, by promoting it on your own website or blog, on Twitter, or through forums that you participate in.

Also: On that fan page, you should be consistently posting valuable and meaningful stuff. Otherwise, what's the point? If you build the page, have a content or entertainment strategy.

The same goes for any Facebook groups you create.

3. Do not post a promotion for yourself on other people's personal profile walls. I hate this. You'll get de-friended or shunned for this type of behavior over time. Also, do not "tag" someone merely to get their attention for something that's not actually related to them. That's the same behavior as posting a promotion of yourself on their Wall.

If you really want to bring someone's attention to something important, then do it in a private message or via e-mail. If that feels disruptive or spammy, or too much like an intrusion, then it is—don't do it.

4. Do not send a private message to your friends, groups, or fans asking them to market or promote your stuff, unless it's something *very* easy they can do (like take 2 seconds to vote for you in a contest).

5 Un-Marketing Principles for All Social Media

1. **Be interesting.** Post updates or links that reflect the unique perspective you have, or that play on themes that fascinate you. Have fun in what you share. See what happens. Experiment. Respond to other people's stories/updates with your own take (but don't be an ass or a proselytizer).

2. **Be helpful.** If someone asks a question or otherwise is looking for assistance, and you're in a position to be helpful, earn some good karma. Remember: You get what you give.

3. **Be open.** It's probably fine to friend or follow people you don't know that well, especially friends of friends. Just watch your privacy controls. Go with your gut; if it feels uncomfortable, then don't do it.

4. **Be a little personal.** We all know there's a line, so don't cross it. But if you share things that don't have any impact on you, or don't touch your life, or that you don't feel passionately about, then you might be a bore.

5. **Be a little vulnerable.** It's much easier to like someone when they have flaws. (Here's a good example of this when it comes to writing bios!)

As you might have noticed, I haven't mentioned anything specific to book marketing or promotion, so it may feel like there's really nothing to do. In part, that's correct. But these are the desired effects over the long-term:

Over a period of months and years, you will have interacted hundreds or thousands of times with all kinds of people. Many people may appear silent, but still observing. So, you will become known to people, even if tangentially. You may have experienced this phenomenon if you've gone to a writing conference, and someone you haven't met before says they like the stuff you post on Facebook or Twitter! That's excellent. You're making an impression. People are remembering who you are.

As your relationships develop, opportunities will open up to you. These may be interviews, guest blogging posts, speaking/teaching gigs, consulting, etc. As people come to know who you are and what you stand for, they'll remember that when faced with an issue or opportunity that fits you. And vice versa. You may uncover people you want to offer an opportunity to.

When you actually have a book coming out, you can share any calls to action that might interest your first circle of fans. E.g., if you have an Amazon pre-order day campaign, you can let people know about it. Or, if you're trying to find people to interview on a specific topic, you can put out a call.

However, this is where we get into some tricky territory, because it involves some form of hard or soft marketing, which most people really botch up on social media.

I'll end with this piece of advice from the Twist Image blog:

> Most people are lazy. They're busy with their day-to-day lives, and they think that the easiest way to get things done is by blasting everyone they know ... They're wrong ... and it's lazy. Even taking the extra time to personalize each email with a name and a sincere note will make all of the difference in the world. Marketing a message should not be an act of laziness, but an act of care and sincerity. Those that take the time to care and are sincere about it are usually the ones that are successful.

Q&A with Jane on Using Facebook
A number of my fellow authors have started fan pages on Facebook. How does an author who is just starting out—and does not have photos and videos to post, is perhaps an introvert to boot—use and benefit from an author presence with the new timeline format?

First and foremost, realize that no matter what Facebook does with your profile page, or how the Timeline evolves, most people are interacting with your posts in their own newsfeed. Very few people visit your profile unless they have a reason to research you or be curious based on something you've posted. That means: Don't sweat your Timeline too much. Yes, do fill out as much information on the about page that you're comfortable sharing (especially for the public view), but beyond being clear about who you are, I don't think the Timeline/profile format is meaningful from a marketing standpoint.

Here are three keys to behavior on Facebook that you need to understand, based on best business practices as well as what I've observed and experienced:

1. Facebook is a place to be informal, fun, and casual with people who have already expressed some level of interest or affinity for what you're doing. If people friend you or "like" you, they've given you permission to be in touch and offer updates. Such people may not have any other alerts or notices about you except for what appears in their Facebook newsfeed. Remember that and also respect it. You're creating an impression each time you post—what do those impressions add up to after a week, month, year? Are you conveying a personality, voice, or image you're comfortable with?

2. Most studies show people using Facebook typically dislike too-frequent updates and are afraid of being directly marketed to. BUT: People on Facebook do enjoy being given special access or insight they might not get anywhere else.

3. There is no "right" content or updates to post on Facebook. It's true that photos tend to get a lot of attention on Facebook, and it's probably a good idea to occasionally post photos—even something as simple as a sunset, your pet, or a meal. But the most important thing is to share things YOU care about, and to express something meaningful rather than dutiful. Never throw up a link or a photo without giving the story behind it, or why it matters to you. People crave meaning. Facebook is an excellent tool for delivering that. It creates a connection.

Also, introversion/extroversion really has nothing to do with your ability to use social media. I think social media is the best thing to ever happen to introverts (and I speak as one of the biggest of all time).

I resonate with your "Un-Marketing Principles" for Facebook use. These actually describe my aim for my newly-established author blog. Is there a benefit to having both an author blog and an author Facebook page? How would you clarify a distinction between them in terms of format, content, purpose?

Absolutely, there's tremendous value in having both. (And let me say, in case there's any confusion, that I don't really differentiate, in terms of strategy, between having a personal profile page on Facebook or having an "official" author page. Ultimately, they both serve the same purpose and can be used in exactly the same way. For me, I prefer to stick to my personal profile, encourage people to subscribe, and make 90% of my posts public.)

But back to the question. Consider: Who, upon visiting your blog (especially a new one!), will either (a) bookmark it (2) subscribe to it (3) remember to visit it again? Typically the only people who visit your blog, at first, are your mother and a couple very close friends. It's not that people don't care—they care a lot—but you have to remind them to visit when you have specific new content.

A few anecdotes from my experience:

I can tell from my own website traffic that there are thousands of people every month who rely on seeing my Facebook link as a reminder to read my latest blog post. In fact, the No. 1 referral to my site is Facebook. Many people who subscribe to me on Facebook (as well as my Facebook friends) also share my posts to their Facebook friends, which substantially increases my audience.

My Significant Other is a huge music fan. How does he keep up with his favorite musicians? Facebook news feed. For him, it's more efficient than following dozens and dozens of different blogs.

I have a former colleague who started a wonderful personal blog. I didn't subscribe to it or bookmark it even though I intend to read every post. I wait for him to post updates on Facebook. Unfortunately, he rarely does that, so I have to catch up every couple weeks when I see some reminder of it. He really ought to be posting a link to Facebook every time he updates the blog. No one is going to somehow not like that—especially since each time he does link/post, he gets a string of positive comments/feedback on it.

And that's key. If you post something that resonates with your audience, you aren't bugging them. You're serving, delighting, informing, entertaining. Maybe even thoughtfully provoking.

Finally, I can't imagine using Facebook as a replacement for a meaningful blog. I don't mean to say everyone should blog, but a Facebook status update doesn't have much in common with a great blog. A status update is very limited in its length and formatting. It's not meant to take more than a few seconds to either read or act on. (And in that, it does have something in common with Twitter!)

Now, if we were talking about Google Plus, we'd have a pretty interesting discussion, because that social network is being used successfully as a blogging tool. But that's a whole other Q&A!

Someone like myself has a business page in part to keep work and private life separate; to have a way to disseminate information and (hopefully, at least!) stimulate exchange. What can you say about the intersection of personal, author and business pages in terms of information-sharing and reach?

There are only two things I'll say about the personal page vs author/fan page.

It's a personal decision, so do what you're comfortable with and makes sense for your audience. It's hard to offer general advice because everyone's overlap/intersection differs.

Maintaining two pages on Facebook increases your workload. It makes no sense to have an author/fan page unless you have a content strategy for it that you will manage on a near-daily basis.

Okay, three things. For the love of god, if you're frequently duplicating posts or content on your personal profile and your author/fan page, *you have totally defeated the purpose of creating separate pages.* Instead, do yourself a favor, and stick to a personal profile, open it up to subscribers, and make some posts public.

Can you offer some specific guidance about best Facebook list practices —how to set them up, classify and manage them—based on your extensive experience?

Yes, lists are exceptionally helpful if you've decided it's better to manage everything from one profile. Facebook will help you to some extent by creating automated lists based on people who went to the same school as you, people who live in the same city as you, people who work at the same company as you, etc. Use those!

For example, if you host an event in your current city, use Facebook automated lists to only invite people who could reasonably be expected to make the trip, as well as "close friends"—another automated list from Facebook that you can adjust.

And speaking about that "close friends" list—that's an important one to closely manage. That way, if you post something quite personal about family, children, or whatever, it's easy to segment that content off to just your inner circle. You can also designate some content only appear to specific individuals.

(Still, though: Never post anything on Facebook you could regret later. You still have to treat it, to some extent, as a public forum. You never know what friends might do with the content you post.)

I also set up lists for people I consider "distant" connections—people I haven't met, but who are still important on a professional level. These people don't have as much access to content I consider personal.

Again, I've mentioned this several times already: Take advantage of the subscriber feature. Allow people to "subscribe" to your profile rather than become your friend. Then you can designate certain posts as public, and they'll appear in your subscribers' newsfeed. This is so useful—and for most authors, it will be just as effective as having a separate fan page.

As a final note: I know many people enjoy the phenomenon of Facebook birthdays, with all the wall posting jubilee. But if you're at all concerned about privacy, remove that from your profile. It's not incredibly safe to have that personal data available, even to an inner circle.

What advice can you offer about the value of attracting blog followers vs. Facebook subscribers—and how to keep from needing to carry on the same conversation on multiple sites??

I think there's value in both. On my own site, I recently changed the sidebar to encourage readers to subscribe to me (and thus my blog posts) on Facebook—more so than my blog's e-mail/RSS subscription. I've had excellent success so far; it just so happens my readers are more likely to be heavy users of Facebook. Also, Facebook subscription is a great alternative to the rather significant commitment of a formal e-mail/RSS subscription to the blog—that's a huge show of loyalty and fandom if someone does that, and it's not great for those with casual interest.

So, yes, that does mean conversations happen on both the blog post as well as Facebook. But you can't control or dictate where people will discuss your content. You go where they go. For me, I'm happy for the conversations to happen in two places, as well as on Twitter. It's not a burden, and it's a good "problem" to have. Either way, you need to show you're active and listening in both places, by responding to questions, liking comments, etc.

That said, if similar questions are being raised in multiple locations, and you've already answered in one place, it can be acceptable to say, "That's a great question, and I answered it at **this link**." Or you can just use the good ol' copy and paste. People appreciate your efforts.

How I Got a Six-Figure Twitter Following and Why It Doesn't Matter

Whenever a former boss would introduce me at an event, he always started by saying how many Twitter followers I have, which is inevitably far more than anyone else in the room. Today, my follower number is roughly 200,000, and it grows by a few hundred every week.

How did my Twitter following reach six figures?

- I was an early adopter. I started my Twitter account (@JaneFriedman) on May 22, 2008.
- I'm active. Except for the first 7-8 months of joining Twitter, I've been actively tweeting since I joined.
- I'm relentlessly focused. Mostly I tweet about writing, media, publishing, and technology.
- I mostly share links that I hope are helpful or insightful.
- I'm somewhat reserved. It's rare for me to tweet more than 6-8 times per day. The way I look at it: Each tweet is a potential waste of someone's time.
- I joined Twitter while I was publisher of Writer's Digest, and I also created the Writer's Digest Twitter account. Writer's Digest now has about 370,000 followers, and for its first two years, I operated its account in tandem with mine. It was helpful to have my name associated with a big brand when I got started.

However, none of that probably matters as much as what comes next.

- I started blogging better (better headlines, better topics, better solutions for writers) and blogging more consistently. (This was during my years at There Are No Rules at Writer's Digest.)
- I ran a weekly blog feature called Best Tweets for Writers. I curated a few dozen of the best online articles (for writers) I'd found via Twitter. The series started around May 2009 and concluded in summer 2011, when I asked Porter Anderson to take the reins, and he created Writing on the Ether.
- Also during this time I was actively live-tweeting conferences and other events, which usually results in a following boom.

My blog content reinforced what I was doing on Twitter, and what I was doing on Twitter reinforced the blog. I created a rather virtuous circle that I believe boosted the follower count. But most important, the Best Tweets round-up wasn't about myself or my own content. It was about drawing attention to other excellent work, which resulted in a lot of mentions, links, tweets, and so on. Some call this link-baiting, and it's a fairly well-known strategy for building blog traffic. If done well, everyone wins.

There was one thing out of my control, which I can't track very well: At some point, I became one of Twitter's "Suggested Users" in the Books category. If I'm still there, I believe my account is listed fairly close to the bottom. If I was being shown higher around 2010-2011, that could also be playing a significant role. But keep in mind, I probably would've never been listed if it weren't for the activity I've just described.

Why the Size of My Twitter Following Doesn't Matter
Some studies show that smaller, more loyal followings are more effective. That aside, here's a big reason why no one needs to be impressed by my following: about 30% of my followers are fake, and another 30% are inactive. Of those "good" accounts that follow me, how many do I actually *engage*? Maybe 1-3 percent.

And now you know not to be impressed by that six-figure number.

The Secret to Twitter That Can't Be Taught

I've found Twitter—and many aspects of social media—somewhat tricky to teach. Why? Here are 3 reasons to start:

1. Using social media is mostly about being YOU, finding your voice, and finding the right audience (those inclined to listen).
2. Your strategy, motivation, or purpose will be different—and it will change—depending on where you're at in your career. That means I can't teach you by explaining what do; my strategy cannot be your strategy.
3. Whenever you set out to use social media as a means to an end (e.g., selling books), that tends to ensure you won't attain your end. It's a very Zen process that doesn't necessarily reward those who "try" the hardest.

In an interview with author Christina Katz about using Twitter, she said:

> I'm not sure that people like to hear that the tools can become intuitive if you use them enough or that you are actually allowed to take a break because folks often approach the tools as marketing channels or bullhorns.

But social media tools are really much more fun and intuitive if you use them for social artistry rather than if you spend all your energy trying to get followers or trying to get folks to buy your stuff.

My experience of using online tools is that you are basically plugging in and expanding your sensibilities the same as when you walk into any room. Writers should think of all of the online tools as an extension of their own nervous system. If you walk into a room, you would get an immediate intuitive sense of the environment. The same is true of Twitter or any online environment. When you connect into to theses contexts, you are not acquiring billboard space. You are entering a context, an environment. Don't over-think how you are going to act. Just do what you would do if you were entering any new room. After a while, you will become "a regular" and people will look forward to seeing you when you show up.

Managing Multiple Identities Online (Avoid)

Inevitably, at some point during author platform discussions, two questions get asked:

- What if I want to write under a pen name, or two (or more) different names? Do I need to maintain multiple identities?
- What if I have different areas of interest that have no connection to each other? Should I have separate blogs/sites/presences for each?

There are several different facets to these problems that need to be unraveled. Let's start with the question of using a pen name.

Pen Names or Pseudonyms

The first question here is: Why are you using a pseudonym? For protection/privacy or for marketing purposes?

If you're using it to prevent market confusion (e.g., you don't want your crime fiction fans to be confused and buy your newest postmodern fiction masterpieces), that's understandable and it's a well-known marketing move to use different names for distinct readerships.

If you're doing it to something from friends or family, or even something from a segment of your audience, you'll expend a lot of energy "protecting" yourself and your readers. You should avoid this whenever possible—it's time consuming and takes away momentum from both writing and platform building. Furthermore, in today's world of diminishing privacy, it is difficult to keep anything a secret for long.

Plus, any work that you cannot directly and openly affiliate yourself with will be a challenge to market, since there will be certain strategies/tactics you can't implement without being identified with the work.

If You Write in Very Different Genres/Categories

This could be an advantage—since readers in either category could potentially be interested in the other things you write, or know people who are. Bringing all worlds (readers) together isn't a bad thing if they can easily find what they're looking for.

When you set up your sites, blogs, or social media accounts, you'll want to include mentions of all the pen names you write under, and have subsections for each, as needed.

When Should You Develop & Maintain Separate Identities?

There are usually 2 areas where I see a definite need to separate and maintain different sites or social media accounts:

- When you write for children (you may need a separate experience/voice for them)
- When you have a professional pursuit that really can't be mixed with your writerly pursuits

In both of these cases, you aren't necessarily hiding anything from anyone (I would expect you're still able to be affiliated with your work no matter where you go), but mixing things up could prove detrimental.

So, overall: Have a holistic presence whenever possible, and avoid identity segmentation. It will be less work in the long run, and you could see benefits from cross-pollination of your interests.

CHAPTER 10
Rights and Legal Issues

||||||||||||||||||||||||||||||||||||||||||||||||||||||||||||||||||||||||||||||||||||||||||||||||||||||||||||||||||||||||||||||||||||||||||||||||||||||||||||||||||||||||||||||||

Most writers fall into one of two camps: people who are (overly) concerned that someone will steal their work, and innocents who don't take time to learn what rights they ought to be protecting.

Here are 5 things every U.S.-based writer should know about their rights (and, by extension, other people's rights). However, keep in mind I am not a lawyer, and this is not legal advice.

1. Your work is protected under copyright as soon as you put it in tangible form. Your work doesn't need to be published to be protected, and you do not have to display the copyright symbol on your manuscript to have it protected. (One of the reasons there is so much confusion surrounding this issue is that the law changed in the 1970s.)

Since your work is copyrighted from the moment you create it, the existence or validity of your copyright doesn't require registration of the work with the U.S. Copyright Office. It's possible to register the work after you find infringement and still be afforded the same protection as if you had registered it earlier.

2. For shorter works (non-books), publications automatically acquire one-time rights unless specified otherwise in the contract. The current law puts the burden on the publication to notify the author in writing if it wants to acquire any rights other than one-time rights (that is, the right to publish the work one time). The law also contains termination provisions that allow an author to regain rights she assigned to others after a specific period.

3. Your work cannot accidentally fall into the public domain. Any published or distributed material on which a copyright has expired is considered to be in the public domain—that is, available for use by any member of the general public without payment to, or permission from, the original author.

It used to be that your work might accidentally fall into the public domain if not protected under copyright or published with the copyright symbol. This is not the case any longer.

4. Selling various rights or licenses to your work doesn't affect your ownership of the copyright. Various rights are all part of your copyright, but selling or licensing them in no way diminishes your ownership of the actual work. The only way you can give up copyright entirely is if you sign a contract or agreement that stipulates it is a "work for hire."

5. You can quote other people's work in your own work, without permission, as long as you abide by fair use guidelines. The downside here is that there are no hard-and-fast rules as to what constitutes fair use of a copyrighted work. Most publishers have their own fair-use guidelines that they ask their own authors to abide by. But, if you're picking up only a few hundred words from a full-length book, it's probably fair use. (Fair use will be discussed more in-depth later.)

Are You Worried Your Work or Ideas Will be Stolen?

I am not an attorney nor do I have any special experience in intellectual property law. Legal professionals are likely to offer a different view than I do. However, I think we all know that asking a lawyer for advice can over-complicate a situation. I've heard lawyers speak at writing conferences on copyright, and everyone ends up paranoid and frightened in the space of an hour.

Many warnings are unnecessary and counterproductive. My goal is to make things simple and give you information based on the actual likelihood something "bad" will happen to you.

The following advice is directed toward writers of prose and poetry. If you are a scriptwriter or playwright, look elsewhere for advice; it's a different world for you.

I'll break down this issue in 3 ways:

1. Protecting your ideas
2. Protecting your unpublished writing
3. Protecting your published writing

1. Protecting Your Ideas

It is not possible under current U.S. law to copyright or protect an idea. (You also cannot copyright a title.) So, how much precaution should you take to keep your ideas secret?

Very little. I guarantee that others have similar ideas; you see it happen all the time in the business. Chalk it up to cultural zeitgeist. While I don't advocate advertising your idea far and yon, or putting flashing lights around it on your blog, the chances that an agent, editor, critique partner, or stranger will:

- steal your idea
- execute your idea better than you
- AND be able to sell it

… are next to zero. It is not worth worrying about. Share your work with trusted advisers, send it to agents/editors for consideration, and talk about aspects of it on your blog. No problem. Unless you are known in the industry for coming up with million-dollar salable concepts, it's not likely you'll experience idea theft.

I love Jeanne Bowerman's take on this fear: Sure, someone can steal your idea, but they can't possibly execute it or interpret it in the same way you can. No one can be you. That is your best protection of all.

2. Protecting your unpublished writing

As explained earlier, your work doesn't need to be formally published to be protected, and you do not have to display the copyright symbol on your manuscript to have it protected. So does it make sense to register your work with the U.S. Copyright Office?

Let's go down the series of events that must happen for a lawsuit against an infringer to make sense:

- Someone must steal your work.
- Someone must develop and package the work (or make it desirable for someone to pay for it).
- Readers have to find it and pay for it.
- Meanwhile the person who did the stealing needs to keep a low-enough profile that the infringement is not detected while still making enough money to make it worth his time.

Most people don't view unpublished writings (or writers) as an untapped gold mine. It's a lot of hard work to profit from a piece of writing (especially writing from an unknown, unproven writer)—isn't it?

3. Protecting your published writing

If you self-publish your work or otherwise begin selling it, then you should officially register it with the U.S. Copyright Office.

Then the question becomes, if you find infringement, is it worth your time to issue a cease-and-desist or otherwise take legal action?

This is where we enter into a philosophical debate. Many believe that obscurity is a greater threat than piracy. I tend to agree. Piracy is more likely to hurt authors who are famous, rather than the unknown authors. However, even bestselling authors have experimented with giving their work away for free—even enabling piracy!—and have claimed to profit even more due to the marketing and publicity effect. (Paulo Coelho is an example.)

There is one area of theft and wrongdoing that is frustrating: People who create and sell e-books on Amazon by duplicating or repurposing other people's content, or using public domain work. But Amazon has significantly cracked down on this activity.

When Do You Need to Secure Permissions?

With more authors self-publishing than ever, I'm hearing more questions about permissions. Unfortunately, it's a tough issue to navigate without having an experienced editor or agent to guide you.

Permissions is all about seeking permission to quote or excerpt other people's copyrighted work within your own. This means contacting the copyright owner of the work (or their publisher or agent), and requesting permission to use the work. Most publishers have a formal process that requires a signed contract. Often, you are charged a fee for the use, anywhere from a few dollars to thousands of dollars.

An Important Preface to This Discussion

Quoting or excerpting someone else's work falls into one of the grayest areas of copyright law. For understandable reasons, you might be seeking a "rule" to apply to reduce your risk or reduce time spent worrying about it.

Therefore, the biggest "rule" that you'll find—if you're searching online or asking people—is: "Ask explicit permission for everything beyond X."

What constitutes "X" depends on whom you ask. Some people say 300 words. Some say one line. Some say 10% of the word count.

But you must never forget: there is no *legal* rule stipulating what quantity is OK to use without seeking permission. Major legal battles have been fought over this question, but there is STILL no black-and-white rule.

So any rules you find are based on a general institutional guideline or a person's experience, as well as their overall comfort level with the risk involved in directly quoting/excerpting work. That's why opinions and guidelines vary so much.

The other problem is that once you start asking for permission (to reduce your risk), that gives publishers (or copyright owners) the opportunity to ask for money or refuse to give permission, *even in cases where the use would actually be considered fair.* So you can get taken advantage of if you're overly cautious. See the Catch-22?

I receive many queries from my readers about fair use, and it's very difficult for me to advise each of them on these matters because every instance of quoting/excerpting may have a different answer as to whether you need permission or whether it would be considered fair use.

There is no rule you can apply, only principles. So I hope to provide some clarity on those principles here.

When Do You NOT Need to Seek Permission?

- **When the work is in the public domain.** This isn't always a simple matter to determine, but any work published before 1923 is in the public domain. Some works published after 1923 are also in the public domain.
- **When simply mentioning the title or author of a work.** You do not need permission to mention the title of someone's work. It's like citing a fact.
- **When you are stating unadorned facts.** If you copy a list of the 50 states in the United States, you are not infringing on anyone's copyright. Those are unadorned facts.
- **When you are linking to something.** Linking does not require permission.
- **When the work is licensed under Creative Commons.** If this is the case, you should see this prominently declared on the work itself.
- **When you abide by fair use guidelines.** If you're only quoting a few lines from a full-length book, you are likely within fair use guidelines, and do not need to seek permission. But this is a gray area.

When Should You Seek Permission?

When you use copyrighted material in such a way that it cannot be considered fair use. In such cases, *crediting the source does not remove the obli-*

gation to seek permission. It is expected that you always credit your source regardless of fair use; otherwise, you are plagiarizing.

A Brief Explanation of Fair Use

There are four criteria for determining fair use, which sounds tidy, but it's not. These criteria are vague and open to interpretation. Ultimately, when disagreement arises over what constitutes fair use, it's up to the courts to make a decision.

The four criteria are:

1. The purpose and character of the use (e.g., commercial vs. not-for-profit/educational). If the purpose of your work is commercial (to make money), that doesn't mean you're suddenly in violation of fair use. But it makes your case less sympathetic if you're borrowing a lot of someone else's work to prop up your own commercial venture.

2. The nature of the copyrighted work. Facts cannot be copyrighted. For that reason, more creative or imaginative works generally get the strongest protection.

3. The amount and substantiality of the portion used in relation to the entire quoted work. The law does not offer any percentage or word count here that we can go by. That's because if the portion quoted is considered the most valuable part of the work, you may be violating fair use. That said, most publishers' guidelines for authors offer a rule of thumb; at the publisher where I worked, that guideline was 200-300 words from a book-length work in a teaching/educational context.

4. The effect of the use on the potential market for or value of the quoted work. If your use of the original work in any way damages the likelihood that people will buy the original work, you are in violation of fair use.

To further explore what these four criteria mean in practice, search online for read this excellent article by attorney Howard Zaharoff that originally appeared in *Writer's Digest* magazine: "A Writers' Guide to Fair Use."

Does this apply to use of copyrighted work on websites, blogs, digital mediums, etc?

Technically, yes, but attitudes tend to be more lax. When bloggers (or others) aggregate, repurpose, or otherwise excerpt copyrighted work—whether it originates online or offline—they typically view such use as "sharing" or "publicity" for the original author rather than as a copyright violation, especially if it's for noncommercial or educational purposes. I'm not talking about wholesale piracy here, but about extensive excerpting or aggregating that would not be considered OK otherwise. In short, it's a controversial issue.

Again, you do not need permission to link to a website.

A Note About Song Titles, Movie Titles, Proper Names, Etc.

You do not need permission to include song titles, movie titles, TV show titles—any kind of title—in your work. You can also include the names of places, things, events, and people in your work without asking permission. These are facts.

Permissions for Song Lyrics and Poetry

Because songs and poems are so short, it's dangerous to use even 1 line without asking for permission, even if you think the use could be considered fair. However, it's fine to use song titles, poem titles, artist names, band names, movie titles, etc.

CHAPTER 11
Advice on the Writing Life

Since college, I've held fast to an existential philosophy that goes something like this: We make time for whatever is important to us. Our actions are the biggest indicators of who we are.

Not surprisingly, when I worked for Writer's Digest, I had little patience for writers who complained about having lack of time. We're all given the same amount of time in a day, and we make choices we must be held accountable for.

Those who don't have time to write:

- Haven't yet made the necessary sacrifices to create time (like giving up TV or sleep)
- (Or) don't yet have the discipline to set aside the time to write
- (And) may be too afraid to make the time (fear of failing or starting at all)

When attending the Midwest Writers Workshop one year, I met Haven Kimmel's mother, Delonda. It was an otherworldly experience since I knew her first as a character in Kimmel's memoir, *A Girl Named Zippy*.

At the time, I was not writing a word. I carried guilt over it—I was an editor and publisher of references for writers, yet felt uncomfortable telling anyone I was a writer. Because I wasn't writing.

As I was confessing my lack of writerhood, Delonda said, with such grace and empathy, "Why dear, you're exhausted." It was among the kindest things anyone has said to me.

Suddenly my own choice came into view. It wasn't a matter of being "good enough" or productive enough or disciplined enough to be a writer. During this period of my life, I focused on Writer's Digest, and when I did, my energy for other things was limited.

It's important to acknowledge and fully realize what choices we are making—either in the short-term or long-term—that impact other things we want to achieve. What sacrifices are we making, implicitly or explicitly?

We can't have it all (at least not all at once). We have to choose.

The Secret to Finding the Time to Write, Market, Promote, and Still Have a Life

One question I can count on, in every setting—no matter the topic, event, or audience skill level—is: *How do you find the time to do all this?*

"All this" refers to writing, blogging, marketing, promoting, social media, website building, blogging, traveling, speaking, etc. The question comes up so often that I wonder what kind of secret people think I'm hiding.

Up until now, I've never had a good answer for people who asked this question. I sleep, eat, watch TV, and have downtime like everyone else. But I've been meditating on what helpful advice I might have that doesn't involve miraculous scientific advances or large inheritances.

Here are five strategies.

1. Decide what you'll stop doing—and I'm not talking about TV. This isn't discussed nearly often enough. Every year, you should make a "stop doing" list. It's a highly personal activity if done right, so I can't say universally to all of you: Stop doing THIS one thing.

However, when I talk about a "stop doing" list, I'm not talking about watching TV, working in your yard, going shopping, or other activities that make life enjoyable—though these things be on your list too. Your call.

What I'm really talking about are projects and activities that probably fall under the rubric of the writing life, but have (1) stopped being fun and enjoyable, (2) aren't pushing you further or growing your skills, and (3) suck up your time without benefit. Sometimes you even have to stop doing things you enjoy because you have to free up time for something more important to you. (For instance, I stopped doing weekly Best Tweets for Writers compilations, even though I enjoyed it.)

These are tough decisions to make, but if you don't currently have the time you need to make progress, you have to stop doing *something*. (Gather more ideas here.)

Finally—and most controversially in this context—*stop reading writing advice*. Like it or not, it's one of the biggest and most attractive distractions in the world, because it usually comes with community, conversations, and relationships. But you can overindulge in it, especially if you're constantly telling yourself you're not "ready" to write. One gets better at writing primarily by doing two things: writing and reading. Mentoring is helpful and essential of course, but only insomuch as you're practicing and producing the work. So get to work.

2. Pay someone to do stuff that you don't like or don't need to learn. This assumes you have more money than time. If not, skip to No. 3.

Long ago, I decided that my time was much better spent on writing and teaching rather than cleaning. So, I hired a cleaning service and I never wash my car. I hire someone to do my taxes. I hired someone to move my website to a new host because, while I could manage it myself, I didn't want the time sink or headache.

Identify activities in your life that give you no pleasure to do, and that you have the money to pay for.

3. Say good-bye to guilt and obligation. This is the hardest thing of all, because we're so attached to our guilt and obligation. This is a book about writing, though, not psychology, so I won't go into the step-by-step of how to rid yourself of these self-imposed problems. But if you're interested in having more time or freedom to write, then you need to examine activities you don't enjoy and continue doing only because you feel obligated to someone. What's the very worst thing that could happen if you stopped?

And, by the way, this applies to social media too. Do you feel obligated to read someone's blog posts every day? Do you feel obligated to acknowledge people on social media sites, to acknowledge every e-mail and Facebook message, to respond to every single blip on your screen?

You don't have to. Respond to the messages and to the people who actually matter to you, or when it's a pleasure to interact, or when you feel grateful, or when you are giving from your abundance and not feeling exhausted by the activity.

4. Be good at what you do. Some of the biggest time wasters are activities you may enjoy, but that you have little skill for. This describes me when I first started blogging in 2001. (I abandoned it, but returned to the form when I was better prepared.)

The paradox here is that you only get good at something by logging a lot of hours doing it. The more you write, the better you get at writing. The more you blog, the better you get at blogging. The more you interact on social media, the better you get at social media. And by "better," I mean that the quality of your work increases, your efficiency increases, and your effectiveness increases.

I attribute most of my apparent productivity to the fact I've become very good at what I do.

If you're not good at what you're doing, then you must decide to:
- Pursue it harder than before and get really good
- Stop doing it so you can get good at something else.

5. Spend the most time on what matters most to you. Obvious, isn't it? But we don't do it. We're constantly doing what other people tell us to do, getting sidetracked by the latest blog post, or otherwise worrying over details that won't matter in the long run. We lose our focus.

As you plan your year, do the following:
- Decide what meaningful productivity looks like on a weekly basis. Does it mean writing 250 words every week, plus two blog posts? Does it mean having meaningful conversations on Twitter? Does it mean making progress on a long-term project? Decide, but under no circumstance should you measure productivity based on what someone else does.
- Figure out how much time it takes you to be "productive" on a weekly basis. If the amount of time scares you, then you've been too ambitious. Scale back to a level where you can be disciplined and consistent.
- Block out sacred time on your schedule for you to get this work done.

3 Ways to Add Meaningful Structure to Your Writing Life

One of the big lessons I've learned as a professor is: Writers need structure.

It was a hard lesson to learn because many of the things I value in life cause me to downplay structure. I value things like:
- Intrinsic motivation (some would say "passion")
- Doing what feels right or comes naturally
- Changing direction upon insight/discovery
- The journey, not the outcome

However, freedom can be our worst enemy. It can lead to paralysis, procrastination, aimlessness, or indecision. And especially for writers who are just starting out, the principles still need to be learned. While we may need room to experiment and explore, we also need meaningful practice and a way of measuring progress.

By way of example, the best writing course I ever took in college was Introduction to Poetry. The professor was well known for being a formalist, someone who required the students to write metrical verse. For those not familiar with the poetry world, this is unusual. Most classes focus on free verse since it's the predominant poetic idiom today.

Some of the best work of my college career came out of that class. It's like what Robert Frost said: "I would sooner write free verse as play tennis with the net down." I found the challenge invigorating. It forced me to think harder about my word choices, and what I wanted to say. It sharpened every writing skill in a concentrated way.

For fiction writers—or all writers—here are 3 ways to introduce structure (or add a little more structure) to your writing life:

1. Daily or weekly creative assignments. Use writing exercise books or worksheets on a daily or weekly basis—but the kind that force you to go outside your comfort zone. One of my favorite resources for unusual, skill-building exercises is *3 A.M. Epiphany* by Brian Kiteley. (He also authored a follow-up with more great exercises called *4 A.M. Breakthrough*.) Here's an example of a terrific exercise:

> Describe a happy marriage over at least 10 years. You will have to dispense with focused narrative, summarizing to a large extent, listing details—the reasons you think this is a happy marriage. Is a happy marriage an enviable marriage? Can a couple be too happy? Inseparable and insufferable? 600-word limit.

For something whimsical, try the *Write-Brain Workbook* by Bonnie Neubauer.

2. Scheduled writing time *with specific tasks*. If you don't already have a set time and place for writing that you *never* deviate from, try this: Pick a 30–60 minute time slot each week that has zero chance of being superseded by other responsibilities. Go somewhere that is a treat for you: a coffee shop, a park, wherever you *love* to go. (If it's more of a treat to stay home, then stay home, as long as you can't be interrupted.) Make this your dedicated time to get the same writing task done *each week*. Never miss it, and always do the *same kind of work*. And see what happens!

3. Weekly and daily goal sheet. This is an excellent tool for a writer who is working daily (or near-daily) on a long-term project, who also may have other responsibilities vying for her time.

Each week, list what you'd be satisfied with accomplishing, given everything else that is happening in your life. Do not overshoot it. The point is to list what you'd be *satisfied* with. Click here to download a sheet I developed that you might find helpful. It includes the following sections:

- What you plan to accomplish in a week
- What else is happening that may affect your ability to get stuff done
- What 1 task you're avoiding that you promise to complete this week
- "Parking lot": This is your free space to list or note what you like. I find it an ideal place to mention stuff I'm worried I'll forget. If I keep it here and know it's safe, my mind is free to focus on my work.

After you have your weekly sheet, at the start of each day, use a single Post-It note (a small one—and only one!) to list what tasks from your weekly sheet you have time for. Then accomplish it!

I recommend saving or filing past goal sheets so you can evaluate when your most productive times are. Sometimes you can gain insight into what motivates you to produce lots of work or your best work.

Reasons to Be Optimistic About Freelancing and Journalism

I consider writing for hire (freelancing and journalism) quite different than creative writing (novels, memoir, etc), because the former necessarily has to pay attention to marketplace concerns, and if not, be gifted into existence or sustainability by patrons, grants, fellowships, and so on.

Journalists don't typically expect—or shouldn't expect—to make a living from their work by just writing what they want and disregarding the market. A creative writer, on the other hand, is usually assumed to be focusing on his art and mostly disregarding trends, though what he writes is of course influenced by what can be sold. For instance, short stories once could bring a writer decent pay, as it did F. Scott Fitzgerald, but one is quite lucky to earn any money from short fiction today. And serials could be very profitable for Dickens during the Victorian Era, but the form later fell out of favor for long fiction. (And serials may now be making a comeback because of their suitability for mobile distribution and consumption.)

Too often we equate content with its container. For much of our lives, quality journalism has appeared in newspapers and magazines, so we equate the decline of that particular industry with the decline of journalism. But the survival of quality writing or journalism is not tied to the future of the newspaper or magazine business. Those are delivery and distribution mechanisms, they are services to readers, and they have become less useful and valuable to us in the digital era.

The challenge, of course, is that we know how to monetize a print newspaper or magazine—and it's easier to charge for their perceived value.

We're still figuring out how to monetize digital forms. But amidst this challenge, I'd argue we're not seeing less quality journalism, we're seeing more, because we have no distribution barriers and low start-up costs in digital publishing.

I'd also ask if we *really* think the system pre-Internet was producing quality journalism, or if we merely prefer the devil we know. In the mid-20th century, media began to be operated by handful of conglomerates with significant control over the mass mediums of radio, TV, newspapers and magazines, a system that was hard for outside voices to access. To be sure, these major media conglomerates are being disrupted by another set of powerhouses (Google, Apple, Amazon, Facebook), but the latter provide us possibilities that didn't exist before: the ability to directly reach a specific, targeted readership and gather a community, which can lead to monetization by individuals and businesses alike.

How long does it take to reach sustainability? It depends on what kind of community you've established and if you offer a compelling value they find deserving of their dollars. Let's look at a few examples of people or institutions experimenting and succeeding in the digital era.

Brain Pickings. In 2006, Maria Popova started her site Brain Pickings, which is a catalogue of "interestingness." Today, her work reaches millions through her website and email newsletter, and it's sustainable through donations and affiliate marketing (more on that below). I recommend watching her talk at Tools of Change (available on YouTube), where she discusses how journalism can sustain itself in the future. Popova is clearly doing what she loves, and has found a business model to serve her art.

The Information. Launched in the fall of 2013, The Information is a subscription-based digital publication that costs $399 per year. It's focused on a niche market, the technology business audience. What is the value or benefit to readers? High-quality stories and journalism that can be trusted (unlike much online content in the tech industry), and an implicit promise that you, the reader, are getting the smartest viewpoints and insights—in a very efficient way, I might add. You don't have to filter through the noise of the many tech journalism sites to figure out what's important.

Stratechery, Ben Thompson. Thompson just recently began a monetization effort for his insightful tech industry blog that offers incentives for people to become members. Those incentives include: the ability to comment on articles, direct email access to Thompson, daily updates, virtual and in-person meet ups, and a private online community.

The Wirecutter. This website offers high-quality product reviews, mainly in the tech/media product space, and sustains itself through affiliate marketing.

Chris Guillebeau. An author and world traveler, Chris's brand centers on the art of nonconformity, and I often recommend writers read his "279 Days to Overnight Success," which details how he made his website and blog a sustainable living in just under a year. He makes money from selling his own digital products and traditionally published books, as well as producing events.

And of course you also have the big guns, Andrew Sullivan and Nate Silver, but they are so often pulled out as models that I won't belabor their trajectories here. I should also point out there are many valuable digital-era operations that give us plenty to be optimistic about when it comes to the future of journalism, such as ProPublica, a nonprofit, and the Pacific Standard, another nonprofit run out of the Miller-McCune Center for Research, Media and Public Policy. (In my mind, nonprofits and for-profits face the same issues of sustainability and have the same challenge of balancing art and business.)

Regarding payment for writers: When The Atlantic Online got in trouble last year for offering Nate Thayer $0 to re-post an article, Alexis Madrigal wrote a very long response about how and why freelancers were offered so little payment for their pieces. Madrigal explains Atlantic's strategy of using *in-house* writers and editors to generate the large majority of content that goes online, because it's a more successful way of getting quality content and higher traffic. The freelance work often contributes very little to the bigger picture, thus the lower investment.

This is a frustrating reality for freelancers. Some argue it's next to impossible to make a living as an online-only freelancer, unless you supplement it with other forms of writing. Felix Salmon sums up the challenge best:

> The lesson here isn't that digital journalism doesn't pay. It does pay and often it pays better than print journalism. Rather the lesson is that if you want to earn money in digital journalism, you're probably going to have to get a full-time job somewhere. Lots of people write content online; most of them aren't even journalists, and as Ariana Huffington says, "Self-expression is the new entertainment." Digital journalism isn't really about writing any more — not in the manner that freelance print journalists understand it, anyway. Instead, it's more about reading, and aggregating, and working in teams, doing all the work that used to happen in old print-magazine offices, but doing it on a vastly compressed timescale.

When I recently interviewed longtime magazine industry insider Bo Sacks for *Scratch*, he discussed how it's survival of the fittest for many publications that have traditionally been supported through advertising. He said:

If you do not have excellence, you will not survive in print. There's plenty of indifferent writing on the web—it's free entry, and it doesn't matter. But quality will out there, too. Really well-written, well-thought-out editorial will be the revenue stream. You must have such worthiness that people give you money when they don't have to, since they can get entertained elsewhere for free.

People giving you money when they don't have to? What might inspire that? The answer lies in focusing on the *why* underlying what you do, the fundamental motivation driving your writing, publication, or business. There's enough choice and community out there that most people only have time and money to devote to things they can feel a part of, or believe in, or simply can't get anywhere else.

Now I'll address some questions I frequently hear on this topic.

There's an abundance of jabber and dreck, and we're more distracted than ever. How is all this low-quality work affecting us?

This question comes up at almost every talk I give these days, and I think each person is asking a different question. It can mean so many different things:

- I am appalled at the quality of work published today.
- I am worried low-quality work will push out the high-quality work.
- What will happen to us as a culture/society if we allow low-quality work to proliferate?
- I am overwhelmed and anxious by all the horrible stuff out there. Will I lose what I love?
- I am tired of people talking about what they had for breakfast.

These are concerns that have been expressed literally since the beginning of publishing. After the printing press was invented, and the world started filling with books, intellectuals worried that the abundance would negatively affect people's consumption of the most worthy content. When novels emerged, they were accused of being light entertainment that would rot the mind. One intellectual, dismayed at the quality of literature being produced in the 1700s, commented:

Reading is supposed to be an educational tool of independence, and most people use it like sleeping pills; it is supposed to make us free and mature, and how many does it serve merely as a way of passing time and as a way of remaining in a condition of eternal immaturity!

Even as literacy spread, and more people learned to read, some were concerned that such a solitary activity would detract from communal life. And it did, but there were other benefits. Elizabeth Eisenstein writes in *The Printing Press as an Agent of Change*:

> By its very nature, a reading public was not only more dispersed; it was also more atomistic and individualistic than a hearing one. ... To be sure, bookshops, coffee houses, and reading rooms provided new kinds of communal gathering places. ... But even while communal solidarity was diminished, vicarious participation in more distant events was also enhanced; and even while local ties were loosened, links to larger collective units were being forged. Printed materials encouraged silent adherence to causes whose advocates could not be found in any one parish and who addressed an invisible public from afar. New forms of group identity began to compete with an older, more localized nexus of loyalties.

An identical passage could be written about the dynamics of the digital age!

When you recognize this overriding pattern, the same concerns arising again and again throughout history, we should take consolation in it. Perhaps, just perhaps, we will manage much as we have in the past. New problems arise, but we find enough solutions to carry on. I don't believe the new problems are any more dire or pernicious than those our predecessors faced.

Finally, when it comes to low-quality operations disrupting high-quality operations (think: Huffington Post disrupting print newspapers), people forget that these low-quality operations often evolve and mature into high-quality operations. This is one of the ideas expressed in Clay Christensen's *The Innovator's Dilemma*. One of the classic examples he uses is how the Detroit automakers scoffed at the low-quality compact cars coming out of Japan in the 1960s. We all know how that story ended, and Japan now makes *all* quality of cars, not just those for the low end of the market. We've already seen how outlets like Buzzfeed are implementing journalistic standards and getting closer to what traditionalists consider quality journalism.

Bottom line: I think arguments about quality aren't productive or taking us anywhere new. There is an audience for all types of quality; know your market and serve the quality that's appropriate—and remember that the price reflects the quality. (If you were paying to read each blog post on my site, I would be approaching it *very* differently, and would spend more than a few hours on each one.)

What are the new business models for writers? How can they make money in the digital era?

This is a big question, and it's why I started *Scratch* in partnership with Manjula Martin. We explore this question, in all its facets, in each quarterly issue and on the blog. It's not a question that can be answered with a formula, nor decisively, because the environment is still dramatically changing, and every author is different in terms of their strengths, available time to invest, and what they are willing to sacrifice to earn a living from writing. One of the major points of my talk was that successful authors often buck the trends or economic models of their time, and find new ways of sustaining their art. They ignore prevailing cultural attitudes that often inhibit innovative thinking.

However, I can point to trends in the market and the different models that are currently playing out.

Serials. I reported at length, again for *Scratch*, on how fiction writers are using platforms like Wattpad, Amazon KDP, and Kindle Serials to build an audience and then monetize it.

Two keys to this model: People get to sample your work for free, which builds trust, and then later on you charge, once you have a devoted reader. This model is prevalent in the digital age and tech world: capturing new users (or readers) with a free or freemium service, then charging the most devoted users (or readers) for the full experience.

Serials do well in a mobile reading environment, and given that we're nearly at 100% mobile adoption in the United States, more and more reading needs to be optimized for that environment. Wattpad has been very successful at this; the majority of reading activity on their platform is mobile-driven.

Crowdfunding. Everyone has heard of Kickstarters by now. Writers have been funding their projects for years through this platform. But to be successful, it requires that you're able to mobilize a community or fan base, who comes to your aid in support of your project. How do you develop that community or fan base in the first place? It could be through serials (described above), blogging, working your ass off getting published and noticed in a variety of outlets online, being on social media, and so on. Successful crowdfunding usually comes after years of putting in the work to develop a readership, rather than at the beginning of a writing and publishing effort.

Advertising and affiliate marketing. If your website or blog has sufficient traffic, you can monetize through advertising and affiliate marketing, where you get a small percentage of sales when people buy something because they were referred by your site. Amazon has the largest and most successful affiliate program, and I am an Amazon affiliate myself, to help cover the costs of maintaining my site.

Donations and tip jars. Maria Popova sustains herself through a combination of donations and affiliate marketing. Many bloggers who otherwise write for free have a tip jar on their site to encourage readers to pay for content that they've found valuable. You won't find a tip jar on my site, but that's mainly because I've monetized successfully in other ways, and also I've been too lazy to incorporate one.

Subscriptions and memberships. People *do* pay for content if they find value in it or can't get it elsewhere. Subscription and membership models work well when you have a very well-defined target audience, with common values and beliefs, where people are motivated to be part of the community, and/or want to directly support your efforts. See also: Andrew Sullivan.

Collectives. There have been experiments, formal and informal, with author collectives, where authors who share similar audiences band together and cross-market and promote themselves to each other's audiences. One of the more recent examples of this is *The Deadly Dozen*, twelve thriller writers who bundled together their work digitally and sold it at a very competitive price. The project hit the New York Times bestseller list, and you can bet that every author now has increased visibility and a new set of readers they didn't have before.

Experiences, services, and events. While at The Muse & The Marketplace, I met author Jamie Cat Callan, who is the author of *Ooh La La! French Women's Secrets to Feeling Beautiful Every Day*. Jamie has begun taking 14 ladies on a tour of Paris in the summer, to learn the secrets discussed in her book.

While such a strategy plays well for nonfiction authors, sometimes it's tougher for fiction writers to make a connection to an "experience" that would be inspired by their work. But places and themes in books can often parlay into discussions, events, and experiences that devoted readers would pay for (or that help sell books), especially if you can partner with one or two others who are writing about the same places and themes.

Good old-fashioned sales. I don't believe the value of content is approaching zero or that it's meant to be free or gifted. Certainly *some* content has a market value of zero and it's often very smart to make *some* content available for free as part of a larger content strategy. My blog, for instance, is 100% free, yet it is one of the most important ways I make money. The value of its content attracts 100,000 visits every month, and ranks at the top of Google searches for how to write and get published. Significant opportunities come from that.

Every decision you make as a writer has to be made with the bigger picture in mind—of how a particular book, article, blog post, or social media effort attracts a certain type of reader, and how you expect to "funnel" that reader to the next experience if they enjoy your work. Genre fiction authors have been expert at this, and have built up incredible communities of fans who end up spreading the word on their behalf. Taking care of your readers means also taking care of your sales, and the digital era has brought us an abundance of models and means to engage and interact with readers, and turn that into a sustainable living.

Michael Bhaskar, in *The Content Machine*, writes:

> More models allow more points of views, more ways of thinking and more ways of existing. This freedom creates a better chance of innovative and different work coming through ... Diversity of models is hence always to be encouraged.

This has not been an exhaustive list of all the ways that writers can make money, either from direct sales or through other means, but I hope it helps get your wheels turning. As I see it, the challenge isn't really about a lack of opportunities or models, but the average person's lack of time to pursue these things, or the lack of stamina (these strategies take time to pay off—it's rarely a quick win), or the desire for a sure success and a low tolerance for failure. Some experiments or models *will* fail, and that's where people often stop and decide "game over." If I had stopped my blog after its first uneventful 18 months, or abandoned Twitter after 18 months, I would say they were both a waste of time. But I stuck with them, and they paid off.

The Greater Challenge

We're approaching an era of universal authorship. Anyone can and does write now, and because of that, the writers who know how to find and engage their readership or community (to tap into the *why*), and who enter into collaborations with other authors and artists, hold an advantage. Future-of-the-book expert Bob Stein has said that if the printing press empowered the individual, the digital era now empowers collaboration.

You can find an expression of this in The Power Law of Participation (go Google it), where you see the qualities of moderating, collaborating, and leading as requiring and producing high levels of engagement with a community—a coveted thing when attention is scarce.

Every writer knows you have to spend time on your writing for it to get better, and to produce something that's special. The same is true of every activity described above, including any social media efforts you pursue. We're seeking long-term sustainability, and it's an organic process that's nearly impossible to rush.

Parting Words

Sometimes we can get so caught up in what we've lost that we don't see what we've gained. We fail to see the opportunities right in front of us because we're focused on the qualities of a system that we find exploitative or antithetical to our values. I'd rather be open to the art of possibility, to recognize the abundance we have. To do this, it helps to focus on the higher motivations of what we do (our gifts) and pursue excellence through our work and play, rather than focus on the outcomes.

For More Reading on This Topic

Search for the following articles and books:

- "Twelve Steps" by Brian O'Leary (blog post): it says everything I want writers to know about the disruption in book publishing
- "A Frank Conversation With the Former Editors of the Washington Post and New York Times," an online interview on the future of journalism
- "The Future of the News Business," a blog post by Marc Andreessen
- *Show Your Work* by Austin Kleon, a *New York Times* bestselling book
- *Make Art Make Money* by Elizabeth Hyde Stevens, a book on how Jim Henson was able to make his art pay.

My Advice for Undergraduate Writing Students

Dear Hopeful Student,

When I applied to undergraduate programs in the early 1990s, I only considered one type of degree: the BFA in creative writing. I've now forgotten why I fixated on such an eccentric degree that only ten schools in the country offered at the time. But it was a fortuitous obsession: I fell in love with my program and soon embarked on a dynamic publishing career upon graduation.

However, here's a simple question, one that never occurred to me as an 18-year-old: what does an undergraduate creative writing degree prepare you for? If you intend to land in another creative writing degree program (MFA or PhD), then the answer is simple. You're practicing and laying important groundwork for more of the same.

But if the degree should prepare you for a career in writing, editing, or publishing—if you intend to earn a living from it—most programs do not help students achieve that through their requirements or extracurricular offerings alone. This is not an accusation as much as it is a statement of fact; BFA and BA writing degrees are like English degrees, with some writing courses thrown in. Required coursework will not force you to be a successful writing professional.

I'm not eager to debate the intrusion (or necessity) of professionalization of undergraduate writing degrees. Rather, I want to speak directly to the students I hear from every day, who seek guidance on how to make a living from what they love: reading and writing.

You've probably heard that it's hard to make writing pay—or even that the best writing, the most artful writing, is at *odds* with commercial success. This is the persistent and dangerous myth of the starving artist, that "real art" doesn't earn money, and it's not possible for art and business to dance. Some creative writing programs divide the art from the business, rather than exploring how each informs the other, and how successful writers across history have proven themselves savvy at making their art pay.

Thankfully, I was lucky to be in a program that didn't perpetuate that myth. Such attitudes don't serve anyone—not you, not the writing programs, and not the world, which needs more writers who can be artful *and* innovative about producing work for an increasingly digital world where attention is the most precious commodity there is.

When I graduated with my BFA in 1998, the Internet was part of daily life, but media had yet to go fully digital. Today, traditional newspaper, magazine, and book publishing jobs are dwindling as the economics of the industry change. More and more people are writing than ever, with or without degrees, for free. As Arianna Huffington has said, writing is the new form of self-entertainment. Questions about how writers earn a sustainable living are at an all-time high. Nearly every writing career is supplemented by some other kind of skill: a knack for copywriting, ability in photography or graphic design, or expertise in a particular field such as science.

Your writing program's requirements should push you to get one cornerstone in place: it should discipline you to write, to write a lot, to write across genres or mediums, and to analyze the techniques of others. Obviously this is one of the whole points of the degree: immersion in the craft.

But you can't stop there, because the writing you're learning to do in a typical creative writing class has little relevance to today's publishing and media industry. Entry-level positions require creativity with digital media, imaginative social media tactics, and an artful approach to online marketing. This isn't to say that the writing itself isn't important—excellent storytelling that can cut through the noise is critical—but good writing skills aren't enough.

So what do you do? Seek opportunities to do more writing and reading on a deadline, particularly in digital media environments. Contribute to print and digital publications, volunteer to copyedit and proofread, learn how to build your own online presence and portfolio of work. Whatever hands-on experience you can get, take it, and take more than you think you can handle. Don't limit your writing experience to the typical classroom workshop environment, where egos can be fragile and stakes are low.

When you're evaluating a program, consider:

- Does the program include courses that acknowledge most reading, writing, and publishing is now done digitally?
- Does the program work with organizations or businesses to regularly offer internships or other opportunities to students? Is internship credit required?
- Do you have (or will you have) more knowledge and experience than your professors in digital media? What do they have to teach you beyond how to write fiction, poetry, and personal essays for traditional print publication?

While I was earning my BFA, I ventured outside the English department, and took classes to learn copyediting and graphic design and layout. I served as editor of the university newspaper and literary journal, which helped me land internships at two book publishers before graduation. I could have done these things just as successfully without being a BFA student, but I gained something of tremendous value from my program: the mentorship of my writing professors, who offered constructive criticism and invaluable professional connections for my career. Each of them had practical experience and insight that contributed to my ability to happily earn a living post-graduation.

If it were up to me, every undergraduate writing program would help their students better understand the economics of the writing life and how authors or artists *do* manage to put together a full-time living from doing what they love. It is possible, but instruction and mentorship surrounding these issues remains rare in traditional programs. So it is up to you, dear student, to demand it from your program and its professors, or find it elsewhere.

My Advice to Young Publishing Professionals

How can young book professionals make a personal brand for themselves?

I would consider two things to begin: First, whatever you're doing for your day job in publishing, does it represent what you ultimately want to be known for? If it does, then you should be describing and showcasing that work on your own personal website, and including highlights in your professional bio, wherever it may be found (LinkedIn, Facebook, etc).

If your current day job in publishing isn't necessarily what you see as your long-term future, then find ways to express or pursue your vision for your career. This might mean committing to online or offline activities (volunteer work, blogging, freelancing, etc), but either way, your personal website and social media presences should probably give preference and priority to that side of your life, rather than the day job. Remember that you're the one who tells the story about your life and career—particularly at your own website—so tell it in a way that attracts the right opportunities to you. The goal is to have a cohesive message surrounding your name and the kind of work you do or want to do.

What are some of the best ways for someone early in their career to get noticed by other publishing professionals?

Be proactive and solution oriented when dealing with challenges. Instead of bringing problems to your boss or team, bring problems plus potential ways to resolve it. Look for the answers yourself, then discuss the complexities or nuances of what solution is best with your mentor or boss. It's also impressive when someone has done their research in ways that add value and depth to conversations, rather than working merely by gut instinct or "this is the way it's always been done." While it's good to ask questions and be informed—especially to do your job right and avoid misunderstandings—avoid asking questions that you could answer yourself by doing a little bit of research or picking up the phone.

What are three things someone looking to move up in the publishing world can do to get ahead of other applicants?

Be better at the tech surrounding media/publishing. Learn HTML and WordPress. Know how to put together an EPUB. Know how to capture decent audio or video. Understand best practices of social media.

Attend every possible publishing-related event you can, even if it costs you money, to broaden your network, meet more people, and have more connections. More connections means more opportunities at jobs.

Treat people well. Your reputation will precede you, and if you become known as difficult to work with, you'll encounter barriers.

What advice do you wish you'd gotten early on in your career?

If you become a manager, you can't be friends with the people you manage—even if you were peers or friends before.

What mistake in your career have you learned the most from?

On a couple of occasions, I made the mistake of trying to tell colleagues how they could do their jobs better—even going so far as to show them a concrete vision of how I'd do things. That has never gone over well and in fact made me a few enemies. No matter how well-intentioned, it just comes off as presumptuous and arrogant (at best).

CHAPTER 12
The Future of Publishing

Most writers are aware that the publishing industry is undergoing a range of transformations, new beginnings, failures, and consolidations. But there's so much change it can be difficult to weed out and understand the most relevant and important changes—especially when hundreds of opinions seem to surround the smallest change.

Here are four trends that writers should keep a close eye on.

1. Publishing Contracts

When I started working in trade publishing (1998), it was very rare that the company's boilerplate contract would change. Obviously it was negotiated in minute detail by every agent that came into contact with it—so contracts differed from author to author—but the process always played out by a certain set of expectations or guidelines.

By the time I left trade publishing (2010), the contracts were being tweaked every 6 months to reflect a changing business environment and new opportunities in digital and multimedia publishing. I'm starting to wonder if there will ever be a "typical" contract again, given the increasing number of variables.

Consider:

- Successful self-published authors can gain leverage in negotiations: Hugh Howey's traditional publishing deal allowed him to keep his e-book rights.
- New digital imprints or start-ups offer very different contracts than established outlets—and rightly so, though some are good contracts

and others are bad. (More on that below.)

- Print publishing deals and distribution rights are becoming more and more like subsidiary rights. In other words, they're not always the most important or profitable right for an author to license.
- Foreign and translation rights will become increasingly important as e-book sales grow in international markets.

Unfortunately, most publishing contracts are closely guarded and not available for public review. So what is an author to do? Here's my advice.

Do your due diligence on *any* **publishing contract you sign.** Fully understand what rights you're granting and if it makes sense for your career and what you're getting paid. If you don't have an agent to negotiate your contract, consider hiring one on an hourly basis.

Think carefully and negotiate hard when it comes to digital-only publishing contracts. Some ebook-only publishers take a healthy share of your profits for doing things you could accomplish on your own. I'm skeptical of many digital start-ups that promise visibility and "talent discovery" when they have no success stories, no better distribution than what's already available to a self-publishing author, and limited (or no) industry experience. If the publisher isn't reaching a greater audience than you could on your own, ask yourself why you want to sign a contract with them. What value are they providing?

Always double-check how and when rights revert to you (the reversion clause). With traditional publishers, rights often revert after sales fall below a specific threshold. With digital-only publishers, rights often revert after specific time period has passed, or upon written notice. Make sure you understand the terms, and always negotiate for a better deal on this particular clause—to make it easier for you to get your rights back. (For more detail, read Dean Wesley Smith's post on rights reversion.)

Don't be afraid to walk away from a deal. Too many authors get caught up in the excitement of a publishing offer, and overlook contract terms that could hurt them in the future. If you can't be hard nosed about negotiations, find someone who can. No deal is better than a bad one.

2. The Evolving Role of Agents

To further complicate matters, your relationship with your agent may be the first contractual obligation you need to consider or reconsider.

Traditionally, an agent takes 15% commission on every book she sells. But what happens when you self-publish some of the titles that your agent couldn't sell? Or what if your agent sells your work to an imprint that pays no advance and even charges you (the author) upfront fees—a scenario that was briefly on the table when Random House rolled out new contracts for their digital-only imprints? Or what if you get the rights back to older titles that your agent sold, and you want to self-publish them on your own?

It's a hornet's nest of complications, but some of the best practices I've seen work off some variation of the following:

As usual, the agent takes 15% commission only on those books they've sold (where there is an advance or the makings of a "traditional" deal).

The agent does not take 15% commission on any type of self-published work by the author. However, if the agent is able to sell subsidiary rights or make other deals with that work, then they get their usual share on those specific deals.

Most agents are not interested in selling your work unless an advance is involved (70-80% of books never earn out their advance). However, agents often assist existing clients on all kinds of deals if there's a longstanding relationship in play. A good agent will be transparent and upfront about how all deals are handled, and will be closely following the evolution of best practices in the industry.

3. The Value and Distraction of Author Platform Building

As far as trends go, the idea of building a platform has been around for at least five or six years now, if not longer. Unfortunately, as time has passed, I'm not sure the discussions surrounding platform—or the common wisdom that gets spread—is any better than it was in 2007, and social media as both marketing tool and creative tool has greatly complicated matters.

The questions that often get asked include:

- When publishers or agents look at a writer's platform, what are their criteria? Is it a numbers game? What numbers do you have to reach?
- Do you need an established blog or website?
- Must you be on Twitter, Facebook, or the social media site du jour?
- Do you need to be a "brand"?

If you're a totally new, unpublished writer who is focused on fiction, memoir, poetry, or any type of narrative-driven work, forget you ever heard the word platform. I think it's causing more damage than good. It's causing writers to do things that they dislike (even hate), and that are unnatural for them at an early stage of their careers. They're confused, for good reason, and platform building grows into a raging distraction from the work at hand—the writing.

Therefore, build your platform by writing and publishing in outlets that are a good fit for you, lead to professional growth, and build your network. The other pieces will start to fall into place. It might take longer, but who cares if you're feeling productive and enjoying yourself? Go be a writer and take a chance on the writing. Writing and publishing good work always supports the growth of your platform—and I'm willing to bet more valuable platform building will get done that way, especially for narrative-driven writers.

Exception to the rule: Nonfiction/non-narrative authors and authors who are self-publishing. Sorry, but you should probably focus on platform as much as the writing.

4. Transmedia & Authorship

Let's start by defining transmedia, and I'll lean on Guy Gonzalez here. He wrote the following in 2010:

> [Transmedia] focuses on the storyworld first, distribution channels second, with the latter determined via a collaborative process that puts the author's creative vision at the center. Most so-called transmedia projects are really just cross-media marketing initiatives and/or brand extensions, driven by licensing deals and a parceling out of rights in a manner that often includes loss of creative control by the author. Star Wars is the go-to example of a transmedia property, and while it has definitely evolved into a legitimate one, it didn't start out that way.

My two cents: Unless you're already a high-profile commercial author, don't worry yourself about transmedia. Yes, you will set yourself up better if you're building expansive storyworlds (think: Game of Thrones), but unless you already have friends and colleagues involved in media—e.g., app development, audio/video production—you're probably not going to be shopping around your transmedia project any time soon.

However, when it comes to platform building (which I just told you to forget!), it does help to think beyond blogging, tweeting, and all the text-based forms of communication, and consider the whole world of opportunities available to you, to produce fun, interesting content that complements your published work. Think John Green's YouTube videos or Seth Harwood's podcasts or Tweetspeak Poetry.

AFTERWORD
A Few Words of Wisdom

We're all so focused on …

- Being as productive as possible
- Crafting the best manuscript possible
- Building the best platform possible
- Appearing as professional as possible

… that we lose sight of who we really are and instead try to follow every commandment that comes along, and behave in a way that will be acceptable to whomever we think is watching and judging.

It's why, in my more humorous moods, I tell people that the best way to get published is to stop caring about getting published.

When you strive so hard and for so long, the whole reason you started writing in the first place—the real joy and motivation for it—gets completely lost. You're so focused on the goal that you've forgotten the journey. You've forgotten to sing and dance, which is the secret to being a wonderful and successful writer.

Unfortunately, much advice the experts offer (that includes me!) don't help you take more joy. (Quite the contrary.) But joy is the one thing you have probably lost along the way, and didn't realize was lost in the first place.

Go find it, and celebrate it daily.

WRITING & PUBLISHING TERMINOLOGY

What are submission guidelines?
Also called writers guidelines, submission guidelines are instructions from editors, agents, or publishers on what submissions they'd like to see from writers, and how they prefer you submit your material. Guidelines briefly describe the publication's or publisher's audience, the type of material published, and the type of material that's *not* accepted.

Reviewing submission guidelines is critical if you want to find an agent or a publisher, and should ideally be combined with studying an agent's client base or a publisher's recent releases. Most agents and publishers post their guidelines on their website.

What does it mean to "market your material"?
It means selling what you write. "Study the market" means study the places where you might submit your work—and you usually start by reading the submission guidelines.

What's an SASE?
Acronym for self-addressed, stamped envelope. A SASE should almost always be included with any snail mail submissions.

What's a query?
A query is a letter to an editor or agent attempting to sell him (or seduce him) on the idea of your book. A typical query is 1-page, single-spaced. Not all publications or agents accept queries. Their guidelines may state

they are closed to submissions, or the guidelines may state that unagented submissions are not accepted.

What's an unsolicited manuscript?

When you submit a manuscript without the publisher/agent requesting it, your manuscript is unsolicited. In such a case, the publisher/agent has not given any indication she will read the work; she and the writer have not previously communicated. Many publishers will not read unsolicited manuscripts; they expect a query first.

What's the slush pile?

Slush pile is a term for all the unsolicited material (queries or manuscripts) received by those in publishing.

What is an agent and what do they charge?

An agent acts as liaison between author and publisher (editor). An agent shops a manuscript around to editors, receiving a commission only when the manuscript is accepted for publication. Agents usually take a 15 percent cut from the advance and royalties after a sale is made.

What is a simultaneous submission?

A simultaneous submission is a manuscript submitted for consideration to more than one publisher or agent at the same time. Some submission guidelines state that simultaneous submissions are not accepted.

Usually "simultaneous submission" refers strictly to manuscripts under consideration—not query letters, which are commonly sent in batches.

Once frowned upon, simultaneous submissions have become a common practice, mainly because of today's lengthy response times. My personal advice: (1) Don't submit to agents or editors who don't accept simultaneous submissions or (2) Allow exclusives for very defined and reasonable time periods given the length of the manuscript or (3) Be sly and don't let on that the material is being considered by multiple parties. Life is too short, and response times too long.

What is a multiple submission?

Technically, this is sending multiple manuscripts or story ideas to a single editor or agent for consideration. Don't do it. But sometimes this term is used interchangeably with *simultaneous submission*.

What is a proposal?

Proposals are used to sell nonfiction book ideas; instead of writing an entire nonfiction book and then trying to find a publisher or agent, you generally write the proposal first.

What is a synopsis?

Synopsis can be a confusing term, since its meaning depends on the context. Synopsis most frequently refers to a brief summary of a novel, but synopsis can also refer to a section of a nonfiction book proposal. Synopsis requirements vary widely. Sometimes you'll hear *synopsis* used interchangeably with *outline*.

What's an advance?

An advance is a sum of money a publisher pays a writer prior to the publication of a book. It is usually paid in installments: for instance, one-half on signing the contract and one-half on delivery of a complete and satisfactory manuscript. The advance is paid against royalty money that will be earned by the book, which means that royalties will not be paid to the author until the publisher has recouped the total sum of the advance from the author's royalties.

What is meant by rights? What rights do you sell, and what rights do you keep?

A writer owns all rights to his literary creation upon putting it in tangible form. He is entitled to decide who shall own the right to print his work for the first time, make it into a movie, adapt it into different formats or editions, and so on.

When selling your rights to a book publisher, the contract you sign will indicate what rights you keep and what rights you grant to the publisher (and when the publisher ceases to hold any rights). Regardless of what rights are granted to the publisher, the author—in most traditional book contracts—will retain copyright and can regain all rights to the work after a specified period. The big exception to this rule is work-for-hire agreements, where the author relinquishes all rights to the work.

RECOMMENDED RESOURCES

I've probably read, reviewed, or at least seen every single advice book, website, and service for writers. I could recommend dozens of resources, but I'll just focus on the most helpful for new writers.

Freelance Editors and Consultants

- Writer and editor Andi Cumbo [andilit.com] offers a range of budget-friendly services for all types of writers.
- For early career writers, especially those working on their first manuscript, consider editor and author Dave Malone, who offers affordable rates and respect for your voice [maloneconsultingonline.com].
- Ginger Moran [gingermoran.com] offers editing for novels and memoirs, and is also a certified coach.
- The Book Doctors offer top-shelf editing services, as well as consulting and publishing assistance [thebookdoctors.com].
- Blurb.com offers a vetted list of freelance editors, designers, ghostwriters, and ebook conversion services. You don't have to publish with Blurb to use their recommended freelancers.

Trustworthy Resources for New Writers

- Especially good for sussing out scams and not-quite-legitimate publishers and agents: Writer Beware. It's also a great 101 site for learning about the publishing industry.
- Self-doubt and motivation (am I good enough? am I wasting my time?): *Page After Page* by Heather Sellers

- On the long-term psychological battle: *The War of Art* by Steven Pressfield
- The kindest servant I know to other writers (poets, take special note), and one of my former colleagues: Robert Brewer [robertleebrewer.blogspot.com]
- Want to start a freelance writing career? Take a class with a stellar coach who helps you get results: Christina Katz [christinakatz.com]
- Writing a script? Jeanne Bowerman & Scriptchat [jeannevb.com]
- Want to share your work with other writers and get feedback? Try one of these online communities: Book Country, Wattpad, or Figment
- Social media training: Alexis Grant [alexisgrant.com]
- If you need to hire legal counsel or consult with a lawyer who specializes in the publishing industry, search online for Alan J. Kaufman.
- Need help with your author website? Check out The Willingham Enterprise (easily found online).

Attention Self-Publishers & Indie Authors

The best information on how to self-publish (whether in print or online) can be found here:

- Self-Publishing 101 at Writer Beware by Victoria Strauss [sfwa.org/other-resources/for-authors/writer-beware/]
- The Book Designer website [thebookdesigner.com]
- The Independent Publishing Magazine by Mick Rooney: to help you vet self- and e-publishing services [theindependentpublishingmagazine.com]
- I also maintain an updated list of DIY e-book resources for authors at my website [bit.ly/epub-resources].

News & Trends

Writers tend to get frustrated and bitter in their attempts to publish—usually because they don't understand how the publishing industry works, or they have expectations that will never be met. Read these blogs to better navigate your way to success and learn about the changes facing the industry: Shatzkin Files [idealog.com] and DigitalBookWorld.com.

Where to Find Market Listings (Places to Publish)

In your quest to find editors, agents, and publishers to query, there are many go-to resources. These are some of the best free listing sites available.

Fee-Based Resources
- WritersMarket.com: best for book publisher listings and magazines
- Duotrope.com: best for literary publishing markets, such as poetry and short fiction
- PublishersMarketplace.com: best for agent listings

Free Listings of Book Publishers
Be aware that most New York publishers do not accept unagented submissions, so sometimes "searching for a publisher" really means "finding an agent."
- QueryTracker.net. About 130 listings.
- Preditors & Editors. Hundreds of listings; been going since 1997. Waves a red flag on publishers to avoid. However, unclear how often the information is updated.
- Ralan.com. About 100 listings, focused on SF/F.
- AgentQuery.com. Bare-bones list (no submission guidelines), but offers embedded links to publishers' sites. Useful to preview the landscape.
- WriterMag.com. If you subscribe to The Writer magazine, you get 3,000 online market listings for free. Vetted list.
- Poets & Writers [pw.org]. Hundreds of listings, serving primarily the more literary side of the writing community.

Free Listings of Agents
- AgentQuery.com. About 900 listings.
- QueryTracker.net. More than 1,200 listings.
- AAR Online. This is the official membership organization for literary agents. Not all agents are members of AAR.

Free Listings of Literary Journals
- Poets & Writers [pw.org]. Hundreds of listings, serving primarily the more literary side of the writing community.

Free Listings of Magazines & Periodicals
- Ralan.com. Several hundred listings, focused on SF/F
- WritersWeekly.com. Offers weekly updates of markets looking for articles, as well as writing opportunities.
- Preditors & Editors. Unclear how often the information is updated.

5 Remarkable Prompt and Exercise Books

After working at Writer's Digest for a decade-plus, I saw more than my fair share of writing exercise/prompt books—plus I also acquired and edited quite a few. Writing prompts have always been an ever-popular tool for writers, regardless of stage of career.

Here I'd like to share what I found to be the most remarkable books—a mix of Writer's Digest titles and other publishers' titles.

The Pocket Muse by Monica Wood. What makes this book so special is the small size, vivid images and playful design, and high-quality production. It's now out of print, though you can get copies used–or opt for the sequel, *The Pocket Muse 2.*

3 A.M. Epiphany & *4 A.M. Breakthrough* by Brian Kiteley. I rarely find the time to use writing prompts, but if I did, these are the books I'd use. Very sophisticated and thought-provoking, I do put them to work in the classroom—for brainstorming nonfiction ideas to write about. Highly recommend to both writer and teacher. (I know both books are popular in MFA programs.)

What If? by Anne Bernays & Pamela Painter. This is one of the original exercise books for writers, published in 1991. It has since been updated, but you're safe sticking with the original.

The Practice of Poetry by Robin Behn. If you're a poet, this is the one to grab. It's another one that's been around forever and doesn't go out of style.

The Writer's Idea Book by Jack Heffron. Last but not least, one of the best-selling titles of all time from Writer's Digest was this exercise/prompt book, authored by one of its editors.

Stay in Touch with Jane

I'd love to hear your feedback on this book. You can send me an email at hello@janefriedman.com with your thoughts, questions, or suggestions for the next edition. If you found the book helpful, I would be immensely grateful if you left a review at Amazon or Goodreads.

You can stay up-to-date on my newest resources and classes—and my thoughts on publishing—through any of the following:

- My active blog and website at JaneFriedman.com
- My monthly e-mail newsletter (sign up at my site)
- Twitter: @JaneFriedman

Thanks so much, and best of luck in your writing and publishing journey.

ABOUT THE AUTHOR

The former publisher of Writer's Digest, Jane Friedman has more than 15 years of experience inside the book and magazine publishing industries, with expertise in the ever-evolving digital media landscape. Jane specializes in educating writers from a measured and nuanced perspective, to help them make the best long-term decisions for their careers. Since 2001, she has spoken at hundreds of writing conferences around the world, and is known for thought-provoking talks on the future of authorship. She recently delivered keynotes at The Muse & The Marketplace, the University of Wisconsin Writers' Institute, and PubSmart.

Her feature articles for writers have appeared in *Writer's Digest* magazine, the AWP Notebook, VQR Online, Digital Book World, Publishing Perspectives, IBPA Independent Magazine, The Huffington Post, Writer Unboxed, *Scratch* magazine, and many other print and online venues.

Her essays have been published in collections by the University of Chicago Press, Seal Press, Milkweed Editions, and McPherson & Co.—as well as Writer's Digest Books, *Writer's Market, Writer's Market UK,* and *Australian Writer's Marketplace.*

Her award-winning blog for writers enjoys more than 100,000 visits every month, and her social media presence is often cited as a model to follow in the writing and publishing community. Currently, Jane teaches digital media and publishing at the University of Virginia, and resides in Charlottesville, Virginia. Find out more at JaneFriedman.com.

INDEX

48242626R00131

Made in the USA
San Bernardino, CA
21 April 2017